Unwin Critical Library
GENERAL EDITOR: CLAUDE RAWSON

GOETHE'S FAUST

Unwin Critical Library

GENERAL EDITOR: CLAUDE RAWSON

Goethe's Faust

JOHN R. WILLIAMS

Lecturer in German,
University of St Andrews

London
ALLEN & UNWIN
Boston   Sydney   Wellington

Allen & Unwin, the academic imprint of
Unwin Hyman Ltd
PO Box 18, Park Lane, Hemel Hempstead, Herts HP2 4TE, UK
40 Museum Street, London WC1A 1LU, UK
37/39 Queen Elizabeth Street, London SE1 2QB

Allen & Unwin Inc.,
8 Winchester Place, Winchester, Mass. 01890, USA

Allen & Unwin (Australia) Ltd,
8 Napier Street, North Sydney, NSW 2060, Australia

Allen & Unwin (New Zealand) Ltd in association with the Port
Nicholson Press Ltd,
60 Cambridge Terrace, Wellington, New Zealand

First published in 1987

British Library Cataloguing in Publication Data

Williams, John R.
    Goethe's Faust. — (Unwin critical library).
1. Goethe, Johann Wolfgang von. Faust
I. Title
832'.6 PT1925
ISBN 0-04-800043-4

Library of Congress Cataloging-in-Publication Data

Williams, John R., 1940–
    Goethe's Faust.
(Unwin critical library)
Includes index.
Bibliography: p.
1. Goethe, Johann Wolfgang von, 1749–1832.
Faust.   I. Title.   II. Series.
PT1925.W54   1987   832'.6   87-9255
ISBN 0-04-800043-4 (alk. paper)

Typeset in 9 on 11½ point Joanna by
Nene Phototypesetters Ltd, Northampton
and printed in Great Britain by
Billing and Sons Ltd, London and Worcester

For Elizabeth, Ivor, Bruno

GENERAL EDITOR'S PREFACE

Each volume in this series is devoted to a single major text. It is intended for serious students and teachers of literature, and for knowledgeable non-academic readers. It aims to provide a scholarly introduction and a stimulus to critical thought and discussion.

Individual volumes will naturally differ from one another in arrangement and emphasis, but each will normally begin with information on a work's literary and intellectual background, and other guidance designed to help the reader to an informed understanding. This is followed by an extended critical discussion of the work itself, and each contributor in the series has been encouraged to present in these sections his own reading of the work, whether or not this is controversial, rather than to attempt a mere consensus. Some volumes, including those on *Paradise Lost* and *Ulysses*, vary somewhat from the more usual pattern by entering into substantive critical discussion at the outset, and allowing the necessary background material to emerge at the points where it is felt to arise from the argument in the most useful and relevant way. Each volume also contains a historical survey of the work's critical reputation, including an account of the principal lines of approach and areas of controversy, and a selective (but detailed) bibliography.

The hope is that the volumes in this series will be among those which a university teacher would normally recommend for any serious study of a particular text, and that they will also be among the essential secondary texts to be consulted in some scholarly investigations. But the experienced and informed non-academic reader has also been in our minds, and one of our aims has been to provide him or her with reliable and stimulating works of reference and guidance, embodying the present state of knowledge and opinion in a conveniently accessible form.

C.J.R.
University of Warwick,
December 1979

CONTENTS

PREFACE

The arrangement of this volume follows the guidelines set out in the General Editor's Preface. I have departed from the usual structure by placing the chapter on the reception of Goethe's Faust before the commentary section, in order to outline some of the main areas of critical controversy before turning to my own analysis of the text. I have also appended a brief survey of the prosody of Faust; the variety of its metres and verse forms is surely unique in dramatic literature, and this is an area that is not often covered fully or systematically in commentaries. The first part of the volume sets out to provide historical information on the Faust legend and on the composition and reception of Goethe's Faust, the second part to provide a guide to the understanding of the work. While the overall unity of Faust is not disputed, the approach adopted is to consider the two parts of the drama as related but fundamentally different parts of the whole: the first as a mimetic tragedy, the second as a historical and cultural allegory, both enclosed within a theatrum mundi framework. It is hoped that this approach will do justice both to the better-known first part of Goethe's Faust and to the relatively unfamiliar sections of the second part.

This volume is written both for the specialist student of German literature and for the interested non-academic reader. A wide knowledge of Goethe's works or of German literature is not assumed; what is assumed is a thorough knowledge, or at least a careful reading, of Goethe's Faust. Quotations from Faust and from other sources (Goethe's correspondence, conversations and other works) have been translated or paraphrased in English, but references have been provided to the original, and line references have been consistently given to the text of Faust. It is therefore convenient if readers have access to a Faust text that prints line numbers. To readers using an English text, the Norton Critical Edition, Faust: a Tragedy, translated by Walter Arndt and edited by Cyrus Hamlin, is particularly recommended, not only for that reason but also because the translation is faithful to the metres and rhymes of the original, and because the edition contains an extensive critical apparatus in English. Stuart Atkins's recent translation (Suhrkamp edition) reproduces the original metres, but does not attempt rhyme. A rhymed and metrical translation of Part One only, by F. D. Luke, is due to appear shortly in the Oxford University Press World's Classics series; Dr Luke has kindly informed me that his version will print line numbers, and will also contain an introduction and notes.

I have used Ernst Beutler's Artemis *Gedenkausgabe* for references to Goethe's works, as the most complete modern German edition of Goethe, with occasional references to the Weimarer Ausgabe where necessary. Students may, however, find volume 3 of Erich Trunz's Hamburger Ausgabe, or its separate printing as *Goethes Faust* (Wegner Verlag), more convenient for reference to the text of the drama. Volume 8 of the Berliner Ausgabe (Aufbau Verlag) is also recommended; while it is less convenient for line references, it contains not only the *Urfaust* and *Fragment* versions but also the paralipomena, together with historical information and notes to the text. Reclam and dtv editions also print line numbers.

It is impossible to ignore completely the vast encrustation of critical literature that has grown around Goethe's *Faust*; it is equally impossible to take account of more than a selection of it in a study like this one. I have referred to a range of criticism in German and English that has seemed to me to offer valuable, interesting, or – occasionally – eccentric readings of the work. In particular, I have drawn attention to recent criticism that has examined the historical and allegorical dimensions of the second part of *Faust* and has, I believe, laid the foundation for a satisfactory overall understanding of a text that has often been too readily regarded as wilfully obscure or haphazard in both its details and its structure.

I have to thank the University of St Andrews for a period of study leave during which this volume was completed. For their help, advice and encouragement during the writing of it, I am most indebted to Jeffrey Ashcroft, Richard Littlejohns, Barry Nisbet, Claude Rawson and, quite particularly, to Francis Lamport. To my wife, Elizabeth, I owe an immeasurable debt of gratitude.

JOHN R. WILLIAMS
St Andrews, November 1986

ABBREVIATIONS USED IN THE NOTES

In the footnotes, references to books and articles are given by means of shortened titles, after the first mention, while full details of titles and publication are provided in the Bibliography. The following abbreviations are also commonly used in the footnotes:

Biedermann	*Goethes Gespräche*, ed. Flodoard Frhr. von Biedermann, 5 vols (Leipzig, 1909–11).
Briefe, HA	*Goethes Briefe*, Hamburger Ausgabe, ed. Karl Robert Mandelkow, 4 vols (Hamburg, 1962–7).
Briefe an Goethe, HA	*Briefe an Goethe*, Hamburger Ausgabe, ed. Karl Robert Mandelkow, 2 vols (Hamburg, 1965–9).
BA	Goethe, *Poetische Werke*, Berliner Ausgabe, 16 vols (Berlin, 1976–81).
GA	Goethe, *Gedenkausgabe der Werke, Briefe und Gespräche*, ed. Ernst Beutler, 27 vols (Zürich, 1948–71).
HA	*Goethes Werke*, Hamburger Ausgabe, ed. Erich Trunz, 14 vols (Hamburg, 1948–60).
WA	*Goethes Werke*, Weimarer Ausgabe, hg. im Auftrage der Großherzogin Sophie von Sachsen, 133 vols (Weimar, 1887–1919).

GOETHE'S FAUST

PART ONE

History, Composition and Reception

CHAPTER 1

The Sources and Transmission of the Faust Legend

Georg Faust, self-styled 'Demigod from Heidelberg', 'Philosopher of Philosophers', 'Magister Georgius Sabellicus, Faustus junior, wellspring of necromancers, astrologer, second magus, chiromancer, aeromancer, second in the art of hydromancy' – Faust, for all his evident talent for self-advertisement, had a very bad press from his own age.[1] To Abbot Trithemius of Sponheim, he was a vagabond, a braggart and a rogue; to the learned monk Conrad Mutianus Rufus, nothing but a boaster and a fool; to the scholar Joachim Camerarius, a windbag of empty super-stition. The city fathers of Nuremberg labelled him 'the great sodomite and nigromancer', the reformer Philipp Melanchthon execrated him as a 'vile beast' and 'a stinking privy of the devil', and the Heidelberg professor Augustin Lercheimer described him as a lewd and devilish scamp, a parasite, glutton and drunkard, who lived from quackery. Even if few of these graphic indictments are based on reliable first-hand experience, and even if the more direct and apparently authentic sources are themselves coloured by prejudice, rivalry, or antipathy – it is still extraordinary that this was the historical figure who would be transmuted into Marlowe's doomed and anguished scholar, let alone into Goethe's restlessly striving individual who proceeds through universal experience and error towards his ultimate salvation.

So elusive a figure is the historical Faust (it was a view common in the seventeenth and eighteenth centuries that he never existed at all), that not only the place and date of his birth and death, not only his academic education and titles, not only his religious affiliation, but even his very names are in doubt. Johann(es), the first name of virtually all the literary Fausts up to Goethe, which was first mentioned in an edition of Melanchthon's aphorisms by Johannes Manlius in 1562, is presumably a posthumous accretion – unless we accept Mahal's surmise that he might have been baptized Johann Georg. Current opinion is that his name was Georg or Jörg Faust, and that the name 'Sabellicus' by which Trithemius knew him was an assumed 'professional' title designed to allude to the Sabines of Italy, a people reputed for sorcery; it is not generally accepted that this was the form of his family name Sabel or Zavel, Latinized in the humanist fashion to Sabellicus. Nor is it commonly believed that 'Faustus' was a similar working pseudonym; it is thought to be coincidental that the Latinized form of a common German family name was a happy choice for a future conjuror or magician – Faustus = fortunate. Nevertheless, if we accept that Sabellicus was an adopted name, we must at least allow the possibility that 'Faustus junior' was also part of Faust's self-advertisement, whether by chance or design.

The general consensus is that Faust was born in Knittlingen, a few miles north of Pforzheim, in or around 1480. Ernst Beutler's argument that he was one Georg Helmstett(er) who studied at Heidelberg between 1483 and 1489, and was therefore born around 1465 in Helmstadt near Heidelberg, is not widely accepted, though Frank Baron has recently revived this hypothesis.[2] Unless we accept it, there is no evidence that Faust received any formal university education; the various ranks and titles with which he adorned himself – Magister, Doctor, Commander of the Order of Knights of St John – were surely bogus. There is no historical authority for the siting of his birthplace at Roda near Weimar in the Spies Faustbook, nor at Sondwedel (Anhalt) in Widmann and subsequent versions (see pp. 6ff.). As for Faust's death, it is believed on the authority of the *Zimmerische Chronik* that he died violently and mysteriously (possibly even explosively, in the course of an unsuccessful alchemical experiment) at Staufen, a few miles southwest of Freiburg im Breisgau, around 1540.

Otherwise, the 'facts' of Faust's life are meagre. He narrowly avoided a confrontation with Trithemius at Gelnhausen in 1506 – according to the abbot, he had been boasting that he knew the works of Plato and Aristotle by heart, and could perform all Christ's miracles. He was, again on the hostile evidence of Trithemius, appointed schoolmaster in Kreuznach in 1507 through the good offices of Franz von Sickingen, but fled when charged with pederasty. He appeared as 'Georgius Faustus, Helmitheus Hedelbergensis', in Erfurt in 1513, and in 1520 he was paid a handsome sum, ten guilders, for casting a horoscope for the Bishop of Bamberg. He may have met the Prior of Rebdorf, Kilian Leib, in 1528; in the same year he was ordered out of Ingolstadt by the city council, and refused entry to Nuremberg in 1532. He probably knew and visited Daniel Stibar, a Würzburg councillor, prior to 1536; and he apparently cast an ominous horoscope for Philipp von Hutten's expedition to

Venezuela, which set out in 1534 – accurately enough, as it turned out, for the venture was disastrous, and Hutten was murdered in 1546. In 1539 Faust's reputation was compared by Philipp Begardi to that of Paracelsus – which was by no means intended to flatter either party.

Virtually all the reports of Faust from before or after 1540 present an unflattering, indeed damning, picture of the man – though with such sparse evidence it would be incautious to conclude that he was therefore as great a windbag, charlatan, rogue, or pervert as the no doubt biased accounts suggest. The very fact that Faust was so well known to his contemporaries is of some significance, however they judged him; and anyone who was paid so generously for a horoscope by the Bishop of Bamberg – a tolerant and humanistic prince-bishop far removed from the ambitiously scheming prelate of Goethe's *Götz von Berlichingen* – must have been more than a mere charlatan or travelling quack. Hans Henning suggests that Faust might have stood midway between the uneducated tricksters and the scholars of his time;[3] and Mahal has suggested a psychological profile of Faust as an autodidact of humble origins, with all the insecurity and resentment of the self-made man, the need for self-assertion and the aggressive antagonism towards established scholars. He could have had theoretical and practical knowledge of medicine, astrology and alchemy; he could have had considerable gifts of hypnosis or suggestion, and with the help of a primitive magic lantern would have been capable of putting on a show to impress a credulous public. Being of humble, even peasant, origins, he would have had neither a university education nor a fixed position, and would have joined the army of wandering self-styled scholars whose livelihood depended on their ability to attract and hold an audience with stories of travel and prodigies, with magic tricks, horoscopes, divinations and conjurations.

Nevertheless, there are no reliable contemporary judgements on Faust that cast him in a remotely favourable light, and it was no doubt his very notoriety that led, in the forty or so years after his death, to the accretion of the most sensational and scandalous anecdotes and superstitions around his name. He attracted like a powerful magnet many of the already mythical attributes of his more prominent contemporaries – Agrippa von Nettesheim, Paracelsus, Nostradamus and even, by a fine posthumous irony, through a poem of Hans Sachs, his arch-enemy Trithemius himself;[4] his name also became associated with many crude pranks and scrapes of the sort previously attributed to figures like Till Eulenspiegel. Above all, in an age conditioned by an obsessive demonology, he became known as the man who, for the sake of knowledge, power, fame, riches and pleasure, had made a pact with the devil. As such Faust was, in a rough and ready way, already an ambivalent and composite figure who represented almost emblematically the contradictions and tensions of the age. He was on the one hand the Renaissance scholar, the speculative seeker for truth beyond scholastic or humanist traditions, the astrologer exploring new worlds on earth and beyond, the alchemist or magus searching for the philosophers' stone, the talisman of the highest philosophical and scientific wisdom; on the other hand, for the Reformation above all, but also for the Counter-Reformation, he was the godless apostate whose presumption and pride had led him, like Icarus, like the Titans, like Lucifer and like Adam, to arrogate to himself powers beyond those properly given to him, to defy God and to ally himself with the devil. At the same time, as Henning suggests, the orthodox or official image of Faust as a renegade intellectual or devil-worshipper did not entirely obscure the popular figure who not only amused and entertained the common people but who, over and above that, might also have been a wish-fulfilment, a fantasy figure who represented an individual's attempt to rise above the social misery, the cultural stagnation and the political frustrations of an age in which the reformed church had become the pillar of a reinvigorated feudalism.

The crystallization of the brew of quarter-truth, anecdote and fantasy that had accumulated from many different sources was the *Historia von D. Johann Fausten, dem weitbeschreyten Zauberer und Schwartzkünstler (History of Dr Johann Faust, the Notorious Magician and Nigromancer)*, the creative compilation of an anonymous author published by Johann Spies in Frankfurt in 1587, purporting to be based on Faust's own writings and claiming to serve as a terrible example and well-meant warning to all arrogant, presumptuous and godless men – as well as a cautionary reminder to the faithful of the snares of the devil. It was the work of a fanatical Lutheran – a Lutheran, moreover, for whom not only anonymity but also the greatest caution in the presentation of his material was necessary. The dedication and preface 'to the Christian reader', and the text itself, are spiced with frequent quotations from and references to the Bible, Luther and Melanchthon; the reader is persistently warned against the boldness and arrogance that are themselves a cause of godlessness, and specifically against the temptation of the serpent (Genesis 3: 5), 'eritis sicut deus', that impels Faust to unbridled speculation and hence to damnation. Theologically, the book represents the strictest Lutheran orthodoxy; it is an exemplary story, as it were the legend of an anti-saint, seasoned with comic anecdotes, or *Schwänke*. For all that, the author and publisher were treading on thin ice, not least because the Historia at several points appears to contain travestied parallels to the life of Christ himself – which is why they were careful to parade their Lutheran credentials before and during the treatment of such dangerous material. Already in 1588 a student of Tübingen University, Johannes Feinaug, was punished for producing without Senate permission a rhymed version of the story; his printer, Hock, was imprisoned. And a decade after the publication of the Historia, Augustin Lercheimer wrote a diatribe against the book as a libel on Wittenberg, Luther and Melanchthon, as a collection of 'vanities, lies and devil's filth', and deploring 'that the fine and noble art of printing, given to us by God for good purposes, should thus be abused for evil'.[5]

The Historia became a best-seller, as indeed was unsurprising with such a potent combination of stern morality and thrilling sensationalism, theology and science, cosmic experience of heaven and hell, crude pranks, travel descriptions, and pornographic adventures in Constantinople, where the 'well-equipped' Faust pleasured the concubines of the Sultan's harem masquerading as the Prophet – in papal regalia. For all the unevenness and occasional tedium of the telling, it was an edifying and entertaining tale, the success of which lay in the very ambivalence of its appeal, in its manifestly orthodox treatment of dangerous and racy material.

The historical Faust was almost totally obscured as the Historia set down many of the canonical episodes and motifs of the Faust legend – Faust's dissatisfaction with conventional scholarship; his pact in blood with the devil, or rather with his agent Mephostophiles (sic); the demon's admission that he, in Faust's place, would do everything in his power to gain God's forgiveness; the master–servant relationship, to be reversed at the expiry of the twenty-four-year term; Faust's questioning of the spirit on theological, philosophical and scientific matters; his cosmic, terrestrial and infernal journeys; the invocation of spirits before an imperial patron; a succession of more or less crude pranks and tricks; the attempt by a pious old man to call Faust to repentance – and Faust's reaffirmation of his pact with hell; the conjuring of a phantom army by Faust; the provision of a succubus in the form of Helen of Troy as his concubine, by whom he has a son, Justus Faustus; and finally Faust's agony of spirit and his truly grisly and terrible end. Moreover, the Historia also laid down the basic structure of the Faust legend, a structure that is inherent in the material itself: the curve of Faust's career from humble beginnings through arrogance and worldliness to the climax of the pact, down through an extensive series of adventures towards his ever more rapidly approaching end.

The immense popularity of the Spies Historia is attested in various ways (quite apart from the case of another Tübingen student, Leipziger, who in 1596 confessed to a pact with the devil in an attempt to relieve his debts; in spite of the fact that he had not actually received any money from the devil, he was 'gated' for six months and ordered to prepare himself for the Eucharist).[6] The Spies version ran to six editions in 1587 alone, and some twenty-two altogether.[7] It spawned a sequel in 1593, the story of Faust's disciple Christoph Wagner and his pact with the demon Auerhahn, and even a sequel to the sequel, the *D. Johann Fausti Gaukeltasche*, purported to have been written by Wagner's pupil Johann de Luna, the earliest recorded edition of which is dated 1607. More to the point of this survey, the *Historia* very soon appeared in a number of translations – into Danish (1588), Low German (1589), Flemish (1592), French (1598), and, some time between 1588 and 1592, English. The English translation is *The Historie of the damnable life, and deserved death of Doctor Iohn Faustus etc.*, 'newly imprinted . . . according to the true Copie printed at Franckfort, and translated into English by P. F. Gent . . . 1592'.[8] It was this version that furnished Christopher Marlowe with the opportunity to transform the Reformation *exemplum* of Faust's blasphemous career into the tragic dissatisfaction of a titanic, if godless, Renaissance scholar.

At this point the transmission of the Faust legend bifurcates, to merge again almost two centuries later with Goethe's *Faust*. Before returning to Marlowe's *Dr Faustus*, we shall resume the history of the German narrative versions of the legend. Apart from numerous editions of the *Historia* and its 'sequels', the Wagner and Johann de Luna stories, a whole substratum of publications which purported to be by Faust, or to have formed part of his library, proliferated during the seventeenth and eighteenth centuries – largely rehashes of earlier cabbalistic writings like the *Clavicula Salomonis*, and often fraudulently backdated for spurious authenticity: *Doctor Faustens dreifacher Höllenzwang*, *D. J. Fausti schwarzer Rabe*, *Fausti Praxis magica*, etc. In the mainstream of Faust literature, three publications stand out as attempts to keep alive the *Volksbuch* tradition.

In 1599 Georg Rudolf Widmann produced a version based largely on the Spies *Historia*, and possibly also on an unknown source. Few critics have anything positive to say about Widmann; apart from anything else, he vastly expanded his version from 227 pages of Spies to some 700, eliminating nineteen chapters and adding thirty-six. What is more, he appended to almost every chapter an interminable 'Erinnerung', or 'Reminder', to his readers, more often than not considerably longer than the narrative itself, in which he sermonizes, quotes sanctimoniously from scriptural and Lutheran authority, parades his own learning, and – as if the narrative itself were not caution enough – manipulates the reader's emotional and moral responses even more crudely than the Spies version does. Of all the changes made by Widmann to the Spies version, the most significant is that he moves Faust's studies from the Protestant University of Wittenberg to the Jesuit College at Ingolstadt, one of the academic centres of the Counter-Reformation – thus, oddly enough, reversing the original shift from south to north of the historical Faust's sphere of activity; the earlier Lutheran critics of Faust had situated him within their own sphere of influence. The disowning of Faust by the Lutheran bigot Widmann is matched by the crude anti-Catholic tendency of his commentaries, where he indulges in the most scurrilous slanders against the doctrines and the hierarchy of the Roman Catholic Church (see the 'Erinnerung' to Chapter 25, part two). And while Widmann is not slow to show off his own learning, the character of Faust as the inquiring scholar takes second place to that of the godless sorcerer who so richly deserves his inevitable damnation.

Widmann's version was not reprinted during the seventeenth century; but a Nuremberg physician, Johann Nicolaus Pfitzer, issued a version based heavily on Widmann, but also drawing on the Spies Historia, in 1674. Pfitzer and his collaborator, Conrad Platzius, a theologian, retained Widmann's tedious glosses, with some variations and additions of their own, and for good measure appended two further studies on magic. Pfitzer stresses the motive of lust in Faust's pact with the devil, and so he reinstates the Helen episode from Spies (which Widmann had consigned to a summary in one of his 'Erinnerungen'), and – what is particularly interesting with reference to Goethe's reception of the legend – he intro-duces for the first time the episode of Faust's lusting after a poor but attractive girl. This girl from the country, in service in a shopkeeper's house, is pursued by Faust, but resists his lechery as long as there is no prospect of marriage; whereupon Mephostophiles procures Helen for Faust as his 'Concubin und Beischläferin'. Even more striking in the light of Goethe's Faust is another anecdote unique to Pfitzer's version, related in his commentary to Chapter 2 of the first book: a student seduces a young girl with the help of presents, unbeknown to her mother. She becomes pregnant, is abandoned by the student, and bears a daughter whom she murders. Two years later she is sentenced to death.

By the beginning of the eighteenth century, the naïve belief in the reality of devils and witchcraft, in the efficacy of exorcism, and in the black arts generally was, at least among the educated élite, if not among the mass of the unlettered population, becoming eroded. Accordingly, the appeal and the power of the Faust story in its narrative form (less so, as we shall see, in the theatrical tradition) was being undermined, whereas the poetic and symbolic dimensions of the legend were as yet

unrealized and unexploited in Germany. The sceptical rationalism of
the age made its mark on the last significant *Volksbuch* version, that of an
author apparently ignorant of the Spies *Historia* and perhaps also of
Widmann, who published in 1725, under the pseudonym of 'a Christian
Believer', a drastically revised and shortened version of Pfitzer. The
'Christlich Meynender' completely omits Pfitzer's commentaries and
glosses, and reduces his source from more than 800 pages to 48. While
by no means approving of Faust's practice of black magic, he contrives
to minimize this element of the legend by passing over most of Faust's
speculative questionings of the devil, thus erasing the image of Faust's
intellectual curiosity even more completely than previous authors.
He retains full disapproval of Faust's 'Epicurean' way of life; but the
scepticism of the author intrudes into his own narrative, making it
difficult to gauge his intention in retelling the legend at all, unless it is
merely to exploit the story for moralizing purposes. A further feature of
this version is that it existed in two different forms. Some editions
continued the anti-Catholic bias of Widmann and Pfitzer, though in an
attenuated form; other editions modified this even further by simply
omitting all references to Rome, popes, monasteries and any specifically
Catholic figures or institutions.

The Faustbook of the Christlich Meynender represents the decadence of the popular narrative tradition of the legend, lacking as it does
the robust, if bigoted, force of previous versions. Nevertheless, it
enjoyed far greater popularity than either Widmann or Pfitzer, almost
rivalling the *Historia* itself as a best-seller in its own age; it had not only
appeared in some twenty-seven editions by 1790, the date of the
publication of Goethe's *Faust Fragment*, but also formed the basis of
innumerable cheaply printed chapbook versions that circulated in the
eighteenth century. However, that century saw the waning of the
Faustbook tradition; indeed, the whole Faust legend had for some time
been discredited and demythologized by the researches and opinions
of sceptics like Gabriel Naudé in 1625, Christian Thomasius in 1701, and
in particular Johann Georg Neumann, who in his researches into the
'so-called' Dr Faust, the *Curieuse Betrachtungen des sogenannten D. Faustens* of
1702, while not denying the existence of the historical Faust, dismisses
him as an insignificant figure, concluding that we would know even less
of this obscure magician if he had not been so frequently played by
'comedians' in the theatre.[9] Indeed, the editors of the stories themselves sowed the seeds of the destruction of the chapbook tradition;
in the last edition of the Wagner story of 1797, the author himself
depreciates his own narrative, and suggests that such superstitious
fantasies do no more than while away an idle hour, since in an

enlightened age no sensible person believes in such sorceries, which have been explained away by natural causes . . . [10]

That writer evidently did not realize, even in 1797, that the Faust legend had been taken up by less rationalistically constricted minds, by creative imaginations that would exploit the powerful poetic, symbolic and aesthetic dimensions of the story, rather than concern themselves with literal truth. But Neumann, although he was writing before the brief recrudescence of the narrative legend as a result of the Christlich Meynender's edition of 1725, was accurate enough in detecting the shift of the Faust story to the theatre. For during the seventeenth and eighteenth centuries, indeed well into the nineteenth century, the story of Faust reached and entertained far broader sections of the population than it had done through the medium of the Faustbooks; it became a firm and favourite stock-in-trade of the popular stage and, latterly, of the marionette theatre. In order to trace this vigorous second branch of the transmission of the legend, we must go back to the English translation of the Spies *Historia*.

It is certain that Marlowe based his *Tragical History of Dr Faustus* on the translation by P. F. of the *Historia*. And if P. F. had already on his own initiative subtly emphasized Faust's intellectual curiosity rather more than the *Historia* did, Marlowe moved his hero further in that direction. The dramatic mode alone precludes as much moral or theological sermonizing as was allowed in the narrative versions; and, in spite of the strictures of the Chorus on a Faustus 'swollen with cunning of a self-conceit', or the Old Man's 'kind rebuke', the dramatist's sympathy with his tragic hero is evident. To be sure, Marlowe's Faustus is a profoundly ambivalent figure – there is scarcely a Faust in literature or legend who is not. And for all his reputed atheism, Marlowe did not dare or did not care to have his Faustus saved; he retains the curve of the Faust story inherent in the narrative of the Faustbooks, and his Faustus is 'damned perpetually'. But the play ends not on the unequivocal call of P. F. 'to euery Christian heart' to defy 'the Diuell and all his works', nor on the fearful words of the Epistle of Peter that conclude the Spies *Historia*, but with the moving epilogue of the Chorus which, while giving due warning against the presumption of 'such forward wits/To practise more than heavenly power permits', also deplores the fate of 'the branch that might have grown full straight' and of 'Apollo's laurel bough/That sometime grew within this learned man'.[11] Marlowe has saved his hero from the final degeneration of the 'swinish and Epicurish life' of the Spies and P. F. versions; his Helen, while she is still a succubus designed to bind Faustus to Lucifer, is the incarnation – or, more accurately, the spirit form – of mythical, Homeric beauty. While she remains a devil in human shape, Marlowe's Helen episode points up the Renaissance image of his Faustus as against the Lutheran image of a lecher who casually indulges his every sexual whim; it also marks an isolated but significant step towards Goethe's conception of Helen as a symbol of classical beauty – even if there is no evident connection between Marlowe's Helen and Goethe's.

Marlowe not only retained many of the popular *Schwank* episodes involving Faust but he (or his collaborator) also chose to counterpoint the Faustian action with scenes of farce and burlesque that are presumably meant to ape and parody the more serious action. These crude prose scenes are historically interesting, for it was these clowning interludes, in their many native transformations, that contributed to the enduring popularity of the subject of Faust on the German stage over the next two centuries.

The decisive shift in the transmission of the Faust legend was the reimportation of Marlowe's dramatized version into Germany by English travelling players who performed Elizabethan and Jacobean dramas on the Continent. These performances, initially in English, though the farcical scenes very soon came to be in German, were quickly absorbed into the repertoire of the popular German stage. From the first recorded performance of *Dr Faustus* in Graz by John Green's players in 1608 until well into the second half of the eighteenth century, the dramatized story of Dr Faust reached even deeper into the popular consciousness than did the chapbook versions.

Our knowledge of these early stage versions is limited to some eye-witness accounts and a series of theatre bills; no script or scenario has survived. From the account by Georg Schröder of a performance in Danzig from 1668, and from various announcements of performances of the Faust play,[12] we can gather that certain distinctive features soon became traditional. Nearly all started with a 'Prologue in Hell', a pandemonium featuring Pluto or Lucifer, followed by a scene in Faust's study, the pact, and by a variety of episodes accompanied frequently enough by fireworks and spectacle, songs, ballet and even circus acts, with much clowning; the role of Marlowe's Robin was quickly usurped by the native clown figures of Hanswurst or Pickelhäring, by Krispin, or, in Austria, by Kasperle. Helen, oddly enough, does not appear in all these versions by any means; instead, Faust conjures various classical or biblical scenes for the Duke of Parma, including Tantalus, Sisyphus, Pompey, Judith and Holofernes, Samson and Delilah, David and Goliath – and, in Schröder's account, Charlemagne. Faust's grisly end is, of course, common to all versions, sometimes followed by a firework display or a ballet. Certain traces of Marlowe survive in these versions: the scene in Faust's study, his dissatisfaction with scholarship, the conjuring of horns on to a courtier's head, and, most distinctly of all, because it was evidently Marlowe's innovation, the tolling of the hours to mark Faust's end – replaced in some late puppet versions by the watchman calling the hours.

Side by side with, and growing out of the stage plays, emerged an even more vigorous tradition of puppet, or more strictly marionette, versions of Faust. It is not possible to date the earliest origins of the puppet play of Dr Faust, though Henning suggests the earliest perform-ance was probably at Lüneburg in 1666; and, while several integral versions of these shows have survived, most of them were recorded during the nineteenth century, and betray in one way or another the impact of the literary versions of Lessing, Klinger, Müller, or Goethe. The Ulm puppet play, which is just recognizable as deriving from Marlowe, is one of the shortest and earliest extant, and therefore presumably all the less overlaid with later accretions.[13]

If the narrative tradition of the Faustbooks fell into decadence in the sceptical spirit of the German Enlightenment, the theatrical and marionette tradition, reaching down to less sophisticated levels of the population, thrived and proliferated, becoming on the one hand increasingly elaborate and on the other hand increasingly farcical. It is scarcely surprising, then, that the 'Literaturpapst' or literary pundit, of mid-eighteenth-century Germany, Gottsched, should view the figure of Faust on the stage with the same stern disapproval as he viewed Harlequin, and that he should declare that the 'fairy tale' of Dr Faust had amused the common herd for long enough;[14] or that Moses Mendel-ssohn, on hearing that his friend Lessing planned a drama on the subject of Faust, should write to him in disbelief, promising himself great amusement at Lessing's discomfiture when the sophisticated theatre-goers of Leipzig burst into laughter at the very mention of the words 'O Faustus! Faustus!'[15]

Nothing could seem further from Lessing's theological and aesthetic principles than the assumptions of the Faust legend; and yet the evidence suggests that Lessing seriously envisaged the rehabilitation of Dr Faust, if only to provide the German theatre with vigorous national material. Moreover, he evidently also intended to reverse tradition by having his Faust redeemed at the end. This was, however, intractable material for Lessing, and it is by no means clear how far he had progressed with his Faust drama when all his working materials were lost with a trunk between Leipzig and Brunswick in 1775. A letter from Freiherr Tobias Philipp von Gebler to Friedrich Nicolai suggests that he had planned two versions, one based on the popular legend and one purged of all diabolism, in which the devil would be replaced by an 'arch-villain';[16] but otherwise the only surviving material is contained in the devils' speed-test scene in the famous seventeenth *Literaturbrief*, the fragmentary 'Berlin scenario', and the not entirely consistent reports of C. F. von Blankenburg and J. J. Engel.[17]

The material in the *Literaturbrief* and the 'Berlin scenario' is, to say the least, ponderous. More interesting are the reports of Blankenburg and Engel, who agree on their account of how Lessing was to solve the fundamental problem, especially acute, surely, for him, of whether Faust was to be damned; for, while Lessing might have agreed with one of the devils of his 'Berlin scenario' on the perils of a man overreaching his intellectual limits by excessive curiosity, he would scarcely have been prepared to see his Faust damned for following his God-given urge for enlightenment. It appears that Lessing intended to solve the problem by means of a device similar to that of Euripides' *Helen*; the Faust tempted by the devils was to be a phantom Faust, his adventures a dream-play only vicariously experienced. An Angel of Providence was to descend just as the devils were singing songs of triumph at Faust's damnation, to tell them that they had not triumphed over humanity and knowledge, that God had not given man his noblest of urges in order to cause him eternal suffering.

This, it seems, was to have been the theological stance of Lessing's *Dr Faust*: an awareness of the dangers of scholarly presumption (humility towards God is a cardinal virtue of Lessing's exemplary pedagogue Nathan), overridden by Faust's imperative to follow his urge for truth, the whole to be directed, as in *Nathan der Weise*, by a beneficent but mysterious providence that remains inscrutable until the last moment. And yet Lessing was clearly uneasy with the diabolistic trappings of the Faust legend; he was unable or unwilling to exploit the powers of darkness creatively or imaginatively, unable to treat magic other than ironically as a quaint form of moral allegory, unable to bridge the gap between an age that accepted the reality of diabolism and one that grasped it symbolically as mythical or poetic truth to express profound perceptions of human and cosmic relationships. We are still some way from Goethe's Mephistopheles, from the sign of the Macrocosm or the Erdgeist. Nevertheless, while Lessing's Faust plans can scarcely have influenced Goethe's *Faust* in any direct way, Goethe's conception was born of the intellectual and aesthetic climate that Lessing had done much to create; and it is no accident that the words of the Lord in the 'Prologue in Heaven' come clearly to mind when we read Lessing's parable on truth. Man's worth consists not in the possession of truth, which would involve passivity, inertia and pride, but in his unremitting quest for truth. If God stood with truth in his right hand, and in his left hand the tireless urge for truth, albeit at the cost of constant and eternal error, and told him to choose, then, says Lessing, he would humbly accept the left hand; pure truth is for God alone.[18]

During the 1770s in Germany, a remarkable rash of literary Faust works appeared, by major and minor authors, stimulated no doubt by reports that Lessing and Goethe were working on the legend, and attracted by the powerful potential of the theme. This is not the place to discuss in detail the Faust dramas of 'Maler' Müller, Schink or Soden, Klinger's Faust novel, or the more sketchy farce projected by J. M. R. Lenz, except to note that both Lenz and Müller planned to save Faust, indeed to have him actually brought back from hell; Goethe was by no means alone among his contemporaries in envisaging Faust's salvation. Also of interest at this time is H. L. Wagner's domestic tragedy Die Kindermörderin (The Infanticide), which is quite free from magical or literally diabolical elements, but which bears such striking similarities to the Gretchen tragedy of the Urfaust that Goethe – rather unnecessarily, as it turned out – accused Wagner of plagiarism. Certainly, the theme of infanticide by an abandoned and distracted unmarried mother is in itself no indication of plagiarism, since there are any number of possible common sources for this material; but there are enough close parallels to bear out suspicions that Wagner had been profoundly impressed by what he had heard of Goethe's draft. Goethe, however, surely overreacted; and there is a world of difference between his lyrical and symbolic treatment of the theme of infanticide and Wagner's prosaic, actual and relatively naturalistic domestic tragedy.

Also worth noting is a drama on the Faust theme which is of no intrinsic literary interest but of some historical curiosity, since it has the distinction of being the first completed Faust drama to show the hero's salvation: Paul Weidmann's Johann Faust of 1775. Not only does Weidmann save his Faust; he also combines, or more accurately he crudely cobbles together, the two plans that Lessing, and indeed Goethe, struggled to reconcile – the domestic, human milieu of bürgerliches Trauerspiel (domestic tragedy) and the metaphysical or supernatural dimensions of the legend. The latter intrudes upon the former in the shape of Faust's good angel, Ithuriel, and his bad angel, Mephisto, who appear on the domestic plane in the guise of his two friends. This ingenious and even original scheme to fuse the human and the cosmic is, however, vitiated by Weidmann's plodding talent and by the crude and maudlin style and characterization of the play. Nevertheless, it is an amusing historical anecdote that a nineteenth-century critic, Karl Engel, caused a sensation by discovering the play, which had originally been published anonymously, and identifying it (wrongly) as the lost version of Lessing's *Dr Faust*.

By now we have overrun the beginnings of Goethe's *Faust*; for by 1775, it is almost certain, the first draft of his play was written down, if only in fragmentary form. The above survey of the sources and transmission of the Faust legend cannot, and is not intended to, give information directly bearing on Goethe's conception and composition of his Faust drama, only to chart the complex history of the Faust material, and to convey some of the resonance of the legend for a young, ambitious and unusually talented poet who was beginning to exploit his creative gifts. For Goethe did not know either the original Spies *Historia* or Marlowe's *Tragical History* at the time he was engaged on the first part of his *Faust*; nor did he know anything of the historical Georg Faust. The Spies version was unknown during the eighteenth century, and Goethe appears to have read Marlowe's play for the first time only in 1818, long after the publication of *Faust I*. What is certain is that Goethe knew and loved, probably from early childhood, the puppet-play versions; in his autobiography *Dichtung und Wahrheit* (*Poetry and Truth*), looking back forty years to his youth in Frankfurt and Strasbourg, he recalls how 'the meaningful puppet-play fable' of Faust 'rang and echoed resonantly' in his mind.[19] He, too, as he recalled it from the perspective of the 60-year-old, had wrestled with all forms of learning – and had soon enough come to see the vanity of it all; he, too, had charged headlong into life – and had always returned more dissatisfied and anguished; he, too, had turned to 'mystical-cabbalistic chemistry'. And all this before the age of 22!

How far Goethe knew the Faustbooks is not entirely clear. We can certainly discount Spies and Widmann, but we know that he borrowed Pfitzer's version from the Weimar library in February and March 1801, and probably also in the previous year. Otherwise, we can only surmise that Goethe in all likelihood knew the more compact version of the Christlich Meynender, either as such or through the many cheap chapbook versions derived from it and sold at stalls, markets and fairs. So, while we can be sure that the Pfitzer version had some part in the writing of the final phase of *Faust I*, we can only assume that some version of the chapbooks informed the early *Urfaust* version and the second-phase *Faust Fragment* (See pp.25 and 30). Otto Pniower, however, has argued strenuously on the basis of textual parallels that, while the Faustbook of the Christlich Meynender, and/or its mass-circulation derivations, might well have stimulated the young Goethe's imagination, it was the Pfitzer edition that he turned to for his literary treatment of the story – and not only for the final phase of work on Faust I, but also for the *Fragment* and even the early *Urfaust* phases.[20]

It is of interest, but almost entirely speculative, to surmise what Goethe's *Faust* owes to its sources. The 'Prologue in Heaven', apart from its obvious debt to the Book of Job, and indeed to the whole *theatrum mundi* tradition, might well be an inversion of the traditional prologue in hell of the popular stage and puppet plays. Faust's opening monologue, with its rejection of the four faculties of academic scholarship, is a remarkable, if vestigial, survival of Marlowe's play through almost two centuries of increasingly garbled adaptation. There is an interesting passage in the Faustbook of the Christlich Meynender about Faust's occult studies; he reads in Zoroaster of 'ascending and descending spirits', which might have suggested Faust's macrocosmic vision of 'heavenly powers' ascending and descending in lines 447 ff. – though there are other interpretations of this passage. The motif of suicide also occurs in the Christlich Meynender version, where Faust tries to kill himself, though in a different context from that in Goethe's drama. Also interesting, with reference to the fearsome appearance of the Erdgeist, and its enigmatic parting words to Faust, is a passage of the Christlich Meynender in which Faust begs the devil to appear in a less horrifying form – whereupon the demon replies that he cannot, but will send Faust 'one who will fulfil all his heart's desires'.

The episode of Faust translating the Bible could be from Pfitzer; and the appearance of the devil in the form of a dog might be from Pfitzer or from the 1725 version. Widmann had already introduced Faust's black dog named Prestigiar, and following versions had taken it over. The figure of Mephistopheles as presented by Goethe is generally believed to have assumed some of the role or function of the clowns Hanswurst and Pickelhäring; among the salient features of Goethe's complex and multi-faceted devil are his irony, his sardonic humour, his earthy cynicism and his gift for clowning. And when Goethe's Mephisto appears at times to advise Faust in his characteristically weary and worldly-wise manner of the folly and futility of his ambitions, this too appears to be a modified survival of the often astonishingly moral sermonizing of the devil of the Faustbooks and the puppet plays; Goethe has evidently taken over and elaborated the traditional dual role of Mephistopheles as Faust's tempter and as his 'unflinching moral taskmaster'.[21] Certainly, the master–servant relationship of the traditional legend is fundamental to Goethe, too.

There is a further feature common to nearly all the traditional versions of Faust, which Goethe does not take up explicitly, but perhaps

retains vestigially – that the spirit does not enter immediately into a pact
with Faust, but claims that he must first seek permission of his master
Lucifer or Pluto. Goethe does have two 'Studierzimmer' ('Study') scenes
in Faust I – even if Mephisto gives no such specific reason for leaving
Faust in lines 1424–5. Goethe makes no use of the Marlovian struggle
between good and bad angels, nor of the 'homo fuge' motif; the only
possible trace of this tradition is in the words of the Spirit Choruses of
lines 1607 ff., and perhaps also the Easter Chorus of lines 737 ff. – the
conditions of the 'Prologue in Heaven' preclude any unequivocally
divine intervention. Goethe does not adopt the various instances in the
narrative and theatrical versions where Faust rues his pact with the
devil, and is tempted to call on God for forgiveness; nor is there any
trace in Goethe of the old man who intervenes in an attempt to save
Faust – though it is possible that Faust's encounter with Sorge (lines
11420 ff.) is a secularized echo of this call to repentance in the
traditional legend. The formal theological dimension of the legend is
secularized and internalized by Goethe into Faust's occasional bouts of
self-awareness and self-hatred and his turning on Mephisto; Goethe has
given his Faust a moral conscience, perhaps identifiable with the
'Urquell' ('primal source') mentioned by the Lord in line 324, in place
of an orthodox fear of damnation – even if the promptings of Faust's
conscience are overriden just as quickly as the fears of the traditional
Faust. Whereas earlier Fausts were made to renounce God and the
Christian faith, and were forbidden the sacraments, Goethe's Faust is
presented as an unbeliever from the start; instead, he pronounces, as it
were, the secular or humanist equivalent of this renunciation by calling
down an awesome curse on all human possessions and values in lines
1583–1606. Goethe does not include any renewal of Faust's contract
with the devil, which was a central feature of Marlowe and the
chapbooks; and, of course, he radically modifies the conditions of the
relationship between Faust and Mephistopheles by introducing a wager
in addition to their traditional pact.

The student scene of Faust I is largely Goethe's own invention,
drawing no doubt on his own experiences at Leipzig University.
However, students had figured in one way or another in the Faust
legend from its beginnings, and the motif of Mephisto masquerading in
Faust's robes and giving lectures in his place is also found in the
puppet-play tradition. The scene in Auerbachs Keller is an amalgam of
derivation and invention; the Faust legend had long been associated
with the Leipzig inn that Goethe knew well, where two murals from the
early seventeenth century (not, as the murals themselves proclaim,
from 1525) depict Faust drinking with students, his companion present

in the shape of a dog, and his exit from the cellar astride a barrel. Goethe has taken over these motifs, as well as further incidents – the conjuring of wine from tables, and the play with grapes and noses – which were present in the traditional legend from an early stage.

The Gretchen episode, as we have seen, might have been suggested by two separate accounts in Pfitzer: the student's seduction of a girl with presents, and the poor but attractive girl who takes Faust's attention. Mephisto's initial reluctance to procure Gretchen for Faust (lines 2621 ff.) might also be an echo of the chapbook and Marlovian tradition that the devil forbade Faust the marriage sacrament, providing him instead with the succubus Helen. However, the whole Gretchen episode is undoubtedly drawn from many sources and stimuli other than the traditional legend: the name of the heroine possibly from the adolescent relationship recalled by Goethe in books 5 and 6 of *Dichtung und Wahrheit*; its emotional content from his abortive affair with Friederike Brion, from the trial and public execution for infanticide of Susanna Margaretha Brandt in 1772 in Frankfurt,[22] and not least from the ballad tradition of doomed lovers, together with the flourishing contemporary idiom of domestic tragedy, which revolved around the theme of the unmarried mother more than any other.

In virtually all its substantial aspects, however, the Gretchen tragedy is Goethe's own free and creative invention. Even the 'Walpurgisnacht' scene, for which Goethe clearly drew on all manner of sources in witch trials and demonologies, has no discernible prototype in the Faust tradition – unless there are echoes of the journey to hell of the Faustbooks. The magic black horses on which Faust and Mephisto ride to Gretchen's prison could again be derived from the chapbooks – or from any number of other sources. Finally, the words of Mephisto at the very end of *Faust I*: 'She is condemned!', and the answering voice from above: 'She is saved!', might well be derived from the awesome warnings to Faust common to many puppet plays. These are delivered in the Ulm version by Mephistopheles, in others by a muffled voice: 'Fauste, praepara te! . . . Fauste, accusatus es! . . . Fauste, judicatus es! . . . Fauste, in perpetuum damnatus es!'.[23]

All the above examples of where Goethe might have drawn on the Faust sources available to him are, of course, from the first part of his drama. As far as Part Two is concerned, we are a long way from the popular, rough-hewn spirit and atmosphere of the legend that Goethe expressly contrived to retain in the first part. No such effort is made in Part Two; indeed, in a scenario for the Helen episode published in 1827, Goethe indicates that Faust's character has by now been recast and 'elevated' far beyond its primitive origins in the old fable.[24] Hence it is only the barest outlines of the traditional legend that Goethe draws on, and around which he creates an elaborate and complex allegory quite different from his treatment of the traditional material in Part One. For this rarefied symbolic action, he chooses only four basic motifs from the legendary sources – the conjuring for the Emperor of the spirits of the ancient world (Act I); Faust's infatuation with Helen, their union and their son (Acts II and III); Faust's summoning of a phantom army (Act IV); and Mephisto's marshalling of the legions of hell – fruitlessly, as it turns out – to receive Faust's soul at his death (Act V).

NOTES: CHAPTER 1

1 For sources and information on the historical Faust and the Faust legend, see Philip M. Palmer and Robert P. More, *The Sources of the Faust Tradition from Simon Magus to Lessing*; Günther Mahal, *Faust. Die Spuren eines geheimnisvollen Lebens*. For broader surveys of the literary transmission of the legend, see E. M. Butler, *The Fortunes of Faust*; Charles Dédéyan, *Le Thème de Faust dans la littérature européenne*; John W. Smeed, *Faust in Literature*.

2 See Ernst Beutler, 'Georg Faust aus Helmstadt'; Frank Baron, *Doctor Faustus: from History to Legend*, pp. 15 ff.

3 Hans Henning (ed.), *Historia von D. Johann Fausten. Neudruck des Faustbuches von 1587*, p. xxiv.

4 See Hans Henning, 'Zur Geschichte eines Faust-Motivs'.

5 See Palmer and More, *Sources of the Faust Tradition*, pp. 119 ff., and Henning, *Historia von D. Johann Fausten*, pp. liii–iv.

6 See J. Scheible (ed.), *Das Kloster. Weltlich und geistlich. Meist aus der ältern deutschen Volks-, Wunder-, Curiositäten- und vorzugsweise komischen Literatur*, Vol. 3, p. 1065.

7 See Henning, *Historia von D. Johann Fausten*, pp. 1 ff.

8 The text of the P. F. version is given in Palmer and More, *Sources of the Faust Tradition*, pp. 134 ff.

9 See Scheible, *Das Kloster*, Vol. 5, p. 479.

10 Quoted by Siegfried Szamatólski (ed.), *Das Faustbuch des Christlich Meynenden nach dem Druck von 1725*, p. xviii.

11 Christopher Marlowe, *Doctor Faustus*, ed. John D. Jump (London, 1962), p. 104.

12 See Palmer and More, *Sources of the Faust Tradition*, pp. 245 ff.; H. W. Geißler (ed.), *Gestaltungen des Faust. Die bedeutendsten Werke der Faustdichtung seit 1587*, Vol. 1, pp. 219 ff.

13 See Palmer and More, *Sources of the Faust Tradition*, pp. 251 ff.

14 'Versuch einer critischen Dichtkunst', pt 1, ch. 5, S. 19, in Gottsched, *Ausgewählte Werke*, ed. Hans-Gert Roloff (Berlin, 1968–83), Vol. 6/1, p. 241.

15 Letter of 19 Nov. 1755. See Lessing, *Werke*, ed. Herbert Göpfert (Munich, 1970–9), Vol. 2, p. 775.

16 ibid., p. 777.

17 ibid., pp. 487 ff., 778 ff.

18 'Eine Duplik', in Lessing, *Werke*, ed. Göpfert, Vol. 8, pp. 32–3.

19   GA. 10. 453–4.
20   Otto Pniower, 'Pfitzers Faustbuch als Quelle Goethes'.
21   See Osman Durrani, *Faust and the Bible: A Study of Goethe's Use of Scriptural Allusions and Christian Religious Motifs in Faust I and II*, pp. 177 ff.
22   On the striking parallels between this incident and the Gretchen tragedy, see Paul Requadt, *Goethes 'Faust I'. Leitmotivik und Architektur*, pp. 218–19.
23   See Palmer and Moore, *Sources of the Faust Tradition*, pp. 268–9.
24   GA. 5. 573.

CHAPTER 2

The Composition and Context of Goethe's *Faust*; The Relationship of the Two Parts

The writing of *Faust* spans the whole of Goethe's creative career, though it lay fallow for long intervals of time, notably between the completion of Part One in 1806 and the resumption of work on Part Two in 1825. His early fascination with the story of Faust goes back to the puppet plays of his childhood in Frankfurt; the final touches were added to the manuscript in January 1832, some two months before his death.

Goethe was born in the Free Imperial City of Frankfurt am Main, the son of a prosperous but undistinguished father and a lively-minded mother, in 1749, at a time when the Holy Roman Empire was in its final stages. He witnessed, and in his autobiography wrote an account of, the coronation of the future Emperor Joseph II as German king in Frankfurt in April 1764. His life covered a period of profound social and political change in Europe, which is clearly reflected in his *Faust*; the barbarous public execution of Gretchen for infanticide, while its fictional setting is the early sixteenth century, is equally applicable to the 'enlightened' late eighteenth century, a period whose legal and social institutions had changed only slowly since the age of the historical Faust. Indeed, it is a disquieting fact that Goethe himself, as a privy counsellor in Weimar, supported the retention of the death penalty for infanticides.

Goethe lived through the time of the Seven Years' War, the War of American Independence, and the French Revolution, with which he struggled to come to terms, acknowledging its causes without ever being able to accept its effects. He saw revolutionary France at first-hand when he accompanied Karl August of Weimar with the Duke of Brunswick's counter-revolutionary allied army into France in 1792; he witnessed that army's decisive defeat by revolutionary forces at Valmy, and the siege that ended the brief Republic of Mainz in the following year. He saw the rise of Napoleon, whom he met on three occasions and with whom he shared a mutual regard, the French invasion and occupation of the German territories, the formal dissolution of the Holy Roman Empire in 1806, and the German Wars of Liberation which culminated in the defeat of Napoleon at Leipzig in 1813; but he was unable or unwilling to share unreservedly the enthusiasm of his contemporaries, especially of the younger Romantic generation, for the liberation of Germany. The last two decades of his life were spent in the political quietism of the European Restoration after the Congress of Vienna, in the German Confederation dominated by the Austrian Foreign Minister Metternich. His final years saw the July Revolution of 1830 in Paris, to which he reacted with frank alarm, and the early beginnings of the Industrial Revolution, to which he adopted a characteristically ambivalent stance of interest and reservation.

Goethe's early studies at Leipzig University (1765–8) were cut short by a serious illness from which he convalesced slowly in Frankfurt; from these years date some of the stimuli, and even some of the dramatic material, of his early draft of Faust. During his second phase of study at Strasbourg (1770–1), he came under the seminal guidance of Johann Gottfried Herder, whose influence on Goethe's creative imagination, and in particular on the early version of Faust, was decisive. After a spell of professional legal work in Frankfurt and Wetzlar, Goethe was invited to Weimar in 1775 as the friend and confidant of the young Duke Karl August. For all his precocious fame as a writer, his appointment as privy counsellor in 1779, and even his title of nobility in 1782, the Bürger Goethe was only slowly, if ever fully, integrated into the formal court society of Weimar. Apart from his status as court poet, his duties included the supervision of the duchy's finances, military, mines, roads and agriculture, involvement in a thriving amateur theatre, and a multitude of other civic and literary activities.

Official pressures, personal entanglement, and above all an increasingly urgent commitment to classical culture prompted Goethe's abrupt escape to Italy in 1786, where he lived incognito as a painter in Rome, travelled the length of the country, and returned to Weimar after two intensely absorbing and stimulating years – during which some work was done on Faust and other major dramas. On his return, his relationship with his mistress Christiane Vulpius, who formally became his wife only in 1806, estranged him from much of Weimar society, while his literary reputation grew enormously. His experience of Italy, and his friendship and literary partnership with Schiller, promoted their struggle to establish a classical culture in Germany during the decade 1795–1805 – the period of 'Weimar Classicism'. These were the years in which he completed the first part of *Faust*, and which also saw the beginnings of his serious scientific research into optics, botany, anatomy and geology. His *Farbenlehre* (*Theory of Colours*), in which he set out to refute Newton's physics, was finally published in 1810. From 1790 to 1817 Goethe was energetically involved with the Weimar Court Theatre as general director, writer and producer.

After the death of Schiller in 1805, Weimar Classicism waned, and for a time Goethe's life entered a relatively sombre phase, during which he produced his tragic and inscrutable novel *Die Wahlverwandtschaften* (*Elective Affinities*). His subsequent life in Weimar became outwardly more formalized and routine, punctuated by visits to the Bohemian spa towns of Karlsbad and Marienbad, by the upheavals of the Wars of Liberation, by the rejuvenating experience of journeys to his native Rhineland in 1814 and 1815, and by occasional emotional attachments. His personal life became more private, even isolated, in his last twenty years, overshadowed by occasional illnesses and depressions which find only infrequent expression in his fundamentally affirmative literary work, by the death of his wife in 1816, and of his ruler and patron Karl August in 1828, by the personal and domestic difficulties of his son August, and latterly by the son's early death in Rome in 1830. Publically and intellectually, however, these years were immensely energetic and productive, involving a prodigious correspondence, interviews with a stream of visitors, a wide range of reading, and a constant output of literary and scientific work. This included studies in botany, zoology, meteorology and geology, his autobiography of the years up to 1775 (*Dichtung und Wahrheit*), the accounts of his Italian journey and the French campaign of 1792, a large and eclectic corpus of lyric poetry, the second part of his major novel *Wilhelm Meister* and, finally, the completion of the second part of *Faust*.

The minutiae of the last decade of Goethe's life were painstakingly recorded by his companion Johann Peter Eckermann, by Frédéric Soret and by other acquaintances; in particular, Eckermann records many of Goethe's conversations and pronouncements on the subject of *Faust*, above all on the second part, which was completed over the last seven years of his life. The reliability and accuracy of Eckermann's record have been questioned, not without cause; nevertheless, it is impossible to ignore or reject this large body of evidence, even if it should be treated with some caution.

Faust, if only because of its sporadic and protracted composition, can be said to reflect only erratically the literary and intellectual fashions and movements of the age of Goethe. Certainly, *Faust I* is unthinkable without the German Enlightenment, or *Aufklärung*, without the eighteenth-century tradition of domestic drama; and yet it is scarcely a typical product of the Age of Reason. The early draft form of the *Urfaust* bears clear traces of the pre-romantic *Sturm und Drang* (Storm and Stress) movement; but while *Faust I* is undoubtedly in many respects a romantic work, and while its final completion overlaps with early German Romanticism, it is not a product of the German Romantic movement as such, towards which Goethe preserved a distant and not uncritical stance. Nor does *Faust I*, on the other hand, reflect, except in very broad terms, the Weimar Classicism against which its final phase of composition was set. Paradoxically, for all the classical features of the second part, it was here that Romanticism left its mark in style, form and structure, in the theatrical irony and extravagance, in the lyricism, and in the often fantastic treatment of the subject. The operatic *Gesamtkunstwerk* of *Faust II* was not without influence on the later music dramas of Richard Wagner; and indeed much of the second part is devoted to the notion of a synthesis of the classical and the romantic, the ancient and the modern. Yet for all its eccentric 'modernity', *Faust II* is equally indebted to the traditions of Baroque theatre and spectacle, of the morality play and the *theatrum mundi*. Above all, however, its allegorical and thematic reference identifies it firmly as a product of its own age, the early nineteenth century.

THE URFAUST:
THE FIRST DRAFT

It is not possible to say when Goethe first set pen to paper on the subject of Faust; but, since he mentions his early work on the play in the same breath as *Götz von Berlichingen* and his novel *Werther*, we can assume from this and from references in correspondence that a first fragmentary draft was written down at various intervals between 1769 and 1775. This 'Frankfurt manuscript' was taken by Goethe to Weimar in 1775, and we are told that he read from it to different audiences over the next few years. It is to this that we owe any knowledge of the early form of the work; for, on completing *Faust I* in 1806, Goethe evidently destroyed his earlier manuscripts, without realizing or remembering that a lady of the Weimar court, Luise von Göchhausen, had borrowed it and copied it some time during the late 1770s. This copy, rediscovered among the Göchhausen papers by the Goethe scholar and editor Erich Schmidt in 1887, was published by him in the same year under the title *Goethes Faust* in ursprünglicher Gestalt nach der Göchhausenschen Abschrift (*Goethe's Faust in its Original Form after the Göchhausen Copy*). It became known as the *Urfaust*.

The *Urfaust* version is not a complete play in itself, and was never thought of as such by Goethe; it represents only the state of composition at the time it was copied down – though this has not prevented its frequent and successful performance on the stage. Very broadly, it comprises the Gretchen tragedy of the final version of *Faust* I, with some variations and transpositions, but without the 'Wald und Höhle' and 'Walpurgisnacht' episodes, preceded by Faust's opening monologue, the first scene with Wagner, a version of the student scene and a version of 'Auerbachs Keller' which is in prose, except for the songs and the first eight lines. The action leaves many questions unanswered; not only the exact circumstances of Valentin's death, and of Faust's adventures between that and the prison scene, but also the crucial details of Faust's introduction to Mephistopheles, and of the nature of the pact between them, are missing. Moreover, Goethe has already in the *Urfaust* introduced a motif that has muddied the critical waters ever since. The parting words of the Erdgeist in the *Urfaust*, 'You are the equal of the spirit that you grasp, not mine!', can reasonably be taken as a reference to Mephistopheles, even as an undertaking by the Erdgeist that it will send to Faust a spirit that he can comprehend. And there is a clear suggestion in the later *Urfaust* prose scene, which corresponds to the 'Trüber Tag. Feld' scene of *Faust* I, that Mephisto was sent to Faust by an 'infinite ... great, glorious spirit'. We shall return to the so-called 'Erdgeist controversy' in due course. Otherwise, while the *Urfaust* is theatrically perfectly viable, and while the Gretchen tragedy arguably works even more compellingly than in its final version of *Faust* I, where it is interrupted and retarded by several interpolated scenes, this prototype version of Part One is still bedevilled by the problem that the university scenes and the love action, the so-called 'Gelehrtentragödie' and the 'Gretchentragödie' ('scholar's tragedy' and 'Gretchen tragedy') are, largely because the former section is so sketchy and episodic, only loosely connected.

The *Urfaust* was the product of the 1770s in Germany, and it reflects as much as anything else the interests and enthusiasms stimulated by Herder and the nascent *Sturm und Drang* reaction against the more mechanistic aspects of mid-eighteenth-century rationalism on the one hand and against the slavish neo-classicism of the Leipzig school on the other. We must guard against over-crude distinctions here; the *Sturm und Drang* is unthinkable without the *Aufklärung* (Enlightenment), and indeed many literary historians will question the very term 'Storm and Stress', which was fortuitously and sensationally applied to certain short-lived aspects of late Enlightenment German literature in the 1770s. And Goethe's Faust drama, even in this initial form, is itself a product of the Enlightenment, of the literary, religious and intellectual emancipation of the middle-class intelligentsia in Germany, with its attendant literary forms – specifically, that of domestic drama.

Nevertheless, the inherent titanism of the figure and theme of Faust, the fascination of the genius or hero beyond the common run of humanity, the arrogant and amoral self-assertion of an intellectual giant, the defiant Prometheanism and the mythical symbolism of the Faust material – these are the elements of the Faust legend that appealed to the young Goethe, rather than the theological and intellectual allegory that, as far as we can judge, Lessing had intended to work into his Faust drama. The creative and literary models of the young Goethe were worlds away from the canonical Gallic neo-classicism advocated, indeed prescribed, by Gottsched and his school, and far enough, too, from Lessing's own reworking of Aristotelian poetics in his theoretical and dramatic works. The colossal impact of Shakespeare on the younger generation of this decade is attested in Goethe's euphoric *Rede zum Schäkespears Tag* (*Speech for Shakespeare's Anniversary*) of 1771, in Herder's Shakespeare essay, and in J. M. R. Lenz's dramaturgy; and it is exemplified equally extravagantly in Goethe's *Götz von Berlichingen* – which overlaps with the beginnings of the *Urfaust*. And while Gerstenberg, Wieland, Eschenburg and Lessing himself had played a major part in the introduction of Shakespeare to the educated German public, it was Herder and the *Sturm und Drang* that championed an informal, anti-classical, 'open' form of drama on what they perceived to be the Shakespearian model: a contemptuous disregard for the dramatic unities; a vision of Shakespearian drama as unvarnished nature, and of Shakespeare as the 'interpreter of nature in all her tongues', as 'only and always the servant of nature';[1] and an exuberant response to the poetic appeal of Shakespeare's apparently chaotic universe, which was fused into an organic whole by the creative power of the poet. Whatever violence it may have done to Shakespeare's aesthetic, this was the model that informed Goethe's early plays and fragments.

It was also Herder who stimulated in Goethe a cultural enthusiasm for German history, turning his attention towards the fifteenth and sixteenth centuries, to figures like Dürer, Maximilian I, Luther and Hans Sachs, to the robust language of the vernacular Bible, to the idiom of *Knittelvers*, to the national past of an Empire that was even then tottering on its foundations, and was only a generation away from final extinction in Goethe's youth. It was this enthusiastic and, to be sure, chauvinistic perception of the religious, artistic and literary vigour of the German

Renaissance and Reformation that Goethe held up as a mirror to his own age; and it produced, among other things, his Götz von Berlichingen – a Shakespearian chronicle drama based on a somewhat fanciful historicism and on the heavily partisan autobiography of the embittered and disillusioned Gottfried von Berlichingen – and his poetic and symbolic treatment of the shadowy figure who haunted the cultural fringes of early sixteenth-century Germany, Faust.

Herder was also responsible for another major influence on the style and content, perhaps also on the structure, of the Urfaust. The Sturm und Drang assertion of nature against sophistication, of creative originality and freshness against academic and derivative formalism, had found its most vivid formulation in Herder's essay 'Über Oßian und die Lieder alter Völker' ('On Ossian and the Songs of Ancient Peoples') which opened the Sturm und Drang manifesto, Von deutscher Art und Kunst (On German Character and Art). This rhapsodic treatise affected contemporary aesthetic values and perceptions and, above all through Goethe, infused the folksong idiom into German poetry of the time. As in his judgement of Shakespeare, it is the 'spirit of nature' that is for Herder the overriding characteristic of the poetry of unsophisticated peoples, of the bards and minstrels, of the sagas and epics, of Homer and Ossian – that is, of poetry before 'art came and extinguished nature'.[2] Uncritical, unsystematic and indeed plain wrong as many of these assumptions were, the effect was radical; and Goethe, encouraged by Herder to pillage the Alsatian countryside for folksongs from the mouths of ancient peasants, also transformed the material he found into the seemingly artless songs that are part of German literature: 'Heidenröslein' and 'Der König in Thule' are two outstanding examples, one of which was actually incorporated into the Urfaust. The story of Faust and Gretchen shows, among other literary influences, the traces of the Sturm und Drang perception of the folk-ballad tradition – in its frank treatment of a classic story, in the 'Sprünge und Würfe', the gaps and leaps in the action, that Herder had recognized as a salient characteristic of popular poetry, the 'aerugo' or patina, the weathering effect of oral transmission.[3] It has, indeed, been suggested that Goethe changed the name of the traditional Johann Faust to Heinrich because 'Heinrich and Margarete' are names redolent of the ballad tradition.[4] For all the metaphysical and theological dimensions of the Faust legend, it was a combination of the lyrical idiom of folksong, the robust vulgarity of the stage tradition and the popular appeal of the chapbook narratives that Goethe was at pains to preserve in his original drafts – in short, what he vividly termed the 'woodcut-like' character of the sixteenth-century fable.[5]

A further major factor that attracted Goethe to the Faust legend was his interest in what he called, in *Dichtung und Wahrheit*, 'mystisch-kabbalistische Chemie' – an early enthusiasm which, he tells us, he was careful to conceal from Herder's sarcastic attention.[6] Goethe's lifelong preoccupation with alchemy and astrology, with the mystical and hermetic traditions of the Middle Ages and the Renaissance, is generally believed to have been stimulated by his close relationship with a pietistic friend of his mother, Susanna von Klettenberg, during the period of convalescence in Frankfurt from the illness that had cut short his studies at Leipzig. Together with this sympathetic companion, who, as Goethe put it in his retrospective autobiographical account, had 'inoculated him with the disease' of cabbalistic science, he explored the hermetic and neo-Platonist writings: Welling's *Opus mago-cabbalisticum*, Basilius Valentinus, Paracelsus, the *Aurea Catena Homeri*, and Gottfried Arnold's *Unparteiische Kirchen- und Ketzerhistorie*. Even the physician treating his illness, according to Goethe, dabbled in herbal medicines and alchemical preparations, which he (illegally) dispensed himself and administered to receptive or interested patients, along with 'certain mystical chemical and alchemical books'.[7]

It is likely that Goethe's interest in Paracelsus, Agrippa and other hermetic writings predates this convalescent period of 1768–9; and, while it was probably during this period that he actually practised experiments in the field of alchemy and proto-chemistry, his interest in and knowledge of alchemy, astrology, neo-Platonism and hermetic mysticism extended through his whole life and, in one way or another, informed much of his creative and theoretical writing – to some degree, at least, Goethe was not unlike Newton. Just how far he ever believed in any literal sense in the truth or efficacy of such theory or practice is difficult to say; what is certain is that, well after his early interest in that tradition as an 'imaginatively serious phenomenon',[8] he retained a strong sense of the symbolism and poetic resonance of alchemy and astrology, and that his use of such material is informed and authoritative, whether he is drawing on it to convey the 'authenticity' of visions and magical incantations (*Faust*, lines 430 ff., 1271 ff.), whether he is using it for overtly satirical or sarcastic purposes (lines 1034 ff., 4955 ff., 6819 ff.), or whether he is exploiting it for allegorical and symbolic reference in his *Märchen (Fairy Tale)*, or in the figure of Homunculus in *Faust II*.

One further literary tradition should be mentioned in connection with the *Urfaust*: that of domestic tragedy, or *bürgerliches Trauerspiel*. This relatively new tragic genre, the literary precipitation of the growing economic power and assertion of the middle classes in the eighteenth century, had found its way into Germany from England and France under the influence of Lillo, Diderot and Mercier; and it was Lessing

who, struggling to establish a native theatrical tradition in defiance of
the prescriptive neo-classicism of Gottsched's Leipzig school, had
devised in his *Hamburgische Dramaturgie* the theoretical framework for
domestic realism in the drama.

It is by no means clear how far Goethe in his *Urfaust* was writing
consciously or unconsciously within the tradition of *bürgerliches Trauerspiel*. For all the homely domesticity of parts of the Gretchen tragedy,
there is not a great deal of common ground, apart from the basic story
of the seduction of a simple girl by a 'gentleman', and of the ensuing
pregnancy, abandonment and infanticide, between Goethe's treatment of the theme and the social drama of his contemporaries.
Certainly, Lessing's criterion of characters who are 'of the same stuff' as
the audience – 'mit uns von gleichem Schrot und Korne'[9] – can scarcely
be applied to Faust, let alone to Mephistopheles. And we see little
enough of Gretchen's family in the *Urfaust* – though Valentin's rigid sense
of family honour and respectability is consistent enough with a line of
domestic autocrats from Lessing's Odoardo Galotti or Wagner's Meister
Humbrecht to Schiller's musician Miller. We know Gretchen's petty-
bourgeois milieu largely by hearsay from her own account, from Faust's
sentimentalized perceptions, or – most briefly, but vividly – from the
censorious gossip of Lieschen at the well. Nevertheless, the milieu and
its ethos are there; and it is precisely the homely idyll of this circumscribed domestic world that attracts Faust's restless and destructive
temperament and creates the collision of divergent social, psychological, intellectual and sexual assumptions that is given powerful expression in the violent imagery of mountain torrent and alpine hut in Faust's
speech of lines 1411 ff. (*Faust I*, 3345 ff.). But if this is domestic drama,
it is domestic drama with a supernatural dimension; and the *Urfaust*
remains a hybrid and fragmentary work, the two distinct elements of
'Gelehrtentragödie' and 'Gretchentragödie' being juxtaposed, and only
to a certain extent integrated.

FAUST. EIN FRAGMENT:
THE PUBLISHED FRAGMENT

The second major phase of work on *Faust* overlaps with a momentous
experience in Goethe's life, his Italian journey of 1786–8. He had
entered into a contract with his publisher Göschen for an edition of his
works; and this was no doubt why, even on his apparently precipitate
departure from Karlsbad for Rome (in fact, a plan long since devised
and cherished), he took with him to Italy a number of uncompleted
projects, among which was the 'Frankfurt manuscript' of *Faust*, or at

least a form of it. It is not possible to establish how much, or exactly
which, new material Goethe wrote in Italy, and how much was written
after his return to Weimar in 1788. It is often assumed, largely on formal
grounds, that the scenes 'Hexenküche' and 'Wald und Höhle', or
parts of them, were completed in Italy; but this is inconclusive, since
Goethe made every effort to think himself back some fifteen years in
order to integrate the new material into the Urfaust version – as he put it
in a letter from Italy in 1788, if he 'smoked the paper', no one should be
able to distinguish the new material from the old.[10]

The Fragment drops the atmospheric little scene 'Land Strase' ('Country Road') that prefaced the Gretchen tragedy in the Urfaust, and, sadly,
removes some of the more robust vulgarities of the student scene.
'Auerbachs Keller' is recast in verse; more significantly, Faust now, in
contrast to the earlier version, takes virtually no part in the pranks,
standing silently by as Mephisto performs them in his stead. The new
'Hexenküche' ('Witch's Kitchen') scene is written in to help to bridge
the Urfaust gap between the university scenes and the Gretchen tragedy;
it also appears to contain, as we shall show in the commentary below,
some allusive references to the contemporary political situation in
France. The most significant additions in the Fragment are: the hundred
lines of dialogue between Faust and Mephisto, corresponding to lines
1770–867 of Faust I; a further twenty-two lines of dialogue after the
student scene (Faust I, lines 2051–72); and the hybrid 'Wald und Höhle'
('Forest and Cavern') scene, which incorporates Faust's violent tirade of
self-hatred that had, in the Urfaust, been placed after the Valentin scene
(Faust I, lines 3342–69). The Faust-Mephisto dialogue still tells us nothing
of the means by which Mephistopheles was introduced to Faust, nor of
the nature of the pact between them.

Otherwise, the most striking feature of the Fragment is that it breaks off
abruptly at the end of the cathedral scene – in spite of the fact that
Valentin's first monologue, and the last three scenes 'Trüber Tag. Feld'
('Dreary Day: Field'), 'Nacht. Offen Feld' ('Night: Open Country') and
'Kerker' ('Dungeon') had already been written in the Urfaust. It seems
that Goethe felt there was a gap in the action at this point that needed to
be filled; it was the gap into which he later wrote the 'Walpurgisnacht'.
The Fragment was published in volume 7 of Goethe's works, the Schriften,
by Göschen in 1790.

FAUST. DER TRAGÖDIE ERSTER TEIL:
THE TRAGEDY, PART ONE

It was largely at Schiller's prompting that Goethe resumed work on the

third and final phase of *Faust* I. As early as 1794, Schiller had begged
Goethe to let him see the unpublished material relating to the *Fragment*,
which he described as a 'torso of Hercules'.[11] It was not until June 1797,
however, that Goethe felt inclined to resume serious work on *Faust*, and
he made a revealing remark in a letter to Schiller of 22 June that year.
Their common interest in the ballad form, he said, had brought him
back to this 'hazy and misty path' – 'diesen Dunst- und Nebelweg'. It
seems it was the impetus of their collaboration on the ballad, one of
Goethe's early *Sturm und Drang* enthusiasms, that led him back to his
Faust material; but this remark also betrays the effort of will and
imagination required, now even more than some ten years previously,
to think himself back into the alien, unclassical material of the Faust
legend. 'Dunst und Nebel', a phrase suggestive of what now seemed to
him the immature and confused time of his initial preoccupation with
the theme, are indeed the very words he uses in the dedicatory poem
'Zueignung', also written in 1797, with which *Faust* opens, and in which
he describes his ambivalent feelings at resuming work on the popular
and romantic subject of Faust: blurred memories and figures from
earlier times rise around him 'out of haze and mist' (line 6).

Schiller had also, as he so often did, urged Goethe to impose on the
episodic and heterogeneous material of his earlier drafts the conceptual
unity of an overall symbolic idea. For all its poetic individuality, Schiller
wrote, the drama required a symbolic dimension; the demands of the
theme were both poetic and philosophical, and, whether he liked it or
not, the nature of the subject would impose on Goethe a philosophical
treatment – his imagination 'would have to adapt itself to the service of
a conceptual idea'.[12] With characteristic critical acumen, Schiller diag-
nosed the inherent problems of the *Urfaust* and *Fragment* versions: the
problem of unity, the imbalance between the tragedy of Faust and the
tragedy of Gretchen, the tension between the representative and the
individual status of the central figure, and the lack of a clear, indeed of
any, metaphysical or symbolic superstructure for the disparate experiences of Faust. And while Goethe may have chafed under Schiller's
insistence that he should submit his poetic imagination to a conceptual
framework; while he may subsequently have declared that there is no
single 'idea' – such as the issue of Faust's salvation – that informs 'the
whole and each particular scene';[13] while he may have protested that,
unlike Schiller, who was one of those 'who work too much from the
idea',[14] he himself had never striven for abstraction, or sought to hang
his works 'on the meagre thread of a single consistent idea' – nevertheless, it seems that Goethe was not unresponsive to Schiller's strictures
and observations. It was no doubt in part due to Schiller's advice that in

1797 Goethe wrote, apart from the opening dedicatory poem, the two scenes 'Prelude in the Theatre' and 'Prologue in Heaven' that encapsulate the dramatic action of Faust within a wider framework.

It was over the next three or four years that Goethe went on to complete Faust I; and we can assume that he had by now some idea of contriving Faust's ultimate salvation, even if the final stages of the process were not to be fully formulated until some twenty-five years later. Above all, what he referred to as the 'great gap ('große Lücke')[15] of the pact and wager scene was filled out in a way which, in conjunction with the issues raised in the 'Prologue in Heaven', leaves open the possibility, if it does not suggest the probability, of Faust's redemption. Also added was the first 'Studierzimmer' ('Study') scene, detailing the introduction of Mephistopheles, and, as a prelude to this, the 'suicide' scene (lines 606–807) and the 'Easter Walk', or 'Vor dem Tor', scene. A further odd, and not entirely happy, change in the construction of Faust I was the transposition of the 'Wald und Höhle' scene to an earlier stage in the Gretchen episode – as it seems, to the time before her seduction by Faust, rather than after, as in the Fragment. The problems and implications of this shift are discussed in the commentary below. The Valentin scene (the brief monologue of the Urfaust had disappeared from the Fragment) was now reintroduced, but before the cathedral scene, not after it as it had been in the Urfaust; and it was extended to include Valentin's death and his denunciation of Gretchen. No doubt the dramatic sequence was thereby improved, since Valentin's curse, and his death, lend added force to the awesome and claustrophobic scene in the cathedral, where Gretchen's guilt and remorse overwhelm her; moreover, this crisis is also now directly followed by the nightmarish 'Walpurgisnacht' – a powerful transition exploited by many producers of the play.

The 'Walpurgisnacht' was a further important addition to the dramatic and theatrical dimensions of the work; the same cannot be said of the feeble satirical intermezzo, 'Walpurgisnachtstraum', or 'The Golden Wedding of Oberon and Titania'. There is, however, some evidence, to which we shall return later, that Goethe originally planned a rather different form and function for the 'Walpurgisnacht', which was to have been integrated more closely with the fate of Gretchen. The remaining principal alteration undertaken in the final writing of Faust I was the versification and revision of the final 'Kerker' scene. This scene was recast in verse, as Goethe wrote to Schiller, in order to mitigate the direct effect of such harrowing material.[16] But if the final version is any less harrowing than the Urfaust scene, this is due not so much to the change from prose to verse as such but rather to the consequential

changes and extensions in the text – the revised version is less starkly
economical in expression than the *Urfaust* scene. Presumably for the
same reason – in order to introduce a note of reconciliation into the
stark human tragedy of Gretchen – Goethe added the theatrical assurance of her salvation in the voice from above, answering Mephisto's 'Sie
ist gerichtet!' with: 'Ist gerettet!'.

For all his intensive work on *Faust* I between 1797 and 1801, it was
another five years before Goethe brought himself to a final revision –
ironically enough, after Schiller's death. Political disruption in Germany,
the Napoleonic invasion and occupation of most of the German
territories, further delayed its publication until 1808, when it appeared
as Volume 8 of the Cotta edition of the Collected Works (*Goethes Werke*).
A further interesting feature of Goethe's work on *Faust* around 1800 is a
poem entitled 'Abschied' ('Farewell'),[17] which, also written in four
stanzas of *ottava rima*, was evidently intended to serve as an epilogue
balancing the formally identical poem 'Zueignung'. Whereas the prefatory poem had described Goethe's mixed feelings at resuming work on
the intractable subject of Faust, the valedictory 'Abschied' expresses
his unequivocal break with the literary and emotional confusions of his
youthful masterpiece. Goethe looks back from the present vantage-
point of his high classicism, from present clarity, to the narrow and
barbarous circle of magic and superstition, to the obscure German past
that had been the creative context for *Faust* I. It is clear from this poem
and from Goethe's correspondence that, for all the care he took to fuse
the new material of this third phase of composition with the earlier
versions, he felt profoundly out of sympathy with what he frequently
refers to as 'this barbaric composition', 'the nordic phantoms', 'nordic
barbarism', 'this witches' product'.[18] What is remarkable is not so much
that Goethe left certain loose ends untied in his final version of *Faust* I –
the Erdgeist question, the 'Walpurgisnacht' and its odd sequel, or the
whole question of Faust's salvation – but rather that he should have
brought it to any kind of completion.

The poem 'Abschied' does not, however, as is often assumed on the
evidence of its first stanza, mark Goethe's intention at the time of
breaking completely with the subject of Faust – though it was to lie
dormant for some twenty years after 1806, and it was indeed fortuitous
enough that the second part was eventually completed. In fact, this
'epilogue' might even have been conceived as a prologue to the
projected second part, for in the following stanzas he talks, not of
abandoning the subject, but only of turning his back on the 'emotional
confusion', on the 'narrow circle of barbarities and magic', and of
redirecting his vision in place and time away from the violent political

convulsions of the present day: eastwards towards Greece, and backwards to the ancient world. This is not only in general terms an expression of Goethe's philhellene high classicism of the decade 1795-1805; it can also be taken as a specific reference to the dramatic fragment also written in 1800, entitled 'Helen in the Middle Ages' (Helena im Mittelalter. Satyr-Drama. Episode zu Faust).[19] These 269 lines of dialogue between Helen, her chorus and Phorcyas correspond to the opening section of the third act of Faust II (lines 8489–802), which was rewritten in 1825–6 when Goethe once again resumed work on Faust.

It is extraordinary to us, now, how patronizingly and dismissively Goethe treated, or at least appeared to treat, the work that has come to be regarded as his undisputed masterpiece; and it is odd to recall that at the time he seemed to regard Faust I as no more important, even as less important, than his preoccupation with classical aesthetics or his scientific research into optics. This is not to suggest that he failed to take Faust I seriously; after all, he did finally complete the project, if only with a considerable effort, and he took great pains to organize the 'barbarous' material and to give the work, which by its very nature tended towards a chaotic linear formlessness, an overall theatrical, theological and metaphysical framework. Critics who detect in the 'Hexenküche' or the 'Walpurgisnacht' sections an ironical or disdainful dimension absent from the Urfaust version may well be correct; but they are judging with the hindsight allowed by the discovery of the Göchhausen manuscript.

Nor can it be conclusively argued that Goethe, in giving the final version of Faust I a quasi-Christian framework, was thereby wholly ironizing or demystifying the religious assumptions that, for him, were largely responsible for the diabolistic trappings of the traditional legend. It is of course true that Goethe was no orthodox Christian believer; it is true that for all his earlier and later admiration for the Reformer, he deplored Luther's vision of a world infested by devils;[20] it is true that the 'old heathen', above all in his commitment to pagan classical culture and civilization, regarded Christianity with more or less baleful mistrust and suspicion – especially in its more extreme manifestations among the younger generation of German Romantics; and it is true that he described the Middle Ages in a letter to Iken as a period of 'monkish barbarism',[21] and in Faust II as a 'benighted age of chivalry and clericalism' (lines 6924 ff.). But Goethe knew and acknowledged – indeed, this recognition underlies the very fabric of Faust II – that he was, willy-nilly, the product of a Western, Germanic and Christian tradition. And for all his nostalgic Hellenism, he acknowledged that ancient Greece was an ideal – an imperishable ideal, but an irrecoverable one. Even at his

Hellenic perihelion, as it were, at the time of his greatest attachment
to classicism and his furthest alienation from Christian and Germanic
traditions, precisely at the time of writing the 'Prologue in Heaven' and
the 'große Lücke' scenes of Faust I, he still retained a sufficient empathy
with Christian systems to use them, in however heterodox and symbolic a manner, for the metaphysical superstructure of Faust. No one
without such an imaginative and empathetic understanding could have
written the scene in which Faust, for all his lack of true faith, is held back
from suicide by the traditional sounds and associations of Easter, the
scene in which Faust seeks revelation from his translation of St John's
Gospel, Faust's 'catechism' to Gretchen, or the passages that reveal
Gretchen's anguished religiosity.

Goethe was to return to Christian models, too, for the final scenes of
the drama because, as he put it, he needed to give a firm delineation to
his poetic intentions if he was not to lose himself in vague spiritual
abstractions.[22] He does not appear to have believed in the literal truth of
his Christian theological material any more than he believed in the
occult or hermetic systems, or indeed in the classical myth, that he drew
on in his Faust; he exploited all these systems for his own purposes, and
more especially Christianity, because it provided a richly resonant and
above all a familiar corpus of iconography and doctrine.

FAUST. DER TRAGÖDIE ZWEITER TEIL: THE TRAGEDY, PART TWO

The history of the composition of Faust II is not nearly as tortuous or as
protracted as that of the first part. Apart from the fragment Helena im
Mittelalter, there is some evidence that Goethe thought out, and might
also have written down, some sections of the last act relating to Faust's
salvation in or around 1800; but between 1806 and 1824 he did virtually
nothing further on the subject, except to dictate in 1816 a scenario
which evidently represents his original conception of the second part.[23]
This is a rather bizarre romance in which the broad lines of Acts I–III are
in part discernible, together with one or two motifs from Act IV. While
the setting is the Germany of Maximilian I, Helen is magically conjured
from Hades within the fairy-tale, medieval context of a castle whose
owner is crusading in Palestine. The son of Faust and Helen strays
beyond the limits of the enchanted castle, and is killed by 'a consecrated
sword'. After the disappearance of Helen and her son, monks attack the
castle, but with the help of Mephistopheles and his three henchmen
Raufebold, Habebald and Haltefest, Faust avenges his son's death and
wins great estates.

It is not until 1825, however, that any serious attempt to resume work is recorded; and once again, the external stimulus was Goethe's preparation of his works for publication by Cotta in the Complete Works, the *Vollständige Ausgabe letzter Hand*. No doubt Eckermann's persistent urgings for a second part were also a factor. In 1825 Goethe worked on some sections of Act V, but this was soon abandoned in favour of Act III; the death of Byron at Missolonghi in May 1824 may well have been the stimulus to modify the Helen episode of the 1816 scenario, and to use the 1800 Helen fragment as the starting point for an episode which, as he later wrote to his friends, spans 3,000 years of history from the fall of Troy to the Greek Wars of Liberation.[24] Completed by June 1826, what was to be the third act of *Faust* II was published separately in 1827 in volume 4 of the *Ausgabe letzter Hand* as 'Helena. Klassisch-romantische Phantasmagorie. Zwischenspiel zu *Faust*' ('Helen: Classical-Romantic Phantasmagoria: Interlude to *Faust*').

From May 1827 Goethe began to work systematically on what he now designated his 'Hauptgeschäft', his 'principal task' – the completion of *Faust* II. Much of the first act (up to line 6036) was completed by January 1828, and these scenes were published that Easter, appended to the text of *Faust* I in volume 12 of the *Ausgabe letzter Hand*; this was the last section of the drama of which Goethe actually saw the publication. By the first weeks of 1830 Act I was complete, and Act II was also written during that year – substantially by June, but with later additions in December. The beginning of Act V (the Philemon and Baucis episode) was ready by May 1831; this was grafted on to the earlier material dating from 1825, and possibly also from 1800. Act IV was written in the first half of 1831, and the whole manuscript was ready by 22 July. It was sealed, though it was reopened, and some alterations were made, in January 1832. *Faust. Der Tragödie zweiter Teil* was published posthumously in 1832 in volume 41 of the *Ausgabe letzter Hand*.

THE RELATIONSHIP OF THE
TWO PARTS

It was no small thing, as Goethe remarked, to complete in his eighty-second year a work conceived in his twentieth.[25] Naturally enough, he saw his whole Faust drama as a single entity, and insisted on more than one occasion that he had carried the second part within him as an 'inner fable' for many years; indeed, we have seen that, even at the point of breaking with the past 'barbarities' of *Faust* I, he was already planning, and even executing in some detail, the classical episodes of the second part. He was, on the other hand, fully aware that *Faust* I and *Faust* II did not constitute a closely unified work in any conventional dramatic or even thematic sense; and he stressed not only the distance between the Faust of the 'old, rude folk tale' and his recasting of the figure in *Faust* I but also the further extension and elaboration of Faust's character in the second part. The first part, said Goethe, had represented a man who, confined and ill at ease within his earthly limitations, considered the highest knowledge and the finest possessions inadequate to satisfy his aspirations, who therefore remained dissatisfied and discontented in all areas of his experience. In the second part, on the other hand, he had aimed to elevate his material beyond this previous 'wretched sphere of experience', and to show such a man in 'higher regions', to lead him through 'more worthy circumstances'.[26]

Such views and intentions may well have been coloured by Goethe's somewhat patronizing retrospective opinion of his youthful work; but time and again he stressed the differences between the two parts in conception and intention. The second part, he wrote, could not and should not have been as fragmentary as the first; it engaged the mind more than the first part, and was designed for the rational reader; the story was more conceptual, wherever the imagination of the poet might lead it. The second part dealt with the 'splendid, real and fantastic' errors of a man, experienced in a 'nobler, worthier, higher' sense than in the 'common' first part. The first part dealt with the specific; the second tended towards the 'generic'.[27] The first part was 'almost entirely subjective'; it concerned a constricted, more passionate individual; the second part was more objective, revealing a 'higher, wider, brighter, less passionate world'.[28]

Whatever Goethe might have meant precisely by these categories, it is clear that he himself regarded the two parts as very different, though by no means separate, parts of a whole. This is not to deny any overall unity or continuity between the two parts, whether structural or formal, dramatic or thematic. Quite clearly, there are echoes and cross-references between them; the figures of Faust and Mephistopheles are common to both parts; the human action is encapsulated within the framework of the 'Prologue in Heaven', even within the 'Prelude in the Theatre', and within the terms of the pact and wager between Faust and Mephisto. The second part represents Faust's experiences in the 'wide world' after the 'narrow world' of Part One, according to the undertaking given to Faust by Mephistopheles in line 2052. But the unity or continuity of the whole, however it is defined, does not alter the fact that the two parts are very different in kind, in structure and characterization, in literary idiom and style, in scope and treatment.

To be sure, Faust I itself was scarcely a conventional dramatic structure; the theatrum mundi framework, the episodic and open construction, the huge variety of language and verse forms, the supernatural elements, the mixture of farce and pathos, the loose ends and the drastic plunges and leaps of the dramatic line, the interpolation of ephemeral and satirical allusions – all this had distinguished Part One from any single contemporary dramatic tradition, in particular from tragédie classique on the one hand and bürgerliches Trauerspiel on the other. Indeed, only a very liberal conception even of Shakespearian drama could be given as the model for Faust I. Nevertheless, the first part, at least in the Gretchen tragedy, can be said to have remained fundamentally within the Aristotelian canon of the theatre, if not in any formal or structural sense, then at least in the sense that it demands, and relies upon, an empathetic emotional response from its audience or reading public. Faust II, on the other hand, demands and relies on a very different reaction; as Goethe suggested, the mind and the intellect, indeed the learning and the education, of the reader are engaged, rather than his emotions. The action is abstract, literary and allegorical rather than sensuous, dramatic and mimetic.

The characterization of the main figures changes accordingly. As Goethe also intimated, the Faust of the first part is a passionate, subjective individual who moves in what Goethe calls the 'Halbdunkel' ('twilight') of a relatively realistic environment. To be sure, the Faust of the first part is a dual personality, both renegade intellectual and young lover; of course he has, over and above his specific human individuality, a representative function. The action is both naturalistic and symbolic; if Faust is not Everyman, he stands in some measure for human curiosity and aspirations, however exceptional his situation and his opportunities. The Faust of the second part, however, while not entirely purged of human individuality, is far removed from the psychologically differentiated and motivated personality of the first part; he is no longer an individual in a dramatic context but an emblematic figure whose epic experiences are not those of any single person but rather those of modern Western man, just as the whole action of Faust II is an allegorical representation of certain areas of Western European history and culture within the scope of Goethe's knowledge and experience. The Faust of Part One had been a recognizable human and emotional figure – that is, within all the limits and qualifications of dramatic and aesthetic reality; Gretchen, even more so, had responded in terms of normal dramatic psychology. There is little of that in the Faust or the Helen of Part Two. Faust appears in a series of roles, each determined by the symbolic or allegorical context in which he moves: as Plutus, as court financier and necromancer, as a travelling philhellene, as a crusading knight, as the military arm of the Empire, as trader, civil engineer and colonist – in short, as a composite historical figure. Helen, similarly, is a composite, symbolic and emblematic figure playing out an extended and complex allegory of the reception of classical culture by the modern Western imagination.

The same principle applies to many other characters. Frau Marthe, Valentin, the peasants and the townsfolk of Part One belong to dramatic naturalism; the Student, too, and even Wagner, for all his function as representative of academic traditions, are situated within a relatively realistic context. The same is scarcely true of the Baccalaureus or of Wagner in Part Two, where their representative function dominates; and the figures of Homunculus and Euphorion, of Chiron and Proteus, of the Emperor and his court, have their symbolic functions within the historical and cultural allegories of Faust II. Mephistopheles, certainly, was hardly a character of conventional dramatic psychology even in the first part; his reactions and his behaviour are determined not by any human motivation but by his cosmic or dramatic function as tempter or clown, adversary or companion of Faust, and his protean role goes far beyond the normal pattern of human or even diabolic behaviour. But in Faust II Mephistopheles also appears in a far wider range of guises and masks adapted to the allegorical context: as court jester, as Zoilo-Thersites, as Avaritia, as Cagliostro, as Sheherezade, as Old Iniquity, as Phorcyas, as Faust's 'military adviser', as his bailiff and agent, and finally once more in burlesque as the Satan of traditional superstition. He also appears as stage prompter, as répétiteur and manipulator of the action. His function as tempter and negator is preserved, as are his roles as mock sermonizer and moralist, as humorist and wit, as jester and cynical commentator; but the scope and variety of these roles are vastly broadened, consistent with the shift of the drama on to a wider 'generic' and symbolic level.

Eckermann suggested – and Goethe evidently concurred in the notion – that the various episodes of Faust II formed self-contained worlds of their own, which were not connected by any dramatic causality, but were linked only as the separate adventures and experiences of the central figure; this, Eckermann added, was similar to the structure of the Odyssey or Gil Blas.[29] The allusion to an epic structure is interesting; for Goethe and Schiller had, at the time of the final composition of Part One, discussed and corresponded on the subject of epic and dramatic poetry in some detail. The dramatic action, they suggest in their collaborative essay on epic and dramatic poetry, is a tightly knit sequence of events that proceeds precipitately towards its conclusion; the broader and more deliberate progress of the epic dwells on the significance of separate episodes, developing them and elaborating them in a way the drama cannot. Drama tends towards naturalism, the mimetic imitation of reality, while the interest of epic is in its broader, more detached narrative perspective depicting an individual's active involvement in wider affairs.[30]

Now, while it is clear that, as well as the relentless causality of dramatic action, the first part of Faust includes episodes of epic breadth, reiteration and 'retardation' – for example, in the 'Vor dem Tor', 'Wald und Höhle' and 'Walpurgisnacht' scenes – it is equally clear that in the second part the epic dimension, as Goethe and Schiller understood it, dominates, and even supersedes, the dramatic. It is true that Faust II, unlike Faust I, is divided into five 'acts'. On the other hand, these five acts have little enough discernible causality in dramatic terms, except on the most tenuous level: for example, that the inflation engineered by Faust and Mephisto in Act I precipitates the bankruptcy and rebellion that allow Faust to intervene and save the Empire in Act IV; or that Faust's intervention in Act IV leads to his enfeoffment with the coastal territories that he develops in Act V – a dramatic link that Goethe did not even think necessary to present on stage. If the dramatic structure of Faust II is sporadic and fortuitous, however, the broad epic structure, based, as I hope to demonstrate below, on the historical allegory informing the action of the second part, is altogether more consistent and satisfactory.

If Part One was influenced in its form and structure more than anything else by the 'open' form of Shakespearian drama, or at least by the Sturm und Drang perception of it, Part Two in many respects manifests the theatricality of the symbolic drama of the Spanish Baroque, the operatic spectacles and transformations, the mannerism and the allegory of Calderón.[31] While remaining essentially theatrical, Faust II stretches the scope and resources of the stage to the limit – and perhaps beyond. Neither development of character nor continuity of dramatic action constitute the principal unity of the second part; perspectives of time and place shift constantly, and the Gesamtkunstwerk draws on a whole range of available forms of entertainment and spectacle: on the trionfo and allegorical review, on pageant, masque, music, choreography and the visual arts.

As I have tried to show, the Urfaust was the product of Goethe's youthful enthusiasms and cultural stimuli. In the Fragment and Faust I, he built on and extended this basic material, he overlaid it with a philosophical or theological framework, but without obscuring it. Historically speaking,

Faust I remains essentially a product of the eighteenth century, of the Germany of Gottsched and Lessing and Frederick the Great, of Europe before the French Revolution, before the Napoleonic invasion of Germany, before the formal demise of the German Empire and before the Romantic movement in German literature. Even if the later stages of its composition overlap with some of these events, it scarcely reflects them, except for some of the political and satirical references in the 'Hexenküche' and the 'Walpurgisnachtstraum'. Indeed, in many ways Faust I predates Goethe's own classicism, even if its completion is almost synchronous with the decade of Weimar Classicism; Goethe himself testified how alien the theme and its treatment had been to him during that decade.

Faust II, on the other hand, is essentially a product of the nineteenth century. It was written after the French Revolution, and, with the exception of the opening of Act III, which is a monument to Goethe's philhellene classicism, after the dissolution of the Holy Roman Empire, after the defeat of Napoleon and the Restoration in France and Germany. It was written on the eve of the Industrial Revolution; it even covers the period of the 1830 July Revolution in France – and Goethe, at the age of 80, watched with great alarm that political upheaval, the shock-waves of which even reached Weimar, though in very attenuated form. Faust II was also written after the main impulse of German romanticism had spent itself, and well after Goethe had seen the high-minded but precarious classicism carefully and energetically nurtured by himself and Schiller run into the sand. Faust II was written by a man of great age, by a mind which, while still capable of 'renewed puberty' and of exquisite, seemingly artless lyrical poetry, tended naturally towards sceptical detachment and ironic scrutiny, towards a playfully serious complexity of vision and expression.

The complexity of Faust II lies not so much, or not only, in the mass of scholarly or recondite allusion that the reader is challenged to recognize and discover in the text, as Goethe plays a part-whimsical, part-serious game of literary hide-and-seek. It also consists in the extraordinary process of reflection and layering that Goethe employs, whereby primary levels of meaning both conceal and reveal secondary or tertiary levels. Thus behind the court of a composite, but by no means idealized, Renaissance Emperor, behind the intrigues and feuds, the hedonism and irresponsibility of a regime on the verge of collapse, we perceive the economic and political state of late eighteenth-century Europe, in particular of pre-revolutionary France. Behind the mischief-making of Mephistopheles, we perceive the charlatanry of a Cagliostro, who was himself for Goethe the very symbol and symptom of corruption and decadence in a frivolous French court. Behind the masquerade of a Roman or Florentine carnival, we perceive a comment on trade, money, wealth and credit in a pre-industrial society.

Behind the arrogant ravings of a young graduate lies a caricature of the solipsistic absolutism of German idealist philosophy; behind Homunculus, the product of Wagner's crazed alchemist's dream, lies a not unhealthy scepticism towards uncontrolled scientific experiment, as well as towards romantic Frankenstein fantasies. At the same time, by Goethe's own testimony, Homunculus incorporates some of his most personal beliefs in human personality or 'entelechy', its existence before physical birth and its survival beyond physical death, as well as his biological credo of morphological evolution, metamorphosis and growth.

Behind the Battle of Pharsalus that marked the end of the Roman Republic, and the Battle of Pydna 120 years earlier that had signalled the end of Hellenic power in the eastern Mediterranean and the rise of that same Republic, we perceive the primal mythical battle that also took place in Thessaly, the struggle of Gods and Titans; and forward in time, all the historical recurrences of that original struggle which, as Erichtho predicts, will repeat itself into eternity (lines 7012 ff.). Gods and Titans, Greeks and Trojans, Greeks and Romans, republicans and monarchists, Guelphs and Ghibellines, aristocrats and sansculottes – the allegories of the 'Klassische Walpurgisnacht' extend from the mythical past to the modern age, to the French Revolution and even to the July Revolution of 1830.

Behind the obstinate bickering of two cranky savants, Thales and Anaxagoras, behind the conflicting claims of neptunist and vulcanist theories, lie not only Goethe's own keen and informed geological and anatomical studies but also his own gradualist political thinking. Behind the third act of Faust II lie 3,000 years of European history. Behind the fantastic encounter between the Greek heroine and the Germanic crusader is an allegory of the reception of the classical heritage by the modern Western world up to and including Weimar Classicism; the historical fate of the classical sites under successive occupations up to the Greek Wars of Liberation; Goethe's own lifelong preoccupation with Hellenic art and literature; and the synthetic reconciliation of classical and romantic, Hellenic and Germanic, pagan and Christian traditions. Above all, there is the recognition that the classical ideal is an irretrievable but infinitely precious heritage in modern Western culture.

Behind the collapse of empire and the insurgence of a rival emperor in Act IV is the Napoleonic occupation of the German territories of the Holy Roman Empire, and the formal demise of that Empire in 1806.

Behind the dubiously engineered defeat of the rival emperor and the restoration of imperial offices we perceive not only the 'Golden Bull' of 1356 by which Charles IV established the constitution of the German Empire but also, in the restoration of a fatally weakened imperial authority, an allegory of the restoration of feudal monarchy in Europe after 1815 in an intricate and precarious system of 'balanced' powers.

Behind Faust's reclamation schemes of Act V, his commercial ventures and his dreams of settlement, we perceive not only a reference to the devastating North Sea floods of 1824–5, and no doubt to other historical precedents, but also more generally the development of modern civil and industrial technology, of world trade and perhaps even of colonialism; the ruthless exploitation of labour and machinery; the destruction of traditional social patterns in the Philemon and Baucis episode; and the utopianism – whether proto-Marxist, capitalist, philanthropic or doctrinaire – of early nineteenth-century social visionaries.

Faust II is, in the phrase of G. C. L. Schuchard, a poetic and symbolic representation of modern man and modern life.[32] But over and above this extended historical allegory, it is also the continuation – and here the continuity of Goethe's Faust must be stressed – of the existential progress of a deeply flawed human individual, of his struggle to fulfil himself by effort and experience. It is the charting of the spiritual development of a man who finally renounces metaphysical speculation and the temptation of miraculous powers in order to affirm the value of limited but constant practical striving for a realizable vision. While Faust dies without achieving more than a provisional glimpse of that vision, his life, which has from the beginning evidently been guided by a providential 'Urquell', is granted the final affirmation of a grace beyond human judgement that does not take issue with a moral balance-sheet of debit and credit. Goethe's Faust, relentlessly and indeed ruthlessly pursuing his destiny through the two parts of the drama, is an eccentric and, for all his ambivalence, ultimately positive representative of Goethe's age, much as the Dr Johannes Faust of the narrative legend had been an eccentric, if negative, representative of his age.

Goethe himself was more than aware of the posthumous exegetical problems Faust II would present. From many references he made to correspondents, we can detect a cautious delight in his anticipation of future efforts to crack the code, to tease out the clues to the secrets he had smuggled into the work.[33] As he wrote to J. H. Meyer, for every problem that is solved, a new problem presents itself, and yet, he hoped, it would give pleasure to anyone alive to the implications of subtle signs and gestures; indeed, such a person, he suggested, might well find in the work more than he had put there.[34] Critics have not been slow to take up this challenge, and Faust II criticism is beset by the suspicion of finding in it more than Goethe intended; but that is the licence of the scholar that he himself anticipated. And in almost his last words on what it pleased him to call 'these very serious jests', Goethe feared a worse fate for his work than critical dismemberment. In such 'absurd and confused times', he feared, his long and honest endeavours with this 'strange edifice' would be poorly rewarded; he imagined that it would perhaps founder and be driven on to the shore, would lie there like a wreck in fragments and, for the time being at least, would be engulfed by the sands of time.[35] The following chapter will be devoted to an account of the critical fortunes and misfortunes of Faust.

NOTES: CHAPTER 2

1   'Von deutscher Art und Kunst', in Herder, Werke, ed. Karl-Gustav Gerold (Munich, 1953), Vol. 1, pp. 885 ff.
2   ibid., Vol. 1, p. 852.
3   ibid., Vol. 1, p. 855 and passim.
4   See Ann White, Names and Nomenclature in Goethe's 'Faust', pp. 71 ff.
5   Letter to Cotta, 30 Sept. 1805 (WA. IV. 19. 65).
6   GA. 10. 454.
7   GA. 10. 372 ff.
8   The phrase is that of F. D. Luke, '"Der nord-südliche Goethe": Some Reflexions on Faust's Dog', pp. 134 and 140.
9   'Hamburgische Dramaturgie', s. 75, in Lessing, Werke, ed. Göpfert, Vol. 4, pp. 578 ff.
10 'Italienische Reise', 1 Mar. 1788 (GA. 11. 578).
11 Letter to Goethe, 29 Nov. 1794 (GA. 20. 42).
12 Letter to Goethe, 23 June 1797 (GA. 20. 363).
13 To Eckermann, 6 May 1827 (Biedermann 3. 394).
14 To Eckermann, 23 Mar. 1829 (Biedermann 4. 79).
15 Letter to Schiller, 3 Apr. 1801 (GA. 20. 855).
16 Letter to Schiller, 5 May 1798 (GA. 20. 574).
17 GA. 5. 529–30.
18 In letters to Schiller and other correspondents (see GA. 5. 634 ff.).
19 GA. 5. 531–8.
20 Biedermann 1. 383, 495.
21 Letter of 27 Sept. 1827 (Briefe, HA. 4. 249).
22 To Eckermann, 6 June 1831 (Biedermann 4. 375).
23 GA. 5. 557–61.
24 Letters to Wilhelm von Humboldt and Sulpiz Boisserée, 22 Oct. 1826 (Briefe, HA. 4. 205, 207).
25 Letter to Zelter, 1 June 1831 (Briefe, HA. 4. 424–5).
26 GA. 5. 573.
27 To Riemer, 1831 (Biedermann 4. 414).

28 To Eckermann, 17 Feb. 1831 (Biedermann 4. 329).
29 Conversation of 13 Feb. 1831 (Biedermann 4. 322).
30 For discussion of epic and dramatic elements in Faust, see Heinz Hamm, Goethes Faust. Werkgeschichte und Textanalyse, pp. 149 ff. It is also the subject of a study by Richard Littlejohns, in Neophilologus: 'The Discussion between Goethe and Schiller on the Epic and Dramatic, and its Relevance to Faust'.
31 See Stuart Atkins, 'Goethe, Calderón and Faust. Der Tragödie zweiter Teil'; Swana L. Hardy, Goethe, Calderón und die romantische Theorie des Dramas, pp. 106 ff., 182 ff. Jane K. Brown's recent study extends the Calderónian or 'non-Aristotelian' principle to both parts of Faust (Goethe's Faust: the German Tragedy, pp. 15 ff.).
32 'Eine poetisch-symbolische Darstellung des modernen Wesens': see G. C. L. Schuchard, 'Julirevolution, St. Simonismus und die Faustpartien von 1831', p. 370.
33 Letters to Iken, 27 Sept. 1827, and Zelter, 26–7 July 1828 (Briefe, HA. 4. 249–50, 292).
34 Letter to Meyer, 20 July 1831 (WA. IV. 49. 292; GA. 5. 664).
35 Letter to Wilhelm von Humboldt, 17 Mar. 1832 (Briefe, HA. 4. 481).

CHAPTER 3

The Reception of Goethe's *Faust*

Because it is the life's work of Germany's greatest poet, because it draws on a specifically German legend, because Faust himself is such a fascinatingly ambivalent figure of such wide symbolic and philosophical potential – for these and no doubt for many other reasons, Goethe's *Faust* has, in the 150 years since its integral publication, become not only a major part of Germany's literary history but also, for better or for worse, what Hans Schwerte, in his review of the uses and abuses of the term 'Faustian', calls a chapter of German ideology.[1] In this sense, the history of the reception of *Faust* in Germany goes far beyond the usual parameters of literary reception; other literary works, the *Divine Comedy*, *Don Quixote*, or Shakespeare's major plays, have undoubtedly had more international influence and esteem, but none, not even *Don Quixote*, has become so central to a nation's image of itself, or to the image it would project of itself, as the story and figure of Faust, and in particular of Goethe's Faust. It is scarcely thinkable that Shakespeare's Hamlet could have been adopted as the mirror of English aspirations and self-questionings, hopes and despairs; yet something like that has been the case with Goethe's Faust in Germany.[2] The present chapter is concerned in the main with the literary critical reception of Goethe's *Faust*, not with the reworking of the Faust theme or legend by subsequent writers; nor is it concerned with the reception or interpretation of Goethe's *Faust*, or of other Fausts, on the stage, in music, painting or films. For material and information on these aspects, readers are referred to the studies of E. M. Butler, Charles Dédéyan and John Smeed in the literary field,[3] to Karl Theens on the Faust theme in music,[4] and to Theens and Hauke Lange-Fuchs on Faust in the cinema.[5]

It was a long time before both parts of Goethe's *Faust* were given an integral performance on the stage. Part One, with much cutting and transposing of scenes, was first performed in the Brunswick Court Theatre in January 1829, and further performances followed in Hanover, Dresden, Bremen, Frankfurt and Leipzig. The first public performance in Weimar was in August 1829; Goethe, for reasons of his own, did not attend it, though he evidently had some part in rehearsals.[6] Early performances of Faust I concentrated overwhelmingly on the Gretchen episode; only in 1856 were the 'Prologue in Heaven' and the pact scene fully integrated in stage performance. Karl Gutzkow produced scenes from the first three acts of Part Two in Dresden in 1849, entitled The Rape of Helen; but not until 1876 were both parts performed integrally, in Weimar under the direction of Otto Devrient.

The early history of the reception of the drama is complicated by its separate publication in four stages – the Fragment in 1790, the first part in 1808, the Helen episode in 1827, and the second part in 1832. The Fragment met with considerable enthusiasm, notably from the Schlegels and Schiller, tempered by the fact that it was a fragment which, even in its incomplete state, was obviously an unconventional and powerful drama. It was hailed as a 'strange torso', a work of original genius, beyond theory and rules, the work of a 'German Shakespeare'. Faust I, with its more complex metaphysical and theological overtones, had a more mixed reception from contemporaries, drawing considerable fire on moral, religious and aesthetic grounds. Faust II was met with wide-spread bafflement, disapproval and even derision; although the appearance of the Helen fragment in 1827 was greeted enthusiastically, the rest of the second part was generally considered to be the product of a genius in decline.

The first part was well received by the near circle of Goethe's friends, though Wieland expressed reservations towards 'this eccentric work of genius', and feared that the 'Aristophanic' vulgarity of the work had damaged Goethe's reputation. Jean Paul Richter acknowledged its poetic power and scope, but had reservations about its philosophical confusions – it was insufficiently critical towards Faust's unbridled titanism. Madame de Staël's judgement was also ambivalent; she was uneasy about the irrationalism of the work, but also fascinated by its imaginative treatment of evil and superstition. In Germany, it was already seen by many as a uniquely German product, as a national poem; Faust was, if not a representative of humanity itself, then at least a German cultural exemplar. Hegel dubbed it the 'absolute philosophical tragedy', Schelling saw it as a 'fount of inspiration'; and the young Grillparzer, conditioned by Schiller's concise dramatic form, was, as he confessed, confused and disturbed by his first reading – though a second reading was sufficient to fire his imagination and to transfer his loyalties 'forever' to Goethe. Grillparzer's reaction to Part Two, how-ever, in common with that of Hebbel, Mörike, Keller and C. F. Meyer, was hostile; after the powerful mixture of poetry and realism in Faust I, it appeared to be little more than a bizarre mythologizing allegory.

Much of the early hostility to the figure of Faust was directed at Goethe himself, who, if he was not identified with his hero, was certainly held responsible for him as his creator. Faust was clearly anathema to religious orthodoxy, both Protestant and Catholic; he was even enlisted by the one church as a negative example of the heresies of the other. Attacks on Faust came from other sources than the church or the moral establishment, however. The survivors of the Aufklärung, Friedrich Nicolai's Berlin circle, deplored its irrationalism and titanism, and regretted that Lessing had not completed his Faust drama; for the politically engagé Jung-Deutschland writers, Goethe was a reactionary figure, a poet who had lost the inspiration and impetus of his youthful radicalism – a decline that was discerned in Faust's progression from the combative rebel of the Fragment to the self-indulgent egotist of Part Two. For Wolfgang Menzel, an influential nationalist writer of the 1830s and 1840s, Faust was the summit of Goethe's poetic subjectivism, the 'apotheosis of the self'; Menzel took violent exception to the fact and the manner of Faust's salvation, describing the whole thing in extreme and not entirely accurate terms as a piece of frivolous machinery, and commenting that, if Faust deserved salvation after his devastation of Gretchen and her family, then every pig that rolls in a flower-bed deserves to be the gardener. Many Biedermeier critics, on the other hand, tended to emphasize the cautionary element in the titanic Faust of Part One, and, while playing down the destructive or criminal side of Faust's nature, also stressed his positive achievements in Part Two, his commitment to practical activity, his constant striving for the better and his acceptance of limited ambitions.

In the welter of conflicting reactions to Faust in the three decades following Goethe's death, Schwerte detects a predominantly negative evaluation of Faust and the 'Faustian nature'. For all the acknowledgement of the poetic and imaginative power of the work, Faust was more than anything else an example of the egotism, ruthlessness, arrogance and pride of the godless individual. Georg Gottfried Gervinus and Friedrich Spielhagen in particular saw Faustian despair as a paralysis of the will, his aimless dissatisfaction as the malady of the age. Spielhagen compared Goethe's Faust unfavourably with Lessing's Nathan, who had unequivocally followed the imperative of duty, who represented a spirit of positive and practical humanity as against fruitless metaphysical speculation and vaulting ambition; Gervinus believed that Goethe had failed, in Part Two, to resolve the dualities of Part One, failed to bridge the gap between thought and action.

F. T. Vischer, the most influential early critic of Faust, whose enthusiasm for Part One was matched only by his disapproval of Part Two, regretted that Goethe had not given Faust the revolutionary features and mission of an Ulrich von Hutten, or made him into an exemplary fighter for reform or German unity in the spirit of the Reformation, instead of the self-indulgent descent into abstruse and pallid allegory and operatic extravagance, and the presentation of Faust as an opportunistic political economist and merchant trader, in the second part. Vischer was also moved to parody Part Two in his occasionally amusing and telling satire *Faust. Der Tragödie dritter Teil* under the pseudonym Deutobold Symbolizetti Allegoriowitsch Mystifizinsky. In this, it appears that Faust's striving has not been quite sufficient to earn him redemption; a spell in purgatory is required before he achieves a state of grace. His penance there is to teach, to instruct the Selige Knaben (Blessed Boys) of the 'Bergschluchten' scene – the worst of which, as he bitterly complains, is that he has to explain Goethe's *Faust II* to them.[7] Goethe's English biographer G. H. Lewes voiced a similar disapproval of the allegories of the second part, while admiring the Helen episode; his somewhat sentimental predilection for Part One is summed up in his comment that 'the kiss of Gretchen is worth a thousand allegories'.[8]

To be sure, there were, around the middle of the nineteenth century, positive assessments of Faust, even of his ruthlessness in the cause of a new industrial era of communications and trade, in keeping with the conviction of scientific progress. As early as 1836, Heinrich Düntzer might be said to have established the tradition of seeing Faust as an exemplar of German, or Germanic, virtues: of German spiritual and intellectual profundity, German courage, tenacity and defiance – in short, of the German *Wesen*. For others, Faust became an incarnation of German mythology, a higher Siegfried, the intellectual hero who represented the speculative spirit of German idealism. Either way, Faust was coming to be perceived as a hallmark of the age, as the symbol of its godlessness or its emancipation from superstition, its enfeeblement or its virility, its Lucifer or its Prometheus; Faust was the touchstone or yardstick for proper or improper human behaviour and attitudes.

After the foundation of the second Reich, Faust was officially absorbed into the German pantheon. Gustav von Loeper's commentary of 1871 identified Faust firmly with the new Germany; the tragic or ruthless element, Faust's guilt or criminality, was passed over or subsumed under a higher purpose. The Faustian material was part of the pagan heritage of German myth; the Faust legend had emotional significance for Germans. Faust became more or less uncritically accepted as the embodiment of German virtues, and Mephistopheles, therefore, as the representative of 'das Welsche' – foreign (notably French and Italian!) cultural values.[9] Certainly, even von Loeper saw the

Faust of Part One as a problematic figure, vainly speculating or attempting to 'storm heaven'; the Faust of Part Two, however, was the activist
who 'stormed the world', the representative not of humanity as such
but of the Germanic, even the 'Aryan', race. Many distinguished critics
of the late nineteenth century followed von Loeper in hailing Goethe's
Faust as the 'second German Bible', relativizing the metaphysical
speculation and tragic experience of Part One and emphasizing the
energetic visionary of a new order in the concluding scenes of the
second part. Karl Goedeke, Erich Schmidt, Kuno Fischer, Wilhelm
Scherer and Herman Grimm were among those 'perfectibilists' who
saw in Goethe's drama the testing and the progressive rehabilitation,
even the purification, of Faustian activism, and who harnessed their
message more or less explicitly to the ideology of the Reich. Not only
Goethe's ambivalent hero but also the more unequivocally diabolistic
Faust of the sixteenth-century legend was rehabilitated as an exemplar
of the 'Promethean' scientific curiosity of the Renaissance, in spite of the
explicit warnings in the text of those accounts against the arrogance and
presumption of Faust's emulation of Lucifer and the Titans: the Lutheran
bigots who compiled these early versions, it was suggested, had been
unable to obscure the positive or heroic dimensions of Faustian titanism,
even if it required a Marlowe to recognize the true greatness of Faust.

In 1918 Oswald Spengler's *Untergang des Abendlandes* (*Decline of the West*) at
once continued, and yet ironically reversed, the Wilhelmine evaluation of Goethe's Faust as the exemplar of modern German culture.
Spengler's pessimistic morphology of Western culture is itself based on
the analogy of Goethe's *Faust*: in his drama, Goethe had anticipated the
'entropy' of Western culture in the 'civilization' of the nineteenth century. The Faust of Part One is for Spengler the positive symbol of man's
speculative inquiry; he is the striving, soaring spiritual urge exemplified
in Gothic architecture, the desire for the infinite that characterized
Western scientific and artistic culture, the Dionysian or 'Faustian' element that distinguished the modern from the Apolline culture of
classical antiquity. This restlessly speculative spirit of curiosity had given
way in the nineteenth and twentieth centuries to the soulless industrial,
imperial and commercial civilization, to the age of 'Caesarism', a sterile
and barren age whose spiritual resources were exhausted. This development, for Spengler, is reflected precisely in the two parts of Goethe's
Faust; moreover, as Hans Kellner has pointed out, Spengler's book even
displays, in its two parts, its introduction and its prefaces, the very
structure of Goethe's drama.[10]

The one-sided distortion of the figure of Faust and the glorification
of the imagined Faustian ideal was continued in the perversion of

Goethe's Faust in the service of National Socialist ideology;[11] and it is scarcely surprising that postwar criticism has been more than cautious in the evaluation of Faust. The coup de grâce was given to all such uncritically heroic perceptions of the Faust figure by the publication in 1947 of Thomas Mann's Doktor Faustus. Certainly, Mann derived his story not from Goethe but from the original Faust legend; but, in so far as his reckoning with German history is presented in terms of the Faustian figure of Adrian Leverkühn, it also represents a reckoning with the reception and perception of Goethe's Faust figure in the hundred years or so after Goethe's death.

It would, however, be a simplistic picture of the reception of Faust if it were assumed that Goethe's Faust was universally idealized between 1870 and 1945, only to suffer a radical revision in the postwar years. As Schwerte has shown, there was a steady alternative current to the prevailing glorification of Goethe's Faust and of Faustian values before and during the Second Reich; and not all critiques of Faust and the Faustian emanated from the church. The anti-perfectibilist tendency to stress Faust's tragic failure, his despair, his egotism and ruthlessness, and the illusory nature of his visions and achievements, gathered impetus in the inter-war years as critics began to question the traditional stereotype of the 'Olympian' Goethe, and thereby also to acknowledge the ambivalence of his Faust drama. The culmination of this revised image of Faust was Wilhelm Böhm's Faust der Nichtfaustische of 1933, in which Faust is presented as a self-pitying sentimentalist, a recidivist criminal and an incorrigible Titan. The work was the tragedy or the satire, not the apotheosis, of the superman; far from being an exemplary or ideal figure, Faust was destroyed by his own hubris and could only be saved by the arbitrary intervention of a predestined and thoroughly undeserved grace.

In postwar German criticism, only the Marxist school remains predominantly perfectibilist or positive in the assessment of Faust. Few Marxist commentators are prepared to see the murder of Philemon and Baucis – one of the great sticking-points of any perfectibilist interpretation – as anything but criminal, as anything but a crime attendant on Faust's bourgeois-capitalist activities; but most are quite prepared to see Faust's final vision not as a satire or a tragic illusion but as a provisional stage in the anticipation of a future ideal society. Faust could not, any more than Goethe, envisage the precise historical conditions under which such a society could become reality, let alone realize it himself; but Faust, in so far as he overcomes his early immature solipsism and titanism, his dabbling in court affairs, his infatuation with an aesthetic ideal and his alliance with feudalism, does finally, in Act V, commit

himself to practical social activity. One of the most enthusiastic perfectibilists, the Soviet critic Otar Dshinoria, is able to affirm Faust's spiritual
progress, his 'titanic will', and to see Faust's final vision as an expression
of 'realistic', that is, of revolutionary, romanticism.[12] Joachim Müller, on
the other hand, an East German scholar who can scarcely be called a
Marxist critic, has moved from a pessimistic or tragic assessment of
Faust during the war years towards a moderately sceptical but more
positive evaluation, and has been taken to task by Dshinoria for his
ambivalence.[13]

The besetting problem of the judgement of Goethe's Faust has been
the urge, or the need, to see the story and figure of Faust as exemplary,
in a positive or negative sense, for successive generations in Germany,
and to attribute to Goethe a vision or gift of anticipation that even he
would scarcely have claimed. It may be that studies like Böhm's, or
Thomas Mann's Faust novel, together with the historical traumas of the
twentieth century, have released Goethe's Faust from his dubious status
as a national symbol, though not necessarily from his function as an
ideological touchstone; as Schwerte suggests, Faust is not dead – the
concept of 'Faustian man' or 'das Faustische', is.[14]

For all that, there is still no very clear critical agreement on many of
the major problems of Goethe's *Faust*, and it is only very broadly true
to suggest that, even in West Germany, anti-perfectibilist interpretations
have dominated. Wolfgang Schadewaldt, Peter Michelsen and Arthur
Henkel have represented the tendency to stress the negative or tragic
implications of Faust's career, and in particular of his final vision –
which for Michelsen is the result of a 'pathological' delusion of the
blind Faust.[15] On the other hand, Emil Staiger, Erich Trunz, Hermann
Reske and Paul Requadt have been closer to a positive, if qualified,
judgement of Faust.[16] Hans Arens's recent commentary on *Faust* I takes a
highly critical stance towards Faust's sententious rhetoric, his self-
deception and his bad conscience, to the extent of comparing him
unfavourably with his 'worthy' famulus Wagner;[17] but we do not yet
know Arens's judgement on the Faust of Part Two. In the Anglo-
American tradition of *Faust* criticism, a more positive assessment of
Faust is discernible: E. C. Mason, E. M. Wilkinson, Stuart Atkins, Ilse
Graham and T. J. Reed are among those who are prepared to accept
Goethe's justification of Faust, of a career in which error and striving,
failure and achievement, are inseparable – while Harold Jantz is an
enthusiastic perfectibilist.[18] Even here, however, Melitta Gerhard, Heinz
Politzer and Wolfgang Wittkowski are among recent critics in America
who insist on an unequivocally tragic judgement of Faust's earthly
career.[19] But the terms 'perfectibilist' and 'anti-perfectibilist' have ceased

to be regarded as adequate or meaningful labels, and most recent
judgements have emphasized the ironies, paradoxes and ambiguities of
Faust's career and his salvation.[20]

Among the unresolved controversies surrounding *Faust* is also the
problem of defining its genre. Goethe insisted on calling the work a
tragedy, or, more strictly, he entitled the two parts *Der Tragödie erster Teil*
and *Der Tragödie zweiter Teil* – though he appeared to exclude the three
prefatory scenes from that rubric, and therefore, perhaps, by implication, also the two final scenes of Part Two. Goethe's actual nomenclature, however, does not indicate whether he himself considered Faust's
fate or career on earth as success or failure, triumph or tragedy – any
more than the transcendental *ex machina* solution of the final scene can
be held to rule out a tragic or pessimistic interpretation of Faust's career
on earth. It is quite likely that he used the term 'tragedy', in the manner
of Euripides, to denote the overall importance or seriousness of his
theme, irrespective of the final outcome and of comic or burlesque
elements in the work; it is also notable that he used the term 'Tragödie'
rather than 'Trauerspiel' – a designation that distinguishes *Faust* from
Clavigo or *Egmont*, which end with the premature destruction of the hero,
and from *Die natürliche Tochter*, which charts the fall of the heroine, and
was perhaps also planned to end with her destruction. Hegel called it
'the one absolutely philosophical tragedy ... the tragic quest for
harmony between the Absolute in its essence and appearance and the
individual's knowledge and will'; and Erich Trunz also sees the tragic
dimension in the inaccessibility of truth for Faust, who can only
perceive the absolute in and through the inadequacy of the real world.[21]
Few critics, certainly, dispute the tragic dimension of the Gretchen
episode, irrespective of the final Voice 'from above'; but opinions are
sharply divided on the tragedy of Faust and the tragic nature of the work
as a whole. Atkins sees it as 'high tragedy' in the classical tradition;
Faust's guilt 'is but the concomitant of finite efforts to live in an
imperfect world nobly and heroically', and the drama is that of a man
who experiences 'triumph in inevitable defeat'.[22] Mason considers that
the 'terrible irony' of Faust's last moments justifies the term tragedy, but
goes on to argue that, like all Goethe's tragic endings, it is 'neither
unmitigatedly tragic nor a real ending'; Faust dies with his spirit
unbroken and 'with a profession of faith in a worthy and noble ideal'.[23]
Erich Heller disputes the tragic element in *Faust*, since Faust's situation is
'unresolvable in tragedy. Nature is fundamentally innocent, and
Goethe's genius is in communication with nature. Hence there can be,

for Goethe, no catharsis.' Restlessness of spirit is both Faust's sin and his salvation.[24]

If the structure of Goethe's *Faust* is perceived as the tragedies of Gretchen and Faust encapsulated within a conciliatory transcendental framework, then the work might be described as a human tragedy within a secularized or quasi-religious mystery play. Erich Franz and Benno von Wiese distinguish thus between the tragic inner action and the outer rubric of the three prefatory scenes and the concluding 'Grablegung' and 'Bergschluchten' scenes.[25] Böhm, Schuchard and other anti-perfectibilists see the human action, at least, as satire rather than tragedy;[26] for Melitta Gerhard, Faust represents the tragedy of post-*Aufklärung* man.[27] Marxist interpretations, seeing in the work a symbolic panorama of human history and progress, incorporating and anticipating new social, political and human values, dispute the tragic dimension except in so far as Faust dies without, or before, realizing his ideal vision. Indeed, Gerhard Scholz sees the principle of the work not as tragedy but as comedy – comedy, that is, in the broad sense as a presentation of human life, the tradition of the mystery play developed into an epic of modern man, into 'Zeitalterdichtung'.[28]

Generally, there is a broad, if often tacit, consensus that Goethe's *Faust* defies any conventional categories of genre definition, in view of the range and variety of its structure, style and theme, of its lyrical, dramatic and epic dimensions. It is *sui generis*, an extended poem in dramatic form, at best containable within such broad terms as 'world play' or 'total work of art': 'Weltspiel' or 'Gesamtkunstwerk'.

The problem of the dramatic and thematic unity of *Faust*, as we have seen in Chapter 2, dates from the very early stages of its composition, when Schiller urged Goethe that the disparate elements of the *Faust Fragment* should be brought together under a unifying idea, a poetic ring or 'hoop' that would encompass such a heterogeneous mass of material.[29] Goethe himself, as we have also indicated above, chose to emphasize the differences between the two parts, and resisted the notion that there was a single 'idea' informing the whole work. Early critics were, by and large, 'fragmentarians', if only because, like F. T. Vischer, they found most of *Faust II* such a bafflingly whimsical and extravagant concoction after the powerful and (relatively) realistic and uniform drama of the first part.

Questions concerning the unity of the work proliferate – whether it lies in the figure of Faust, in the polarity or dialectic between Faust and Mephistopheles, between good and evil, striving and error, or in the issue of the wager in heaven, of the pact and wager on earth; whether there is any continuity of dramatic action between the two parts, indeed

even within Part Two itself; whether unity lies in the philosophical idea
of the work, however that is defined; whether it lies in the structure or
literary organization of the work; or whether the only unity discernible
lies in the fact that it is the product of a single, admittedly original,
unpredictable and multi-faceted imagination.

Early critics like Kuno Fischer, for all that he subscribed to the 'perfectibilist' notion that the drama represented the testing and progressive
rehabilitation of a restlessly titanic 'Weltstürmer', discerned no unity
in Faust other than that it reflected the creative and personal development of its author. Croce, Staiger and Emrich are among twentieth-
century critics who insist on the radical differences, even the discrepancies, between the two parts. Staiger attributes its lack of overall unity or
uniformity to its composition over more than sixty years of Goethe's
creative career, and Emrich argues that Goethe in no sense intended the
second part as a continuation of the first; the 'Anmutige Gegend' scene
that opens Faust II signals an entirely different kind of activity for Faust in
an entirely different world, on an entirely different aesthetic level, from
that of Faust I.

The 'unitarians', represented by Gundolf, Rickert, Viëtor and Korff,
see the consistency and unity of the work in the development of Faust
from the subjective and egotistic individual of Part One towards his
more public and objective achievements in Part Two: the unity of the
drama is conceptual, not formal or literary. Rickert even denies any
radical break in the character of Faust or in the nature of his striving
between the two parts; in both, it is a question of the temptation of
Faust, who progresses, in Goethe's words, through 'an ever higher and
purer activity to the end' towards his salvation – even if this activity is
threatened on the one hand by Faustian excess, and on the other hand
by the weakening of the active impulse (see p.212).

More recent studies have tended to move away from the search for
the philosophical unity of an overall idea in Faust towards an analysis of
its structural and aesthetic unity, of the formal 'architecture' of the
work.[30] This has been demonstrated in the symmetry of its construction, in the encapsulation of the human drama within the transcendental perspectives of the 'Prologue in Heaven' and the final scene
'Bergschluchten' ('Mountain Gorges'), and of these in turn within the
theatrical fiction of the 'Prelude in the Theatre', which is itself prefaced
by the poet's own personal dedication. Symmetry has been discerned
in the parallelism between the two parts, the balance of the private
world of Part One against the public world of Part Two, and in the
reiteration of, or parallels between, scenes and figures: Wagner and
the Student/Baccalaureus; the 'Hexenküche' and 'Rittersaal' scenes;

'Walpurgisnachtstraum' and 'Mummenschanz'; the return to Faust's study in Act II; the two 'Walpurgisnächte', northern and classical; 'Wald und Höhle' and 'Hochgebirg'; Gretchen and Helen. Recurrent themes and motifs, verbal patterns and 'echo structures' have been shown to bind the fabric of the drama – expansion and contraction, ascent and descent, reality and illusion, light and dark, veil and clouds, gold and treasure, creativity, and a whole number of literal verbal prefigurations and parallels. Harold Jantz has even detected a numerological symmetry in the whole work: the relation between Parts One and Two, and the sequence of episodes within the two parts, is based on the ratio of the Golden Section, on tripartite divisions and on further numerological subtleties.[31] Boyle suggests that, while Part Two has a historical rather than a dramatic continuity, there is also a symmetrical structure of ascent and descent that pivots on the central moment of Faust's union with Helen.[32] Fowler has also traced a pyramidal structure in Part One, a rising and falling action that turns on the central 'Gartenhäuschen' scene;[33] and Lamport traces a unifying structure over both parts of the drama, suggesting that Goethe's systematically anachronistic treatment of the linear time sequence creates a synchronic unity that is like 'a vastly extended version of a classical dramatic form'.[34]

While an individual critic's perception of the nature of Goethe's Faust as fundamentally 'perfectibilist' or 'anti-perfectibilist' might determine the interpretation of any number of other problems and questions posed by the work, such broad labels cannot do justice to the range and shades of critical opinion, which can scarcely be rehearsed in this chapter. Some of the main lines of opinion on the many still controversial points of detail will be touched on in the course of the commentary below – the Erdgeist controversy, the 'Walpurgisnacht' and 'Walpurgisnachtstraum', the 'Mummenschanz', the Mothers, Homunculus, Euphorion, Faust's final vision and his salvation. It might be appropriate here to look finally at some of the main developments over the last fifty years on what is generally recognized as the least accessible area of the work – the symbolism and allegory of Faust II.

Broadly, Faust criticism of the nineteenth and early twentieth centuries occupied itself with selective areas of the second part – the Helen episode, Faust's final hours, his death and the question of the pact and Faust's salvation. The intervening material of Acts I, II and IV was regarded, as a heritage of Vischer's disparaging critique, as the eccentric and abstruse product of at best a whimsical, or at worst a feeble, poetic imagination. The mode of allegory itself – as which Part Two was accurately enough perceived – was unfashionable, regarded as an inferior literary form, wooden and abstract, literal and superficial. Indeed, Goethe himself had formulated the sharp distinction between allegory as a 'translatable' system of concepts, and symbolism as an inscrutable, 'untranslatable' expression of ideas.[35] For Wilhelm Emrich the idiom of Faust II is essentially symbolic, in the Goethean sense, rather than allegorical; it is a work whose meaning is decipherable only through the painstaking analysis of a complex network of highly personal symbolic imagery – the meaning of which can, in turn, only be discovered by the 'genetic' study of Goethe's private symbolism, of precedents and parallels across the whole of his creative oeuvre. Emrich's seminal and encyclopaedic study of the symbolism of Faust II, which first appeared in 1943,[36] has dominated much of the critical reception of Part Two since then, and the symbolic studies of Werner Danckert and Gottfried Diener owe much both to Emrich's methodology and to his concept of the 'inscrutable' symbol – even if they also rely heavily on the apparatus of depth psychology and Jungian archetypal symbolism.[37]

Emrich's study, which remains an authoritative guide to Goethe's symbolic thought and expression, has, however, been questioned on more than one count. Apart from the sheer complexity of reference adduced by Emrich, which is not made any more accessible by a scarcely lucid style, it has been objected that such a genetic approach to the symbolic code of Faust II can obscure the meaning or reference of the immediate literary or dramatic context of the symbolism by referring constantly beyond that context. Moreover, Goethe's (and Emrich's) theoretical distinction between allegory and symbol has also been questioned. Charles Hayes, for example, has challenged the distinction, accepted, at least in Germany, for some 150 years, between the unlimited resonance and profound inscrutability of symbolism on the one hand and the simple, unequivocal, one-to-one correspondence of allegory on the other.[38] It is not a question, Hayes claims, of an essential difference between the 'subtle' symbol and the 'superficial' allegory, between the intrinsic reference of symbolism and the extrinsic meaning of allegory; both are more or less equivocal, more or less inscrutable. The degree of discrepancy between concrete image and abstract meaning is irrelevant; allegory is a systematic pattern or structure of related symbols.

This questioning of a theoretical or essential distinction between symbol and allegory has allowed Faust II criticism to emerge from the shadow of Emrich's highly qualitative distinction, and from a long tradition of dismissive reaction to 'mere' allegory. Dorothea Lohmeyer, for example, whose revised study of the first three acts of Faust II goes into the finest detail of the complex symbolic references, treats the term allegory as a working definition, rather than as a literary form in contradistinction to symbol.[39] It has allowed critics to treat the allegorical sequences of Faust II, and the historical references they contain, more even-handedly and without value judgement alongside the grandiose literary symbolism of the work, and to see the latter as an integral part of the former. It has also introduced a certain degree of lucidity into Faust II criticism, which was in danger of becoming at least as obscure and baffling as the work itself is supposed to be.

Katharina Mommsen, whose study of illusion and reality, art and nature, in the first three acts of Faust II is based on the historical and cultural traditions of the Goethezeit, has also dissociated herself from literary critics who, as she puts it, have set out to see the work 'from ever loftier perspectives'.[40] Most recently, Heinz Schlaffer has polemically rejected the tradition of 'symbolizing' criticism epitomized in Emrich's esoteric study, and has interpreted Faust II as a primarily socio-economic allegory of the nineteenth century. He argues (somewhat patronizingly) that while nineteenth-century critics were correct in diagnosing Faust II as allegory, they were unable to come to terms with it, on the one hand because they regarded the allegorical mode itself as inferior, and on the other hand because they were unable to bring sufficient historical perspective to bear on the work: the century that attempted to solve Goethe's puzzle was unable to recognize itself as the key to it.[41] Schlaffer's method, which reveals valuable insights into the structure and meaning of Faust II, can be and has been itself questioned on the grounds of its sporadic, one-sided and highly selective approach. Schlaffer concentrates single-mindedly on Faust II as a prefiguration of nineteenth-century economic, cultural and political imperialism; and, while Schlaffer is by no means in line with the orthodox Marxist tradition of Faust criticism, he shares the tendency of all ideological criticism to see the work not so much in terms of its own age but in terms of future historical developments. Schlaffer is also inclined to dismiss the poetic qualities of Faust II, anything that appears to express Goethe's lyrical, emotional or mystical response to nature, as verging on kitsch.

The situation is not dissimilar to the reception of Patrice Chéreau's production of Wagner's Ring cycle at Bayreuth in 1976. The storms of protest that greeted his politicized allegorical interpretation of a revered masterpiece emanated largely from those who felt that the 'poetic', 'mythical' or 'symbolic' dimensions of Wagner's music drama had been neglected or violated; a close scrutiny of the text, however, reveals that Chéreau had hardly violated the spirit of the work or Wagner's own intentions. It is also ironical that Goethe himself should have been

responsible for an evaluative theoretical distinction between allegory
and symbol that has been harnessed, one way or another, to his own
Faust II, a work that appears to incorporate in great profusion elements
of both modes as he understood them.

It was not possible to take any full account in the commentary below
of some very recent books on *Faust*. Jane K. Brown's study of the whole
work is a highly literary and aesthetic approach that sets out to see both
parts synchronically as a single coherent and continuous text, in
contradistinction, for example, to John Gearey's earlier genetic or
diachronic study of 'the making' of Part One. For Brown, the first part is
treated as a text dating from 'about 1800', the second part is an 'extended
reflection on Part I', and the whole 'a veritable Chinese box of plays
within plays' that is best seen in relation to the non-Aristotelian
tradition of European drama.[42] Benjamin Bennett has published a study
of '*Faust* and the Regeneration of Language' that sees *Faust* as Goethe's
response to a sense of crisis in the linguistic and cultural tradition of
Western literature, as his version of what Bennett calls 'an *antipoetic*
possibility' of regenerating poetic language.[43] Nicholas Boyle's introduction and commentary to the first part of *Faust* is a reading of Part One as a
coherent tragic drama in itself that begins not with the three prefatory
scenes, but with Faust's opening monologue, and ends on the 'redemptive conclusion' of the final 'Kerker' scene: Part One is a complete play
that does not require either the prefatory framework or Part Two for its
interpretation.[44]

The present study is an attempt to approach the text pragmatically
in order to do some justice both to the poetic dimensions in the
symbolism of *Faust* II and to the historical allegory that underlies the
story of Faust, in the hope that some comparatively (*nota bene: comparatively*) neglected areas of the second part, notably Acts I and IV, may
receive fuller attention. In this respect, a distinction is made between
the relatively concentrated dramatic realism of the first part and the
broader epic canvas of the second, while it is borne in mind that the
two parts are linked, not only by certain structural correspondences and
configurations, but also by the overall personal, theatrical and metaphysical framework of the three prefatory scenes, by the pact between
Faust and Mephistopheles and the dialectical relationship resulting
from it, and most of all by the career of Faust, by the sum-total of
his spiritual, intellectual, emotional, political, aesthetic, military and
industrial experience.

NOTES: CHAPTER 3

1 Hans Schwerte, *Faust und das Faustische. Ein Kapitel deutscher Ideologie.*

2 For a comprehensive, though very tendentious, survey of the critical reception of Goethe's *Faust*, see Rüdiger Scholz, *Goethes 'Faust' in der wissenschaftlichen Interpretation von Schelling und Hegel bis heute. Ein einführender Forschungsbericht.*

3 Butler, *Fortunes of Faust*; Dédéyan, *Thème de Faust*; Smeed, *Faust in Literature.*

4 Karl Theens, 'Faust in der Musik'.

5 Karl Theens, 'Geschichte des Faust-Motivs im Film'; Hauke Lange-Fuchs, 'Ja, wäre nur ein Zaubermantel mein!'. *Faust in Film.*

6 See Julius Petersen, *Goethes Faust auf der deutschen Bühne*, p. 18; Marvin Carlson, *Goethe and the Weimar Theatre*, p. 300.

7 Friedrich Theodor Vischer, *Faust. Der Tragödie dritter Teil. Treu im Geiste des zweiten Teils des Goetheschen Fausts gedichtet von Deutobold Symbolizetti Allegoriowitsch Mystifizinsky.* Act I, sc. 2.

8 George Henry Lewes, *The Life and Works of Goethe*, Vol. 2, p. 433.

9 See Schwerte, *Faust und das Faustische*, pp. 148 ff.

10 Hans Kellner, 'Figures in the Rumpelkammer: Goethe, Faust, Spengler', pp. 149–50. See Oswald Spengler, *Der Untergang des Abendlandes*, 2 vols (Munich, 1918–22).

11 For a survey of National Socialist reception of *Faust*, see Günther Mahal, 'Der tausendjährige Faust. Rezeption als Anmaßung'.

12 Otar Dshinoria, 'Das Ende von Goethes "Faust"'.

13 Joachim Müller, 'Die tragische Grundstruktur von Goethes Faustdichtung'; Müller, 'Fausts Tat und Tod'.

14 Schwerte, *Faust und das Faustische*, p. 240.

15 Wolfgang Schadewaldt, 'Fausts Ende und die Achilleis'; Peter Michelsen, 'Fausts Erblindung'; Arthur Henkel, 'Das Ärgernis Faust'.

16 Emil Staiger, *Goethe*, Vol. 3, pp. 444–5 and *passim*; Erich Trunz, HA. 3. 476 and *passim*; Hermann Reske, *Faust. Eine Einführung*, pp. 189 ff.; Requadt, *Goethes 'Faust I'*, pp. 382 ff.

17 Hans Arens, *Kommentar zu Goethes Faust I.*

18 Eudo C. Mason, *Goethe's Faust: its Genesis and Purport*, pp. 342–3; Elizabeth M. Wilkinson, 'Goethe's Faust: Tragedy in the Diachronic Mode'; Stuart Atkins, *Goethe's Faust: a Literary Analysis*, pp. 254 ff.; Ilse Graham, 'Kompromittierung und Wiedergutmachung. Ein Versuch zu Fausts Schlußmonolog'; T. J. Reed, *Goethe*, pp. 78 ff.; Harold Jantz, *The Form of Faust: the Work of Art and its Intrinsic Structures*, pp. 56 ff. See also Pierre Grappin, 'Faust aveugle'.

19 Melitta Gerhard, 'Faust. Die Tragödie des "neueren" Menschen'; Heinz Politzer, 'Der blinde Faust'; Wolfgang Wittkowski, 'Irrestorable Destruction and Tragic Reconciliation in Goethe's Faust'.

20 Thus e.g. Ehrhard Bahr, *Die Ironie im Spätwerk Goethes. Studien zum 'West-östlichen Divan', zu den 'Wanderjahren' und zu 'Faust II'*; Alfred Hoelzel, 'The Conclusion of Goethe's Faust: Ambivalence and Ambiguity'. Hoelzel also provides a detailed résumé of recent opinion.

21 See *Hegel's Aesthetics*, trans. T. M. Knox, Vol. 2 (Oxford, 1975), p. 1224; Trunz, HA. 3. 474.

22 Atkins, *Goethe's Faust*, pp. 274–5.

23 Mason, *Goethe's Faust*, pp. 341–3.

24 Erich Heller, 'Goethe and the Avoidance of Tragedy', p. 47.

25 Erich Franz, *Mensch und Dämon. Goethes Faust als menschliche Tragödie, ironische Weltschau und religiöses Mysterienspiel*, pp. 11 ff., 233 ff. and passim; Benno von Wiese, *Die deutsche Tragödie von Lessing bis Hebbel*, Vol. 1, pp. 143 ff.

26 Wilhelm Böhm, *Faust der Nichtfaustische*; Schuchard, 'Julirevolution, St. Simonismus und die Faustpartien von 1831'.

27 Gerhard, 'Faust: die Tragödie des "neueren" Menschen'.

28 Gerhard Scholz, *Faust-Gespräche*, pp. 20 ff.

29 Letter to Goethe, 26 June 1797 (GA. 20. 365).

30 See esp. Requadt, *Goethes 'Faust I'*.

31 Jantz, *Form of Faust*, pp. 164 ff.

32 Nicholas Boyle, '"Du ahnungsloser Engel du!": Some Current Views of Goethe's Faust', pp. 137 ff.

33 F. M. Fowler, 'Symmetry of Structure in Goethe's Faust, Part One'.

34 F. J. Lamport, 'Synchrony and Diachrony in *Faust*', p. 127.

35 'Maximen und Reflexionen', nos 1112–13 (GA. 9. 639).

36 Wilhelm Emrich, *Die Symbolik von Faust II. Sinn und Vorformen*.

37 Werner Danckert, *Goethe. Der mythische Urgrund seiner Weltschau*; Gottfried Diener, *Fausts Weg zu Helena. Urphänomen und Archetypus*. For a recent, strictly Freudian, interpretation of *Faust*, see Rüdiger Scholz, *Die beschädigte Seele des großen Mannes. Goethes 'Faust' und die bürgerliche Gesellschaft*.

38 Charles Hayes, 'Symbol and Allegory: a problem in literary theory'. For a similar, but less radical, revision of Goethe's definitions, see Bengt A. Sørensen, 'Altersstil und Symboltheorie. Zum Problem des Symbols und der Allegorie bei Goethe'.

39 Dorothea Lohmeyer, *Faust und die Welt. Der zweite Teil der Dichtung. Eine Anleitung zum Lesen des Textes*.

40 Katharina Mommsen, *Natur- und Fabelreich in Faust II*, p. vi.

41 Heinz Schlaffer, *Faust Zweiter Teil. Die Allegorie des 19. Jahrhunderts*, p 7.

42 Jane K. Brown, *Goethe's Faust*, pp. 15 ff. and passim. See also John Gearey, *Goethe's Faust: the Making of Part One*.

43 Benjamin Bennett, *Goethe's Theory of Poetry: 'Faust' and the Regeneration of Language*, pp. 16 ff. and passim.

44 Nicholas Boyle, *Goethe: Faust, Part One*, pp. 21–2, 114 ff.

PART TWO

Commentary to the Text

CHAPTER 4

The Prefatory Scenes

The three prefatory scenes to Faust, which, it should be noted, are evidently intended to preface the whole work, not simply the first part, might be described respectively as the lyrical, dramatic and epic prolegomena to the drama. The 'Zueignung' records the poet's private feelings at resuming work on a project that belongs to his increasingly distant youth. The 'Vorspiel', ostensibly a discussion of the theatre, its relationship with and its obligations to the public, also contrives to suggest the fiction that the subsequent action is the very performance now being worked out by the three principals of a somewhat rough-and-ready travelling company. The 'Prolog' provides a cosmic dimension in which not only are momentous issues raised concerning good and evil, man's place in the divine scheme, his destiny and his salvation *sub specie aeternitatis*, but also the earthly life of one man, Faust, is shown to be not without the sanction and protection of a higher power, unbeknown to him. As in some classical and Baroque drama, an individual human destiny is observed by, and is to some extent even the plaything of, forces beyond himself – an actor in the great theatre of the world.

'Zueignung': Dedication
The elegiac dedication is best appreciated if it is set against the companion poem that was not included in the published work.[1] The subdued minor key of this introductory poem is complemented by the resolute affirmation of the valedictory 'Abschied', in which Goethe turns his back on the nordic phantom-world of Faust I – though it might be noted that this break with his youthful immaturities and confusions, apparently so decisive around 1800 when he began work on the opening scenes of the Helen episode, was later modified to a more even-handed treatment of classical and romantic elements in the final working-out of Faust II. The tone of 'Zueignung' is intensely introspective, retrospective and ambivalent; as such it is strikingly similar to the mood and expression of much of Goethe's early Weimar poetry, to the brooding uncertainties and tensions of poems like 'Ilmenau', 'An den Mond', or 'Warum gabst du uns die tiefen Blicke'. It also forms the same

kind of contrast to the affirmative 'Abschied' as the pre-Italian poetry
does to the celebration of clear plastic forms and colours in the *Roman
Elegies*, in which the 'mists of the dismal North' are banished from the
poet's imagination.

'Zueignung' conjures a vision of blurred contours and figures, of
shadows and echoes, of past experiences and enthusiasms. It is clearly
programmatic, evoking Goethe's early work on the Faust theme,
together with those with whom he lived and to whom he read his
material, and hinting at the great effort of will and imagination required
to feel his way back into his theme. It is generally thought that 'Leid'
('sorrow') in line 21 of most editions was an error for 'Lied' ('song'); but
the former is not inappropriate, and was possibly left uncorrected quite
deliberately by Goethe. Yet the final stanza affirms the poet's reluctant
resolve to resume work on the alien, but not wholly uncongenial,
material; and it ends with a mystical paradox on the relative reality and
tangibility of past and present.

'Vorspiel auf dem Theater': Prelude in the Theatre
Possibly derived from the *Shakuntala* of Kalidasa, the Sanskrit classic
which opens with a verse 'benediction' followed by a prelude in the
form of a dialogue between a producer and an actress, possibly also
based on Elizabethan dramatic prologues, the 'Prelude in the Theatre'
has long been a controversial scene.[2] The function of the 'Vorspiel' is
ironic; it is to reveal, at least for the moment, the theatricality of the
subsequent action, even to the extent that what follows is presented as
the work of the Theaterdichter of the 'Prelude' (it should be borne in
mind that he is, as the scene-heading suggests, a poet-*playwright*). Even
the following 'Prologue in Heaven', as Requadt has argued, is presented
as his creation: as the writer is the creator of the theatrical world, so the
Lord is the playwright of the 'world theatre'.[3]

There is a long tradition that the Lustige Person (Clown) is played by
the same actor as Mephistopheles; and this doubling is frequently
extended to the roles of the Director and the Lord, and the Writer and
Faust. The parallels between these figures are indeed striking enough;
the relationship between Clown and Writer in the 'Prelude', between
down-to-earth pragmatism and sententious idealism, between ironic
subtlety and humourless egocentricity, is not far from the dialectical
relationship between Mephistopheles and Faust – though the Clown
admittedly lacks Mephisto's sterile negativity and diabolism. The Director is in charge of the theatre, as God is of the world; he is responsible
for its very existence, he runs the show and is concerned with its overall
appeal to the public. To be sure, he has a troublesome task; his public

may not be accustomed to the best of all possible worlds, but they have read 'an awful lot' (lines 45–6) – this, by no means the only reference to the eighteenth-century intellectual climate in these opening scenes, could well be a jibe at the secularized scepticism of an enlightened audience, as well as a rueful reflection on the reading craze of a contemporary public and on Goethe's own experiences as director of the Weimar Court Theatre.

Much of the argument about the 'Prelude' has concerned its relation to the rest of the drama; indeed, Oskar Seidlin has argued that it has no such connection, and was originally written as a prelude to Goethe's sequel to The Magic Flute.[4] Seidlin's thesis is largely based on lines 231–8, which appear to refer more appropriately to a comic Singspiel spectacle than to the first part of Faust, and on some lines of the Clown from some draft material that might suggest the figure of Papageno.[5] This is scarcely conclusive; and a further argument against the applicability of the 'Prelude' to the whole Faust drama – namely, that the scope of the action described by the Director in lines 239–42 ('From heaven through the world to hell') is not consistent with the subsequent action – can be dealt with simply enough. It is true that Goethe's Faust ends not in hell but in heaven; but Goethe could at this stage hardly have known precisely how he was to end the work some thirty years later. And quite apart from the fact that we do see the jaws of hell, at least, gaping in the penultimate scene of Faust II, a draft scheme for Faust dating from around 1800 does indeed conclude with an 'epilogue in chaos on the way to hell'.[6]

The 'Vorspiel' is Goethe's ironic apologia for the unconventional scope and nature of the subsequent drama – though we do not have to share August Wilhelm Schlegel's somewhat dismissive view that it represents his 'Scheidebrief vom Theater', his abandoning of the exigencies of the stage.[7] It is a half-comic, half-serious means of craving the audience's indulgence for the inadequacies of a stage performance, a warning to expect, and not to be offended by, the bewildering mixture of spectacle, lofty sentiment, magic, human emotion, comedy and tragedy, clowning and mystery, that will follow. It is, in dialogue form, the equivalent of Goethe's protest that his work, which encompasses such a richly colourful and diverse spectrum of life, cannot be hung 'on the meagre thread of a single idea'.[8]

The assumption that the Writer represents the views and beliefs of the author Goethe is no longer tenable, if it ever was. Indeed, his humourless and sententious rhetoric is arguably more heavily ironized than either the anxious commercialism of the Director or the sceptical pragmatism of the Clown; the comic stage 'business' suggested between lines 132 and 133, where the Writer evidently indulges in some histrionic posturing, is evidence enough of this. And yet we should not dismiss the sentiments of the Writer simply because of his loftily arrogant conception of an art undefiled by any concession to the claims of banal reality or to the practical demands of theatrical performance. While much of the Writer's declamation, especially lines 134–57, reads like a parody of the aesthetic solipsism of Goethe's problematic poet Torquato Tasso, the implication is, as Benjamin Bennett reminds us, that truth, in life as in the theatre, is made up of all three perspectives: 'neither a complete self-limitation within the strictly practical (the Director), nor even a deep appreciation of ironic subtlety (the Player) is alone sufficient'.[9] These restrictions must be countered or complemented by a creative striving for ideal harmony, even at the risk of error or failure; here, too, in the tension between the extravagant aspirations of the Writer and the sceptical realism of the Clown, in the dynamic relationship of striving and error, the integrity of the 'Vorspiel', the 'Prolog' and the drama as a whole is evident.

The final words of the Director, possibly an echo of the prologue of the Chorus in *Henry V*, prepare the audience for the following scene: if the 'Vorspiel' had presented the stage as a world, the 'Prolog' presents the world as a stage.

'Prolog im Himmel': Prologue in Heaven

Entirely without irony are the majestic opening hymns to creation sung by the archangels, who describe the harmony of the cosmic order in regular strophes: the wider cosmos (Raphael), the earth (Gabriel) and the elements (Michael). They evoke the 'Kette/Der tiefsten Wirkung' (lines 261–2) that Faust for a moment will imagine he has grasped in his vision of the Macrocosm. It is a matter of debate whether the cosmic order described here is Ptolemaic or Copernican, geocentric or heliocentric; the reference to the orbit of the sun and the harmony of the spheres in lines 243–6 suggests the former, while the image of the spinning earth in the second strophe might suggest the latter. Arens argues persuasively that the cosmology presented here is neither, but is Pythagorean, in which earth and sun revolve around a central fire.[10] Moreover, the Pythagorean universe also supposes a tumultuous cosmic sound, inaudible to human ears but heard by the angels – and, interestingly, also by the spirits of the scene 'Anmutige Gegend', where the sun rises with a great tumult (stage direction after line 4665). At the same time, as Arens points out, 'Klang', 'Donner' and 'Tönen' are sounds commonly attributed to the planets and the cosmos in the imagery of much seventeenth- and eighteenth-century devotional poetry.

The calm reverence of the archangels is broken by the entry of Mephistopheles, who parodies the angels' lines, mocks their lofty expression, even pokes mild fun at the Lord and, in lines that at once echo and travesty the philosophical assumptions of the Age of Reason,[11] expresses his contempt for the ultimate miracle of God's creation, man. The appearance of the devil among the Lord's retinue is, as Goethe acknowledged, based on the Book of Job (1: 6–12). And the similarities between the biblical account and Goethe's 'Prologue' are indeed striking, even down to the wager offered by Satan to the Lord – the formulation of which in the Lutheran version is much closer to Goethe than in the Vulgate or the King James Bible version: 'Aber recke deine Hand aus, und taste an alles, was er hat: *was gilt's*, er wird dir ins Angesicht absagen?' (my emphasis). Nevertheless, the situation of Job is quite different from that of Faust: an innocent, godly and happy man is visited by arbitrary misfortune, whereas a godless, arrogant and frustrated Faust voluntarily concludes a pact with hell. But the idea that Satan himself can unwittingly perform God's will, that evil can work for good, is fundamental to both.

In the course of this disturbingly familiar and human exchange between God and devil, the main lines of the 'theological' issues bearing on Faust's earthly career and his ultimate salvation are laid down. However, the issues raised here do not cover the whole question of Faust's salvation, which can only be seen in its full perspective by taking into account Mephisto's introduction to Faust, their pact and wager, the final scenes of *Faust II*, and indeed the broad lines of the dramatic action. From the 'Prolog im Himmel' alone, it appears that the Lord is entirely confident of Faust's salvation – indeed, it might seem, and it is frequently assumed, that he here goes as far as to promise or guarantee it. But the Lord's figurative expression, even his very syntax, make this less than certain.

When the Lord tells Mephisto in lines 308–9 that he will 'soon' lead Faust into the light, it is unclear whether he means the light of heaven – salvation – or whether he here implies that he will, some time in the course of Faust's earthly life, grant him clarity, an awareness or wisdom, that will lead him out of his present confusion. Certainly, such clarity is something that Faust can scarcely be said to achieve in the course of his life, or at most only to a relative degree; but the following metaphor of lines 310–11, that a tree will eventually bear blossom and fruit, would seem to apply more appropriately to the course of a man's life on earth than to his posthumous salvation or transfiguration. Nor do the Lord's words in lines 327–9 specifically guarantee Faust's salvation; lines 328–9 express the somewhat circular or tautologous dictum that a *good* man is conscious of the right way. More crucially still, the understanding of line 327 depends on an inherent ambiguity in the reference of the German word 'wenn' in this context: it is syntactically quite unclear whether it is to be understood as 'when' or as 'if'.

As Arens comments, anything but divine clarity reigns in Goethe's heaven; and Arens has gone some way to meeting this problem by suggesting that the Lord must change his mind after line 311, and that he modifies his plans for Faust. That is, he shifts from his undertaking to grant Faust 'clarity' towards an agreement to allow the devil to try to seduce Faust from his true path, from his 'primal source', or 'Urquell'.[12] At all events, it cannot be claimed with any certainty that the Lord in the course of this scene promises or guarantees Faust's salvation – only that the Lord appears quite confident that the devil will not be able to drag Faust down his path to damnation. Indeed, it is perfectly likely that Goethe quite deliberately and consciously introduced ambiguity and uncertainty here, leaving the issue poised between providence and free will, if only to give himself freedom in the future course of the drama.

Nevertheless, the Lord does appear here to lay down the criteria for Faust's salvation, which include three principles. These are, that human striving is inseparable from error; that man has an 'Urquell' – a no doubt deliberately vague term suggesting some form of divine spark, goodness, or conscience in man; and finally, that evil has its positive function in the order of things, that the devil must, in his own manner, work creatively within God's scheme by goading men out of their inclination to sloth and indolence.

The broad paradox of this extraordinary arrangement between God and Mephisto is that the devil should offer a wager or challenge that he can scarcely win, since his very function is to work to fulfil the divine will. It is true that no actual wager appears to be contracted here; but the Lord does respond clearly enough to Mephisto's challenge. And the paradox of the situation is further compounded later, in the second 'Studierzimmer' scene, when Mephisto, who has admitted to Faust his positive function for good in the scheme of things (lines 1335–6), nevertheless undertakes a wager that he cannot possibly win. That is, while it is his function to spur men out of sloth into activity, while he must, in his function as devil, contribute dynamically to God's purpose, he still accepts Faust's challenge to him to do the opposite – to reduce Faust to a state of indolence and satiety.

If Mephisto must, willy-nilly, work in this way for good, then Faust must surely be saved; indeed, his salvation would appear to be all the more secure since the devil himself must provide the impetus for Faust's striving. For, as the angels proclaim in the final scene in heaven, unremitting striving is a condition of man's salvation (lines 11936–7). The question here seems to be not so much 'How is Faust to be saved?', but rather 'How, under these conditions, could Faust ever be damned?'. There are two factors that qualify this paradoxical situation.

First, it must be borne in mind that what the angels sing is: 'Wer immer strebend sich bemüht,/Den können wir erlösen'. Striving, unremitting effort, a constant awareness of and reaching for ideals and ambitions beyond his grasp, a refusal to lie down on a 'couch of indolence' – all this does not guarantee a man's salvation; it earns him the possibility of redemption, it leaves him open to the operation of a loving grace beyond his understanding – and, of course, beyond the understanding of the devil. Secondly, it appears that Mephisto, at least, perceives an alternative possibility of Faust's damnation – one which is, moreover, evidently allowed for in the Lord's words, if not in the specific case of Faust, then at least in general principle. That is, if Mephisto can seduce Faust's spirit from its 'Urquell', if he can lead him downwards on his path, then he might, by a sufficient expenditure of diabolical resources and energy (the 'große Aufwand' that Mephisto, in line 11837, despairingly concedes has been wasted), involve Faust in such a morass of crime, guilt and sin as to put him beyond the pale of redemption. And as we shall argue later, the means by which Mephisto intends to do this is by harnessing Faust's own titanic appetite for experience, his very insatiability. As far as the debate in the 'Prolog im Himmel' is concerned, and irrespective of any real or imagined wager between the Lord and Mephisto, it is sufficient for the devil's purpose that he is given the opportunity or the permission to tempt Faust.

After the Lord's confirmation of the devil's role in his creation, the scene returns to the cosmic certainties with which it opened, with the Lord's affirmation of the dynamic permanence of creation and of the force that will both inform Faust's earthly career and determine his eventual salvation: love. This stage heaven then 'closes' in a scenically mechanical manner (stage direction after line 349), thus sustaining the fiction of the itinerant theatre in the 'Prelude'; and Mephistopheles, defiantly insouciant of his humiliating relegation to the function of an ethical cog in the mechanism of creation, characteristically retains the last word as he in turn patronizes 'the old man' in an impudent aside to the audience.

NOTES: CHAPTER 4

1 GA. 5. 529–30.
2 For an extended analysis of this scene, see Alwin Binder, *Das Vorspiel auf dem Theater. Poetologische und geschichtsphilosophische Aspekte in Goethes Faust-Vorspiel*.

3   See Requadt, *Goethes 'Faust I'*, pp. 40 ff.
4   Oskar Seidlin, 'Is the "Prelude in the Theatre" a Prelude to "Faust"?'. Jost Schillemeit has recently argued that the scene was originally written for the opening of the rebuilt Weimar Theatre on 12 Oct. 1798 ('Das *Vorspiel auf dem Theater* zu Goethes *Faust*. Entstehungszusammenhänge und Folgerungen für sein Verständnis').
5   GA. 5. 541 (no. 2).
6   ibid. (no. 1).
7   'Vorlesungen über dramatische Kunst und Literatur', no. 36, in A. W. Schlegel, *Kritische Schriften und Briefe*, ed. Edgar Lohner (Stuttgart, 1962–74), Vol. 6, pt 2, p. 279.
8   To Eckermann, 6 May 1827 (Biedermann 3. 394).
9   Benjamin Bennett, '"Vorspiel auf dem Theater": the Ironic Basis of Goethe's *Faust*', p. 453.
10 Arens, *Kommentar zu Goethes Faust I*, pp. 50 ff.
11 See Durrani, *Faust and the Bible*, pp. 27 ff.
12 Arens, *Kommentar zu Goethes Faust I*, pp. 59 ff.

CHAPTER 5

Faust, Part One

THE UNIVERSITY SCENES

'Nacht': Night

The opening monologue is the classic formulation of the Faustian situation; while only a distant echo of Marlowe's version, it is remarkably close to it in spirit. The four faculties are contemptuously dismissed, as is the whole apparatus of conventional scholarship – teaching, titles, learning itself – as a means to truth, to knowledge, or to their effective application to the human condition. It is unprofitable to argue over the precise age of Faust at this point, though he is traditionally understood as a man of advanced age. It is not certain that Goethe, in modifying the 'Doctor and Professor' of the *Urfaust* to 'Magister and Doctor', intended to reduce either Faust's age or his academic status; it would be anachronistic to assume that 'Doctor', in sixteenth- or in eighteenth-century usage, was junior to 'Professor'. Faust has been teaching for some ten years, and yet he must lose thirty years in the witch's kitchen to become the young lover of Gretchen. This would indicate a lengthy and arduous period of study, some twenty years or more, before his teaching career even began – long enough, perhaps, to reach the limits of conventional book-learning.

Faust's bitterness here is not only due to frustrated ideals, nor is it exclusively the result of the frustrations of scholarship itself; he clearly resents not only the futility of pure and applied learning but also the material rewards they fail to offer, the power and status they fail to confer. His turning to magic – as yet, we infer, only to white or 'natural' magic, a not entirely heretical step in Faust's own time – is the compounded result of frustrated personal and scholarly ambition, the impatient hubris of a man who considers himself beyond the common run of humanity, who is ruthlessly prepared to risk himself and others in order to gain immediate access to knowledge, and therefore to power, by means of magical revelation rather than through the never-ending accumulation of book-learning. Faust's terminology draws on the mystical vocabulary of alchemy – 'Saamen und Würckung Krafft' ('seeds and active energy') is itself a term from hermetic writing; and his whole ambition is that of the magus who seeks the direct revelation of ultimate knowledge, the philosophers' stone. His agnosticism and frustration are not those of the devoted scholar – that figure is caricatured and lampooned in Wagner – but rather those of the titanic Stürmer und Dränger whose impetuous ambition has brought him up against what Goethe, in the poem of that title, terms the 'Grenzen der Menschheit' – man's physical and intellectual limitations.

Oddly, the first attempt Faust makes to escape the restrictions of his study is to turn not to magic but to nature. The first of his four attempts in this scene to claw his way out of the impasse of accidie, frustration, dissatisfaction and despair – by turning to nature, to the Macrocosm, to the Erdgeist and to suicide – is an appeal to the moon, an intensely lyrical expression of the nature-mysticism that expects renewed vigour and strength from contact with the natural world. Both Werther and Egmont seek solace and refuge from the perplexities and confinement of their condition by a rhapsodic identification with the creator in organic nature; and Faust will briefly experience a similar, if less exuberant, response in the opening monologue of the 'Wald und Höhle' scene. Here, in the study, his vision is, like Egmont's in prison, a nostalgic wish-fulfilment, not so much a resolute 'Antaeus' experience as an Ossianic lament, a plea for a disembodied spirit-existence in nocturnal nature, for the baptismal therapy of bathing in moonlit dew. It is a passage that resumes a whole complex spectrum of Goethe's own early lyrical nature-mysticism as well as traditional literary and folkloric symbolism. The moon was perceived by the young Goethe as a melancholy friend and comforter, as the bringer of healing dew, as the companion of departed souls and as the source of light in darkness; here, for Faust, it is the agent of hoped-for release from the dusty obscurity of his study.

His appeal, however, is illusory; and here already, the violent manic-depressive swings of Faust's morale are evident.[1] Just as Werther alternates between ecstasy and despair, between the freedom of nature and the 'cage' or 'prison' of his own existence, so Faust's vision returns to the sterile and macabre paraphernalia of his alchemist's den, his 'dungeon', into which the light of heaven penetrates only in a dim and refracted form. This is Faust's early, negative judgement of the relative human experience of truth or light; much later, in the imagery of the opening scene of Faust II, he will recognize the positive symbolic value of human perceptions of the absolute in the analogy of the rainbow within the waterfall. Here, he turns from nature to magic, to the work of his own contemporary Nostradamus, for guidance in the occult sciences.

The sign of the Macrocosm that Faust contemplates is, in literal terms, an astrological diagram representing the harmony of the universe, the interrelationship of the heavens, man and the earth, symbolized in the lines of affinity between the planets, the human organs and the metals or elements. In this abstract scheme Faust imagines he perceives 'die wirkende Natur', active nature in its cosmic totality (lines 440–1); and he describes his vision in the ecstatic language of revelation, as a glimpse into a Swedenborgian realm of spirits, of light and of sunrise.

The precise terms of the vision Faust describes in lines 447–53 are not immediately clear. It is almost always associated with Jacob's vision of a ladder stretching from earth to heaven, with God's angels ascending and descending (Genesis 28: 12) – in spite of the fact that no such ladder features in Faust's vision. There is, moreover, in the biblical account no mention of the golden vessels of Faust's vision, nor of the harmonious sounds that accompany it, nor indeed of the total harmony of interacting forces in creation that Faust evokes. We have already mentioned the reference in the Faustbook of the Christlich Meynender to Faust's reading in Zoroaster of 'ascending and descending spirits' – though this supplies only one single motif of Faust's vision. Erich Trunz gives several possible sources for the imagery of these lines – writers such as Jakob Böhme, Johannes Kepler, Georg von Welling, or F. M. van Helmont, whose pansophic writings themselves drew on biblical imagery of mystical expression;[2] but it is Harold Jantz who has supplied what is hitherto the most satisfactory interpretation of this vision.[3] The 'Himmelskräfte' of line 449 are not, for Jantz, angels passing buckets to each other 'after the manner of a celestial fire brigade', but rather 'powers of heaven' – that is, the twelve zodiacal constellations that rise and set in the sky, through which the 'golden urns' (a Miltonian metaphor for the planets) pass along the ecliptic, and whose influence, penetrating from heaven through the earth to the sound of the harmony of the spheres, extends to man himself. This interpretation, which does justice to almost every item in Faust's vision of cosmic harmony, of 'a perfect dynamic whole composed of . . . interrelated harmonious parts', is not universally accepted; but it remains the most elegant explanation of a passage that Goethe himself had possibly not worked out in over-scrupulous detail.

Faust turns away from the sign of the Macrocosm because it is only a sign, an abstract construction of the human mind; it is not a direct revelation of the harmony of macrocosm and microcosm, but an arcane system into which he reads a spectacular vision – a vision of which he remains only an enthralled spectator. Goethe's draft scheme for *Faust* defines Faust's ambition as a more dynamic one, as an 'ideal striving for active involvement in and empathy with the whole of nature';[4] and Faust's following words (lines 455 ff.) express in physical terms his urgent need to drink at the wellsprings of life, at the breasts of nature – admittedly a confused jumble of metaphors, but entirely characteristic of Faust's imagery in these early scenes. Leitmotifs of liquid, streams, breasts, springs and drinking alternate vividly with metaphors of thirst, aridity, dust, dry leaves and bones, just as images of light and dark alternate both in Faust's figurative expression and in the scenic changes themselves.

From the cypher of the Macrocosm Faust turns to that of the Erdgeist (Earth Spirit), from a vision of universal harmony to the very force of life. And even more than the vision of the Macrocosm, the antecedents and the nature of the Erdgeist have produced a huge mass of commentary. Paracelsus' 'archeus terrae' or Giordano Bruno's 'anima terrae', Welling, Swedenborg and other cabbalistic writers have been cited as possible sources for the name of Goethe's spirit, and Arens also refers to Herder's image of a 'vital earth spirit', a 'großer lebendiger Geist der Erde'.[5] It is, however, commonly held that whatever the origins of its name, Goethe's Erdgeist is very largely his own freely invented pantheistic symbol or personification of the vital forces of nature. Mason has controversially suggested that in turning from the universal vision of the Macrocosm to the terrestrial spirit, Faust is allying himself with the demonic; the Erdgeist, while not a spirit of evil in any traditional or absolute sense, is nevertheless 'sinister, ambivalent, ruthless and dangerous, so that in turning to it Faust is taking an imprudent, temerarious, ominous, reprehensible step, as he would not be doing if he adhered to the Makrokosmus instead'.[6] Indeed, Mason claims, the ambivalence of this chthonic spirit of earth reflects Goethe's 'serious misgivings about his own vitalistic pantheism' – to be compared with the ambivalence of Werther's alternately ecstatic and horrified perceptions of the creative and destructive processes of God-immanent nature, or the perception of a chain of creation and destruction that Goethe described in his review of Sulzer in the Frankfurter Gelehrte Anzeigen of 1772.[7] Hence, Mason argues, Faust's choice of the Erdgeist leads him into an alliance with Mephistopheles, away from the detached and spiritual contemplation of the heavens towards the active rough-and-tumble of sensual worldly experience.

It is of course true that there are clear indications in all three versions of Faust I that Faust, at least, associates Mephistopheles with the Erdgeist, to the extent that he perceives and treats the devil as an emissary of the spirit. It is also true that the spirit appears to Faust in flashes of flame and in a terrifying configuration. Yet few critics have been able to accept Mason's bold hypothesis that the Erdgeist is a 'Luciferian' phenomenon, preferring to see the spirit as ethically neutral, creating and destroying indifferently as the vital principle, the active energy, in creation. Above all, the superb lines in which the Erdgeist characterizes its own activity, weaving the living raiment of God on the whirring loom of time, are ill-fitted to support any real or close affinity between it and the sterile negativity of Goethe's devil. Some critics, indeed, have even associated the Erdgeist not with Lucifer but with God, who appeared to Moses in the fire; but against this Requadt represents a large body of opinion in claiming that the Erdgeist mediates 'vertically', as it were, between God and the world, and 'horizontally' in ethical terms between good and evil, creation and destruction.[8]

Nevertheless, it is certainly true that Faust's encounter with the Erdgeist is ominous and momentous in that it leads, directly or indirectly, to his alliance with Mephisto; for, whether or not Mephisto is actually sent to Faust by the Erdgeist, it is his inability to come to terms with the spirit that causes Faust's morale to plunge into suicidal despair, and leads him eventually into the state of titanic dissatisfaction in which he will curse all human values and be prepared to conclude a pact with hell. 'You are the equal of the spirit that you grasp, not mine': these lines (512–13) appear to lead Faust, at any rate, to imagine that Mephisto is an emissary of the Erdgeist. But Faust's limited perspective can hardly take account of the transcendental situation of the 'Prologue in Heaven', in which he is the object of a theological experiment. Unless we accept this discrepancy between Faust's limited awareness and the audience's or reader's superior knowledge of the agreement in heaven as a deliberate part of Goethe's intention, the conclusion must be that Goethe did not resolve the Erdgeist problem of the early versions when he came to write the final version of Faust I, but rather that he simply overrode it by means of his new conception in the prologue.

Faust's defiant riposte to the Erdgeist (lines 514–17) is futile; his assertion of himself as 'Ebenbild der Gottheit' ('image of the deity') will be modified successively in lines 614, 618 and 652–3 in a curve of despair resulting from his rejection by the 'great spirit'. It is the annihilating sense of inadequacy at this failure that will lead Faust, by way of his frustrated attempt at suicide, to his pact with the 'lesser' spirit, Mephistopheles.

Faust's visionary histrionics are succeeded by bathos with the entry of his famulus Wagner, who is the comic travesty of academic pedantry. But for all the caricature of Wagner, he does represent an intellectual

tradition and position. In sixteenth-century terms, Faust and he stand
for the extremes of the mystical and humanist traditions respectively, as
it were the arcane extravagance of Paracelsus on the one hand and the
(admittedly heavily caricatured and distorted) sobriety of Erasmus on
the other. In eighteenth-century terms, they are respectively the extremes of Sturm und Drang and Aufklärung, emotionalism against rationalism, irreverent titanism against sober study, nature against history,
creative genius and the spirit against rhetoric and the word, intuitive
response against arid textual scrutiny, mercurial impatience against
earnest and plodding endeavour. The 'creeping pedant' Wagner sees
the arid sources of scholarship as the founts of wisdom – here Faust's
imagery of thirst and liquid is travestied by Wagner's pedantry. Wagner
can also be said to stand for the optimistic ideology of the Aufklärung,
which is here guyed as perfectibilist conceit: the study of the past is
pleasurable because it demonstrates the extent of human progress, 'wie
wir's dann zuletzt so herrlich weit gebracht' (lines 572–3). It is no
accident that these two sententious lines are cast in alexandrines.

    The contest between the two is an unequal one; the young Goethe of
the Urfaust, while by no means entirely identifiable with Faust here, was
closer to his mysticism than to Wagner's barren scholasticism, and
Faust's replies are devastatingly formulated by a superior intellect that is
able to browbeat his timid colleague into submission. Many critics draw
a distinction between the role of Wagner as comic buffoon in this early
Urfaust dialogue and the less starkly caricatured partner of Faust's Easter
walk in the 'Vor dem Tor' scene that was written some time between
1798 and 1801; in the later scene, it is argued, Wagner is no longer the
butt of Faust's sarcasm and ridicule, but rather a respected colleague
and confidant – one who, moreover, provides a sober corrective to
Faust's extravagant flights of rhetoric and fantasy. Indeed, not all critics
have seen even the Urfaust confrontation as entirely one-sided; Arens
has noted that Faust's contempt of rhetoric is itself, ironically enough,
delivered with all the elaborate mannerism, hyperbole and lofty
metaphor of the orator, while Wagner's own words are relatively simple
and unadorned.[9] Ultimately, however, while some scholars may be
tempted to side with the 'worthy' Wagner, if only out of a sense of
professional solidarity, against Faust's overwrought rhetoric, the effect
of this scene is comic, and the butt of the ridicule is, clearly enough, the
hapless famulus. Goethe himself suggested in his overall scheme that
the advantage in this confrontation lay with Faust, that in this dispute
between 'formless content' and 'empty form' the advantage was with
the former.[10]

Many features of Faust's second monologue reiterate the positions of his opening monologue in extreme form. The overwhelming sense of restriction and oppression, the curbing of passionate ideals and convictions by the weight of commonplace experience, the discrepancy between hope and fulfilment, imagination and reality, lead to a downward plunge of Faust's morale. His vision of 'Sorge' – care, worry, responsibility – in lines 644 ff. is a powerful early evocation of an insidiously corrosive and paralysing germ in human experience; at the end of his career, it is Sorge alone of the four grey women who will attack and blind the ageing Faust. His earlier defiant assertion that he is 'God's likeness', 'more than Cherub', becomes inverted in lines 652–5: he is the image not of God but of the worm to which the Erdgeist compared him (line 498). And lines 656–85 list an inventory of Faust's study that almost exactly repeats the motifs of the opening monologue: smoke, dust, moths, dim light, desk, books, paper, bones, instruments – the inherited paraphernalia of a futile science.

From this develops a further extreme of negation, the resolve to commit suicide. And yet, characteristically, Faust expects from death a further mystical experience or revelation, much as he did from the Macrocosm or the Erdgeist; his vision of death is expressed in terms of moonlight in darkness, of new horizons, new oceans, a new dawn, new spheres of activity. Faust's perception of death, like his previous vision of the cosmos and of nature, is a mystical vision expressed in a luxuriant lyricism, in Faustian images of wings and flight, of the strait gate of rebirth and liberation, of thirst and drinking.

Opinions are sharply divided on the source and the nature of the Easter hymns that break in at this point and distract Faust from his suicide attempt. They have been understood as a direct divine intervention in the dramatic action, or alternatively, on the not entirely reliable testimony of Mephistopheles in lines 3270–1, as a diabolical intervention; more sober commentators understand them as emanating from a nearby church. While Trunz, for example, sees in these hymns a profound lyrical and musical expression of the Easter mystery, Arens bluntly asserts that the only line free from ironic speciousness is the one that cannot be attributed to Goethe: 'Christ is risen'.[11] Durrani's view of the irony here is more balanced: 'To make religion, which claims to mediate between man and God, stop Faust from striving after the supernatural and instead kindle memories of childhood and a love of this life in him is unquestionably a highly ironic device ... Verses celebrating heaven have had the paradoxical effect on Faust of stimulating an interest in life.'[12]

We are not, however, asked by Goethe to accept the sacrosanct meaning of the Easter message as such, nor does Goethe invite the reader or audience to assume Faust's acceptance of it. Lines 765–8 indicate quite clearly that Faust is unresponsive to the theological truth of the Christian mystery of resurrection and redemption; he is, on the other hand, highly susceptible to the symbolism of rebirth and regeneration implicit in the Easter message. It is no accident that lines 775–8 evoke a natural landscape of spring and growth; and Faust will reiterate this Easter rebirth in man, nature and religious doctrine even more vividly in the following 'Vor dem Tor' scene (lines 903 ff.).

Faust is also susceptible to the memory of the naïve and unquestioning faith of his childhood, when simple perceptions and responses were not yet overlaid and qualified by the agnostic scepticism of the inquiring mind. To be sure, this is a sentimental impulse; but it is scarcely strange or ironical, as Durrani suggests, that religion should satisfy Faust at this point, 'when visions of celestial harmony and the Earth Spirit were unable to do so',[13] since it is not religious faith that brings Faust back from suicide, nor does religion satisfy him here. A brief respite has been gained from despair; but, after a short interlude, it will return in even more devastating form to bring Faust to his pact with the devil.

'Vor dem Tor': Outside the City Gate
This scene provides a contrapuntal contrast to the previous one, as we move from the dark and solitary confinement of Faust's cell to bright daylight, human society, colour and bustle; it is the public reality of the vernal festival, the 'Frühlingsfeier' that Faust's youthful memories evoked in the previous scene. The structure of the opening episode of the scene – a review or parade of figures across the stage – is a technique that will recur, in increasingly elaborate and allegorical forms, in the 'Walpurgisnachtstraum', in the carnival masquerade of the first act of Faust II and in the marine pageant of the 'Klassische Walpurgisnacht'; here, it is a review of a relatively naturalistic social spectrum, which is also the reader's or audience's introduction to the domestic and social milieu of Gretchen. The Girls of the Town, the Soldiers, even the Old Woman with her matchmaking, are types that correspond roughly to the individuals Gretchen and Lieschen, Valentin and Frau Marthe; and the Peasants' ballad, 'Der Schäfer putzte sich zum Tanz' (lines 949–80), is thematically not unrelated to the story of Faust and Gretchen.

Faust's lyrical opening speech is full of colour, light, movement, imagery of thaw and growth, rebirth and revival, hope, release and freedom. The loving-cup he accepts from the Peasants is the very reverse of the solitary ceremony he very nearly enacted in his study the previous night; here even Faust appears to enjoy the honour and status he so bitterly found wanting in his life in the opening monologue. And yet any impression that Faust himself finds release or satisfaction in this landscape, this homage, or this company is surely misleading, or at the very best momentary. His acknowledgement of the Peasants' respect is brief and perfunctory; his enjoining them to praise not him but heaven for their health and welfare (lines 1009–10) is equally laconic, and surely sardonic; and his brutal account to Wagner (lines 1034 ff.) of his and his father's obscure alchemical and medical practices reveals only the shameful bad conscience of the once idealistic healer who has been reduced by failure and disillusionment to a bitter cynicism and a contempt for human credulity. Even his declaration in line 940, where he might appear, quite uncharacteristically, to profess his pleasure and satisfaction at being a man among his fellow-men, is open to question. Nearly every text of Faust, from the original 1808 Cotta edition onwards, with the exception of Trunz's Hamburger Ausgabe, has a colon, not a full stop, after line 939; Petsch's edition of 1926 and Beutler's Gedenk-ausgabe even set line 940 in quotes.[14] In other words, line 940 is scarcely likely to be intended as a profession of Faust's own sentiment, but rather as his outsider's perception of that of others – a perception, moreover, that only serves to emphasize his own feeling of isolation and alienation.

Wagner's naïve veneration of Faust and of scientific tradition triggers a renewed outburst of Faustian frustration. Faust's remarkable speech of lines 1064–99 is constructed around two fields of imagery, light and flight; his grandiose evocation of the landscape under the setting sun only fires his fantasy of escape, of wings to lift him into a sphere of constant sunlight. Requadt has perceptively shown how the final images of his speech recapitulate its thematic structure – the lark climbs out of the 'ocean of error', the eagle soars and wheels horizontally in the upper air, and the migrating crane follows its instinctive drive towards the distant horizon. The banality of Wagner's reply sets off Faust's celebrated declaration of the two souls within his breast, the pull of the spiritual and the physical, the ideal and the real, the mystical and the practical, the infinite and the finite – the almost endless resonances of this fundamental polarity can hardly be exhausted by enumeration. It is a duality that Faust will only begin to resolve, or rather come to terms with, when he ceases to conceive it as an irreconcilable polarity, and comes to realize that the phenomena of empirical reality are the symbolic reflection, the 'Abglanz' of absolute values. It is the duality that will torture Faust throughout the Gretchen episode, and will blight his relationship with her, as he is torn between love and lust, shame and sensuality, his conscience and his appetites, and his two personae, that of the renegade intellectual and that of the young lover.

The nature of the spirits that Faust invokes in lines 1118 ff. is open to debate. If, as many commentators agree, this is a reference to a neo-Platonist notion of a sublunary sphere inhabited by demons, then the import is clear enough – it is an appeal that is almost immediately answered by the appearance of a black dog that will indeed, in its transformation as Mephistopheles, provide Faust quite literally with a 'magic cloak' and lead him away to a new and colourful existence. But Faust's appeal might refer to the fulfilment of the higher side of his dual nature – it might, as Mason puts it, represent 'the upsurging of the divine side of his nature'.[15] If this is so, then the prompt appearance of the dog is a richly ironic response to his wish, for the spirit it conceals is not going to draw Faust's spirit 'upwards to high ancestral spheres' (line 1117). The fact that Wagner takes these spirits as evil, and glosses them in terms of a sort of medieval weather forecast, does not provide any helpful guidance, since he consistently misconstrues the nature and direction of Faust's ambitions. At all events, it is scarcely the 'higher' or 'divine' side of Faust's nature that will be catered for by the spirit that appears in the poodle.

'Studierzimmer' I: Study I

The 'Vor dem Tor' scene, which opened in bright sunlight, closes with the onset of dusk and mist, preparing the return to the narrow but cosy confines of Faust's study. It also closes with an element of burlesque in Faust's and Wagner's antics with the dog; and the comic note survives into the following scene, counterpointing the solemnity of Faust's efforts to divine the love of God in and through the Gospel of St John. It is again difficult to sift the ironies here: are we to accept at face value Faust's earnest search for enlightenment or revelation from the gospel? Or is the whole scene a burlesque, as F. D. Luke has suggested, reflecting the classical Goethe's inability, during the final phase of work on Faust I, to treat the nordic phantom-world of demonic black poodles, spells and spirits, indeed even the magus figure of Faust himself, with his 'bland philosophising' and his '"Sturm und Drang" rhetoric', as the 'imaginatively serious phenomena' that he had originally created in his early youth?[16]

Certainly, it is hardly possible to regard the passages in which Faust conjures the poodle as anything other than, in Luke's words, 'a piece of higher slapstick' – though if it is, it is slapstick informed, as always, by Goethe's broad knowledge of cabbalistic rites and magic formulae. But we should hesitate before we conclude that this comedy infects or

invalidates the seriousness of Faust's attempt to find revelation through
the scriptures, or that his translating the Bible is no more than a
secondary device to prompt the poodle's baying. As Durrani shows in a
detailed survey of opinion, there is no consensus on this question;[17] but
there is little reason why we should not take seriously Faust's attempt to
seek revelation in another book of mystical authority in this new mood
of sober introspection and awareness of his 'better self' and of love
towards man and God (lines 1178–85). As he previously sought revelation in Nostradamus, so he now seeks it one last time in the inscrutable
opening of St John; his translation of the gospel is more than simply an
aesthetic or intellectual exercise. In the opening passages of this scene,
the struggle between Faust's mood of intense and even pious introspection on the one hand and the distracting interventions of the poodle on
the other, is reflected in the metre and verse form; lines 1178–1209 form
four eight-line strophes which alternate between the smooth regularity
of the lines expressing Faust's new-found, if temporary, peace of mind,
and the restless dactylic rhythms of the lines describing the poodle's
interruptions.

Faust's rendering of the *logos* progresses in a semantic crescendo from
'word' to 'deed'; clearly, with his contempt for scholarship, Faust
cannot be content with the mere word. Nor is 'Sinn', which has been
variously understood as 'sense', 'meaning', 'mind', 'intention', sufficiently active or creative for Faust's restless imagination. 'Kraft',
energy, is a more dynamic version, but falls short of realization; 'Tat',
the deed, alone satisfies his subjective reading of the text. At this point,
we may assume, the poodle's baying becomes violent; but it is not at all
clear whether we should understand this as an expression of the spirit's
disapproval of Faust's preoccupation with holy scripture, as an attempt
to distract him from it, or whether it is the devil voicing his full approval
of Faust's efforts. For not only is Faust's vitalistic and heretical 'translation' quite at odds with the Christian message, as Durrani has
demonstrated,[18] but action, 'Taten', is precisely what Mephistopheles
aims to provide for Faust: active involvement in life, not abstract
contemplation, 'joy and deeds' in place of 'reason and learning' – that is,
the kind of involvement that can, indeed will, bring with it the error and
guilt that the devil must exploit if he is to have any chance of Faust's
damnation. And at this point, where Faust invokes the deed, Mephisto
is ready to reveal himself.

The subsequent exorcizing of the devil from the poodle is burlesque
hocus-pocus; it has little of the tense drama of the Faustbook conjurations or Marlowe – or of the furious passion of Faust's earlier invocation
of the Erdgeist. Faust evidently commands the authoritative textbooks

of magical conjuration, above all the *Clavicula Salomonis* and Paracelsus.[19]
His invocation of the four elemental spirits, salamander, undine, sylph
and kobold, is ineffectual; only the crucifix (lines 1300–9) and the threat
of invoking the trinity (1318–21) appear to command the infernal spirit.
The motif of the devil flinching before the cross, which Goethe had
exploited in the *Urfaust* scene 'Land Strase', here finds its way back into
the text in more rhetorical form.

With the emergence of Mephisto in his guise as a wandering scholar,
the element of comic burlesque is not removed entirely, but is
considerably modified; for all the guarded irony and verbal fencing
between him and Faust, we gain as good an insight into Mephisto's
nature and function from his own mouth at this stage as we do
anywhere else in the drama. The question of his name is skirted round;
he himself never mentions it in the whole drama, and it is Faust who
characterizes him as Beelzebub ('Fliegengott'), Mephis ('Verderber')
and Tophel ('Lügner').[20] His own self-characterization of lines 1335–6 as
'Ein Teil von jener Kraft,/Die stets das Böse will und stets das Gute
schafft' ('A part of that force which ever wills evil and ever creates
good') is certainly consistent with the Lord's definition of his role in the
'Prologue in Heaven'; and yet, if these lines are to be taken at their face
value, it puts the spirit who *always* wills evil and *always* creates good in a
most frustrating and indeed paradoxical position. It appears that the
devil is, willy-nilly, a part of God's scheme, that he must, like a rat in a
maze, unwittingly (or more accurately, in full consciousness and in spite
of himself, since he appears fully aware of his position) pursue his
ordained role. This would certainly accord with his own rueful admission of the frustrations of his *métier* as he explains them to Faust in lines
1362–78; but we are still clearly expected to believe, on the evidence of
the 'Prologue in Heaven', that Mephisto has accepted a challenge from
the Lord that he cannot, under these conditions, possibly win. Such
contradictions and paradoxes have led critics to suggest various alternative explanations. We could assume, for example, that Mephisto is lying
to Faust here, and presenting himself tactically as a relatively harmless
devil; we might draw a distinction between Mephisto's nature, which is
evil and negative, and his cosmic function, which is to work positively
for good; or, in Arens's rather elaborately ingenious interpretation, we
could imagine that when Mephisto speaks of 'das Böse' he means that
which *men* call evil, but when he speaks of 'das Gute' he slyly means
what *he* understands as good – namely, evil.[21]

Mephisto's subsequent self-characterization is rather more straightforward: he is the negator, the destroyer, the evil one (1338–44). But
to Faust's facetious question of line 1345, he goes on to formulate a

cosmogony that clearly contradicts the Lord's definition of evil and the devil as subordinate forces in creation; it is an account in which the primeval darkness from which light was born still asserts its equal claim, an account that sees the universe in terms of a constant struggle between opposing principles of equal status – good and evil, God and devil, spirit and matter, light and dark. Mephisto's cosmogony is one which accords up to a point with the biblical account of creation, in that darkness preceded light; but he distorts the biblical version by insisting that light was born of 'Mother Night', not created by divine fiat. His cosmological theory is Manichaean in its dualism, or more precisely it represents an *inverted* Manichaeism, since it supposes that light invaded and usurped darkness, not vice versa.

It has also been noted that Mephisto's account of the relationship between light, darkness and matter appears to be consistent with Goethe's own theory of optics, in which light and dark are in a constant struggle, and yet are interdependent: light is only perceived in its effects on objects.[22] Closer still, however, is a passage from *Dichtung und Wahrheit* in which Goethe recalls his personal religion during the 1768–9 Frankfurt years of his association with Fräulein von Klettenberg. This was a weird mixture of neo-Platonist and cabbalistic notions gleaned from Gottfried Arnold, according to which, after the fall of Lucifer, evil was concentrated into 'that which we perceive as matter, what we imagine as heavy, dense and dark, but which . . . is just as absolutely powerful and eternal as the Father'.[23]

Mephisto's strange cosmology and his own role in it appears, then, to draw on various traditions – on the Manichaean heresy of light and dark, good and evil, spirit and matter, as equally powerful principles; on the orthodox notion of the devil as tempter, negator and destroyer; and on Goethe's own conception of good and evil as twin polarities. That is, evil is not an absolute principle, but, as he formulated it in his Shakespeare essay of 1771, that which we call evil is only the obverse of good; each is a necessary condition of human existence, as the *zona frigida* and *zona torrida* are necessary conditions of a temperate zone.[24] Faust also summarizes the essential sterility of Mephisto's nature in lines 1379 ff. – he is the cold and malign adversary not specifically of God or man but of the creative force, 'der ewig regen . . . heilsam schaffenden Gewalt'.

The rest of the scene is taken up with further burlesque elements from folklore and occult traditions: the pentagram, the rules of etiquette governing the behaviour of demons, the limits of their powers, and the devil's command over the lower animal world of rodents, amphibians and insects. It remains unexplained why Mephisto leaves Faust at this

stage; we have suggested above that it might be a vestigial survival from
the Faustbooks, or even from Marlowe, where Mephistophilis also
leaves Faust to seek instructions from 'great Lucifer'. This is unnecessary
in Goethe's version, since the separate identities of Mephistopheles on
the one hand and Satan or Lucifer on the other are blurred; and there is
only a vague hint in line 1418 that some kind of preparation is required.

In order to effect his escape, Mephisto exposes Faust to the blandish-
ments of a Spirit chorus (1447 ff.). There is no critical certainty on the
precise nature of these Spirits, either here or in their previous (1259 ff.)
and subsequent (1607 ff.) interventions; indeed, it is not entirely clear
whether they are the same spirits on each occasion. Certainly, Mephisto
claims them as his own, as 'die Kleinen/Von den Meinen' in lines
1627–8; lines 1269–70 also suggest some form of bond between them
and him, and they again function as part of his purpose in lines
1447–1505. On the other hand, they appear to warn Faust of the
poodle's nature in lines 1259 ff., and their lament at Faust's destructive
curse on 'the beautiful world' (1607 ff.) is scarcely Mephistophelean.
And if the arcadian vision with which they distract Faust in lines
1447–1505 is indeed an 'ocean of delusion', it is a remarkably positive
delusion; these hypnotic and seductive lines conjure the vision of a
bacchic, erotic arcadia, a classical vision articulated in a classical metre
(adonics), but expressed with all the assonantal and acoustic fluidity
of modern rhymed verse.

Trunz sees these Spirit choruses as reflecting Faust's inner thought
processes, while Requadt suggests that they operate on the narrow
divide between Faustian wish-fulfilment and Mephistophelean
temptation.[25] Whatever their nature or origin, their function appears to
be to encourage Faust to quit his study and plunge into the world of
'Lust und Taten', into the hurly-burly of life – in which sense they might
be said to represent both Faust's own impulses and Mephisto's strategy
for him.

'Studierzimmer' II: Study II
In this second study scene, Faust's morale plunges once again, and in
a remarkably short space of time. It requires little prompting from
Mephistopheles for him to express his drastic sense of surfeit with life
(1544–71); and it takes only a little more provocation to call forth his
awesome curse on all human material and spiritual values (1583 ff.).
This curse is the secular equivalent of the traditional Faust's resolve to
turn from God to Lucifer, the point at which he is prepared to hazard
anything to escape despair. It seems entirely characteristic of Faust that
he should invert and extend the Pauline trinity of Christian virtues into

his own fourfold version: he curses love, hope, faith – and patience. Requadt and Durrani, however, point to a passage from the Pauline epistles (I Thessalonians 1: 3) in which all four of Faust's 'virtues' are enumerated by the apostle; and there is also a maxim of Goethe's that defines patience as the quintessence of the three Christian virtues.[26] With this universal curse, as E. E. Papst suggests, Faust does not simply arrive at the threshold of concluding a pact with the devil; he has already crossed that threshold.[27]

Exploiting the Spirits' warning, Mephistopheles plays on Faust's own sense of the futility of his titanic impulses – the allusion to Prometheus in line 1636 is hardly accidental – and, with a mixture of enticement and provocation, he approaches the nub of his own conception of a pact: the master–servant relationship. The actual hard-and-fast pact or contract between Faust and Mephisto has often been disregarded by critics, who have seen it as being of very secondary importance beside Faust's later wager or challenge that Mephisto cannot reduce him to a condition of self-satisfied torpor. No doubt the reason for this is that, in the event, Mephisto's contract does not seem to be worth the blood it is written in; the devil's indignant claims to his 'hard-won right' (line 11833) are overriden by a higher authority. Hence, critical opinion has centred more on the elaborate wager that presupposes Faust's unremitting striving as a condition of his salvation. Exclusive attention to the wager, however, leads back to the fundamental paradox of Mephisto's position vis-à-vis Faust. For if, as the Lord decreed in the 'Prologue in Heaven', it is the devil's cosmic function to preserve men from absolute sloth, from 'unbedingte Ruh' – which we may surely equate with Faust's 'couch of indolence' – then why does Mephistopheles enter into a wager with Faust in which the crucial condition is that he must reduce Faust to just such a state if he is to win Faust's soul?

The first thing to bear in mind here is that Faust appears to have no great concern for the world beyond, for the consequences of either pact or wager: 'Das Drüben kann mich wenig kümmern' (line 1660). Moreover, he appears utterly contemptuous of the devil's gifts; he is educated enough in magic and superstition to know that they are illusory and meretricious – this is surely the sense of the controversial lines 1675–87. Much ink has been spilt in the argument as to whether the sentence beginning 'Doch hast du . . .' and ending 'wie ein Meteor, verschwindet' (lines 1678–85) is affirmative, conditional or interrogative. For the question mark after line 1685, which was introduced into the Weimarer Ausgabe by Erich Schmidt, is of dubious authority; both the 1808 edition and the Ausgabe letzter Hand have a full stop here, and successive editors have modified the punctuation according to their

reading of the passage.[28] But, however we construe the syntax, whether
we understand that Faust eagerly craves the devil's ephemeral and
gimcrack distractions or that he is sarcastically disparaging such worth-
less pleasures, it is clear that Faust promises himself no lasting satisfaction from them, and that he settles for them only as a *pis aller*, as a
desperate last resort. For Mephisto, however, this is quite sufficient –
Faust's own motives are for him irrelevant.

The paradoxes and ambiguities of this issue are presumably due to
the fact that Goethe could not, or was unwilling to, conclude the
traditional twenty-four-year pact for his Faust, since he had already at
this stage of writing envisaged Faust's salvation – or, at the very least, he
wished to leave the matter open. As Mason puts it, 'not only has Goethe
substituted a wager for the traditional hard-and-fast pact between Faust
and Mephisto: he has also ... completely eliminated the clear-cut,
uncompromising religious and ethical issues of the original Faust
legend and put in their place something so impalpable and ambivalent
than one is tempted to find it merely vague and almost meaningless.'[29] I
would take issue with Mason's use of the term 'substituted'; as I shall
argue, it is rather that Goethe has *added* Faust's wager to, or superimposed
it upon, Mephisto's pact – to the extent that the latter is often ignored
by critics as unimportant, as a mere gesture by Goethe towards the
traditional legend.

But it is also Mason who has suggested, with brilliant simplicity, a way
out of the contradictions of Mephisto's position. That is, Mephisto does
not take *Faust's* conditions at all seriously:

> The only thing that matters in his eyes is that Faust has committed
> himself to him *on any terms*. Ignoring those conditions, he sets about
> procuring Faust's damnation by the good, old-fashioned, and well-
> tried method of involving him in guilt, crime and sin – just like any
> other normal devil; not by the strange, paradoxical method of trying
> to make him so contented that he might feel inclined to say to the
> passing moment: 'Verweile doch, du bist so schön!' [Stay, you are so
> fair].[30]

There are several factors that support this interpretation. First,
Mephisto nowhere in the course of the drama invokes Faust's conditions for the wager – not in the Gretchen episode, nor in the Helen
episode, nor at Faust's death; he speaks only of his contractual bargain,
of the 'noble soul that pledged itself to me' (line 11830). Secondly, the
strategy that Mephisto adopts throughout the drama is entirely consistent with this purpose; far from trying to satisfy Faust, he goes out of

his way to keep him dissatisfied, to blight his hopes and ideals, and 'to contrive disastrous outcomes for all his ventures, thereby indeed goading him on to further ceaseless activity and striving, as the Lord had intended'.[31] Thirdly, this strategy is also consistent with Mephisto's vicious monologue at the end of the pact scene (lines 1851–67) – a passage which is all too frequently disregarded, and one in which, we may safely assume, Mephisto shows himself in his true colours, since he has no reason to dissimulate as he might in Faust's presence. Here, Mephisto makes it quite clear that he intends to damn Faust by Mason's 'good, old-fashioned, and well-tried method'. He will feed Faust with illusions and trivial banality, with 'Blend- und Zauberwerken' and 'flache Unbedeutenheit'; but, far from satisfying Faust's highest aspirations, he will simply be fuelling his insatiable appetite for experience, and will thereby involve him in such a morass of guilt that he will be beyond the pale of salvation; he will have seduced Faust from his 'Urquell' and dragged him down his path to perdition. And the trump card that Mephisto imagines he holds here, the dynamo that will, he believes, drive Faust inexorably towards his own damnation, is Faust's very insatiability. As Mephisto concludes, with diabolical confidence, such a man does not even require the devil's services to drive him to damnation: 'Und hätt' er sich auch nicht dem Teufel übergeben,/Er müßte doch zugrunde gehn!' (1866–7).

Nevertheless, Mephisto is not prepared to take any such chance; and this is where we ignore the pact at our critical peril. Faust's lofty tirade about bidding the passing moment stay is unimportant to Mephisto. Not only are such sentiments incomprehensible to him, but he has already laid down his own clear terms: a master–servant relationship, to be reversed after Faust's death. He waits patiently for Faust's rhetoric to spend itself, and returns insistently and legalistically to his contract, to the document by means of which, in binding himself to Faust, he has also bound Faust to him for the rest of his life.

We might conclude, then, that at least one of the intractable problems of this scene and its relationship to the 'Prologue in Heaven' can be resolved by distinguishing between the perspectives of the different parties involved – Mephisto, Faust and the Lord. Mephisto's perspective is partial and limited; he is aware of his creative function for good, indeed, he appears to admit it to Faust – and yet he must be committed to the aim of dragging Faust down his path to perdition. Faust's perspective is on the one hand more limited than Mephisto's, in so far as he is quite unaware of the issues discussed in the scene in heaven – indeed, he seems indifferent to any such perspective. On the other hand his perspective is superior to Mephisto's in that he has a

relationship with his 'Urquell', he is aware of and believes in his higher
spiritual urge, aware of a conscience that will, for all the confusion and
criminality of his subsequent career, assert itself sufficiently to prevent
him from falling hopelessly into the devil's clutches. What is more,
Faust knows that this side of his nature is something that Mephisto's
sterile and partial perspective does not allow for and cannot comprehend. The Lord's perspective embraces both the others: he allows for
the perpetual error involved in human striving, and he also sanctions
the creative function of the 'Schalk' ('rogue') in his cosmic scheme.

To distinguish fairly clearly between Mephisto's pact and Faust's
wager would at least explain Mephisto's tactics in entering into a wager
that, by definition, he cannot win; but it does not resolve the paradox of
a devil who, while working to drag men down his path to damnation, is
also fulfilling the divine will by aiding them to meet the precondition of
their salvation, which is unremitting effort and striving. Both Faustian
striving and Mephistophelean negation are involved in Faust's progress
towards salvation. Faust defies the devil to satisfy his highest desires and
ambitions, contemptuously confident that he will be unable to do so;
Mephistopheles, pedantically but realistically insisting on a signed
document, is content with his master–servant contract, confident that
Faust's abandoning of reason and learning, together with the impatient and insatiable titanism of his appetites and his resolve to run the
whole gamut of human experience, will be more than sufficient to lead
him into perdition: 'So hab' ich dich schon unbedingt' (1855). At this
point in the drama, as in the 'Prologue in Heaven', Goethe leaves the
issue poised on the knife-edge between human free will and divine
providence.

Once the contract is signed, there is a subtle shift in the relationship
between Faust and Mephistopheles. Hitherto, Mephisto has been by
turns provocative, obsequious and coaxing, using Faust's rhetoric and
his unstable temperament to his one sole end – the signing of the
contract. His replies from line 1760 onwards are bolder, more confident, a mixture of sceptical common sense and cynical mockery; there
is no doubt that in terms of argument and tactics Mephisto is, or at least
imagines himself to be, in control of Faust. In lines 1741 ff., Faust reiterates the sense of inadequacy and disillusionment that has driven him
to accept the pact with Mephisto as a *pis aller*: his rejection by the
Erdgeist, the inaccessibility of nature, and the failure of his speculative
ambitions. He explicitly turns his back on knowledge, on 'Wissen' or
'Wissensdrang'; he promises himself only a restless frenzy of desperate
activity. Faust has abandoned his ambition of a totality of knowledge
for a sum-total of experience; he has turned from contemplation to

activity, to the hurly-burly of human experience from which he promises himself distraction rather than pleasure, experience rather than
revelation.

And yet this welter of haphazard experience that Faust envisages here
contains within it, as yet unbeknown to him, the possibility of relative
satisfaction and partial achievement. This programme allows Mephisto
the opportunity to lead Faust into perdition; but it also provides the
basis of a career in the course of which Faust will move from a position
of hopeless despair through a curve of progressive awareness – expressed, as we shall see, in a series of monologues that lift him and the
reader or audience above the confused sum of experience that the
drama offers – that culminates in his confession to Sorge, in which he
acknowledges constant dissatisfaction and resolute commitment to
this-worldly activity as the fulfilment of human destiny. And it is the
drive of this dissatisfaction that will in the end render Faust accessible
to redemptive love. By line 1775, the ground-rules of the Faust–
Mephistopheles relationship have been laid down; it is now up to the
two players to make what they can of the cards dealt to them.

At this point, Mephisto disconcertingly falls into his role as sermonizing moralist. In his high rhetoric of lines 1765–75, Faust envisages
a totality of experience against which Mephisto delivers a piece of
characteristically worldly-wise advice – advice which is, moreover,
entirely consistent with Goethe's theory of optics and its metaphysical
analogies. For Goethe, light and dark were separate, indivisible phenomena; colour was produced not by the splitting of white light but in
the intermediate zone between light and darkness, by the overlapping
of the two, by the relative opacity of the medium through which objects
are perceived, and by the nature of the background against which they
are perceived. This 'coloured zone' between polar absolutes is also, for
Goethe, analogous to human experience – an intermediate sphere in
which light and dark, good and evil, God and devil, overlap and interact
in a dialectical tension. This symbolism will recur in the grandiose
imagery of the opening scene of Faust II; but it is also applicable to
Mephisto's advice to Faust that he can never fully comprehend either
pure light, the realm of God, or absolute darkness, the realm of the
devil, let alone the totality of both. Man experiences only the alternation
or overlapping of these polarities: 'Day and night' (lines 1780–4, my
emphasis).

Mephisto also mocks Faust's pretensions to 'wholeness' by referring
him to the fantasy-world of art; only the rhetoric of a poet (lines 1789 ff.)
could encompass such a totality. His scoffing at this point is not so
much a gratuitous contempt for Faust's pretensions but rather part of

his strategy to encourage and entice Faust to plunge into life and grasp
the opportunities it offers, to abandon the 'barren heath' of speculation
for the lush green pastures of worldly experience (1830 ff.). The final
irony of this scene is that Mephisto, dressed in Faust's academic robes,
should then play the professor – not only in the following scene with
the Student but already here, where he defines reason and learning,
which Faust has so frivolously rejected, as man's highest gift (lines
1851–2). In the following lines Mephisto, emerging in his true colours,
describes the programme of tawdry banality with which he confidently
expects to ensnare Faust as if with birdlime; and the very force that he
will harness to that purpose is Faust's own insatiability.

The Student Scene

With this scene, the high drama and metaphysical paradoxes of the pact
scene are replaced by burlesque satire as the university scenes draw to
a close. The exuberant Urfaust version of this scene, generally believed to
have been one of the very first scenes to be written, and no doubt
derived directly from Goethe's less than respectful reaction to his own
academic studies at Leipzig, was extensively rewritten for the Fragment,
omitting some of the devil's more homely – and more robustly vulgar –
advice to the Student on how to find his way in university life, but
adding the satires on the faculties of jurisprudence and theology to
those on the faculties of philosophy and medicine. In the Urfaust, this
scene follows immediately after Faust's confrontation with Wagner –
both Wagner and the Student are the butts of Goethe's youthfully
exuberant mockery of conventional scholarship. The one demonstrates
the aridity of bookish learning, while the other, by his very ignorance
and naïvety, bears out Faust's own cynicism towards the supposed
glamour of knowledge and learning.

But the glory of this scene lies in its uninhibited comic satire, in the
rich ironies of Mephisto's gleeful assumption of Faust's role, and in his
purveying to the Student in a deceptively paternalistic manner Faust's
own jaundiced perception of academic study. He amplifies and glosses
the disillusionment Faust has expressed with the four faculties in his
opening monologue by introducing the Student to the constricting
tautologies of logic, the meaningless phrases of metaphysics and the
scholastic dogmatics of theology. Mephisto's advice is a characteristic
mixture of cynicism and common sense as he mocks the pretensions
and futilities of scholarship, while at the same time giving the Student a
glimpse into the truly incalculable complexities of the human mind
(lines 1922–35) and instructing him sagely on the organization of his
studies (1954–63). He concludes his résumé of the rewards of the

unscrupulous application of the pseudo-science of medicine with words that, while they appear at face value entirely free from diabolical undertones, are in fact only a reformulation of his earlier advice to Faust to quit speculation and plunge headlong into life: 'All theory is grey, and green the golden tree of life' (2038–9).

But this is quickly followed by a more overtly diabolical parting shot in the form of a quotation from Genesis 3: 5 – the temptation of the serpent that, by eating of the fruit of the tree of knowledge, men will become as gods, knowing good and evil. As in the case of Faust, Mephisto sees that simply by harnessing man's insatiable curiosity he can work mischief; and he only warns of the dangers of unbridled curiosity, *sotto voce*, when the Student's back is turned. The unexpected and disconcerting results of his own advice the devil will only discover, to his own discomfiture, in his re-encounter with the graduate student (Baccalaureus) in the opening scene of the second act of *Faust II*.

'AUERBACHS KELLER' AND 'HEXENKÜCHE'

These two scenes bridge the major episodes of *Faust I*, the university scenes and the Gretchen episode; and while neither contributes very much to the dramatic action, save for Faust's rejuvenation in the Witch's kitchen, they both have a structural and thematic function in the drama. They contribute to the colourful episodic pattern of the work as part of Goethe's intention to preserve the popular flavour of the Faust legend, its prank episodes on the one hand and its sorcery and black magic on the other. They represent the first stages in Mephisto's programme of trivial banality in the petty-bourgeois world beyond the university – a programme in which Faust plays a notably passive role, but which changes direction abruptly when he seizes the initiative on meeting Gretchen. Further, the two scenes form a symmetrical pairing: if 'Auerbachs Keller' is the unedifying conclusion to the university scenes, 'Hexenküche' marks the equally unpromising introduction to the Gretchen scenes.

'Auerbachs Keller': Auerbach's Cellar in Leipzig

As a student in Leipzig, Goethe had known the tavern that from an early stage had been associated with the Faust legend; and the motif of Faust conjuring grapes and wine, even the play with grapes and noses, had also been a feature of the earliest versions of the legend. Whereas in the *Urfaust* scene Faust himself performs the magic tricks, in the published versions Goethe underlines Faust's unenthusiastic response to what

Mephisto has to offer him in this squalid milieu by making Faust an almost mute spectator throughout. Here Mephisto holds the stage, demonstrating to Faust both his contempt for human ignorance and bestiality (animal metaphors and allusions figure largely) and his delight in moving unsuspected among men, confirming his scathing characterization of 'the petty god of earth' in the 'Prologue in Heaven' (lines 280 ff.). While it is not universally accepted that these are drunken students (Arens, for example, denies this strenuously, arguing that the scene represents the less attractive aspect of the town life of 'Vor dem Tor'),[32] it is not unreasonable to assume that they are; critics have detected in the names of Frosch, Brander and Altmayer, in references to drinking ceremonies and to 'Hans Arse from Rippach' (lines 2189 ff.), clear allusions to university slang and student lore.

Apart from its lively dialogue and characterization, Goethe's main contribution to this Schwank episode lies largely in the two songs, and in the political and social comment that he slips unobtrusively into the scene. Brander's song of the rat is a coarse and ribald counterpart to the emotional intensity of Gretchen's later song at the spinning-wheel; Mephisto's song of the flea is a more subtle and mischievous comment on the patronage and sycophancy of absolutist court life – though it is unlikely that at this stage Goethe had in mind any anticipation of the political instability and decadence in the imperial scenes of Faust II, either with this song or with the reference to the tottering foundations of 'our beloved Holy Roman Empire' (lines 2090 ff.). He also suggests a considerable degree of social tension in the remark that greets the entry of the two travellers (lines 2177–8) – though the younger writer of the Urfaust formulated the resentful hostility of the drinkers rather more radically. For the most part, however, the episode is a rumbustious, if squalid, genre scene which, while deriving principally from the Faust-book tradition, might also owe something to the Boar's Head Tavern episodes of Henry IV; and it ends with the traditional image from the Auerbachs Keller murals, of Faust riding out of the tavern astride a barrel.

'Hexenküche': Witch's Kitchen

This scene was most probably written during and after Goethe's Italian journey; and for many critics it reflects his overwhelming commitment to classical values and his revulsion from the nordic phantom-world that is so grotesquely presented here. In dramatic terms, it charts the arousing of Faust's sexual responses as the preparation for the Gretchen episode; and Faust's sensuality is shown here as characteristically dualistic. His feelings for Gretchen are a compound of love and lust, of emotional involvement and ruthless sexual egotism, of sentimental attraction to the narrow confines of her domestic world and a restless urge for wider experience; and the two motifs of this scene, mirror and potion, represent the dual response of his two selves. The vision of female beauty in the magic mirror is the projection of his idealizing sensuality, while the Witch's potion does not simply rejuvenate his physical appearance – it also stimulates his sexual appetite; as Mephisto remarks for the benefit of the audience, this aphrodisiac potion will restore his youthful potency to the extent that every woman will seem like Helen of Troy.

This coarse comment has led many critics to associate the figure of naked beauty in the mirror with the Helen of Part Two; but any thematic or dramatic link here is very tenuous. It is quite true that there are several very striking parallels between the 'Hexenküche' and the conjuration of Helen in the second part;[33] and Faust will indeed, in lines 6495–7, briefly recall this same vision. However, the very fact that he recalls it as a 'phantom image', a 'Schaumbild', of Helen's beauty suggests that the 'Hexenküche' apparition is by no means to be identified with Helen but is rather Faust's first experience of sexuality; the unreal, magical vision in the Witch's mirror precedes and prefigures Faust's Gretchen experience much as the spectral appearance of Helen in the dumb-show of Act I precedes and prefigures his encounter with Helen in the third act.

Faust is initially as contemptuous of the paraphernalia of witchcraft as he was of the antics in Auerbachs Keller, and almost equally detached from his surroundings. Nevertheless, rather than follow Mephisto's ironically 'sensible' programme of rejuvenation by means of a banal and limited but vigorous and healthy life (lines 2351 ff.), he consents with an ill grace to the easier magical alternative. At this point, a bizarre interlude develops in the by-play between Mephistopheles and the Monkeys that guard the Witch's kitchen, which at first sight appears nothing more than a piece of meaningless and inconsequential chatter. Closer attention, however, reveals it as a satirical allegory reflecting the momentous historical events that coincided precisely with the composition of the scene.

Initially, the purport of these exchanges (lines 2390–428) between Mephisto and the Monkeys seems quite unspecific; references to 'coarse soups for beggars' (2392), to the centrality of wealth and poverty in human affairs (2394 ff.), and to the world as the fragile rolling sphere of Fortuna (2402 ff.) might be simple generalized comments on the human condition. However, with the resumption of the banter after line 2447, it becomes clearer that the flawed crown that breaks in two is an allusion to the precarious monarchy of France; and the 'sweat and blood' with which the animals urge 'King' Mephisto to weld it together might well refer to the taxation and repression by means of which the regime tardily attempted to shore itself up. In this light, the earlier references also assume more specific form – to the poverty and hunger of pre-revolutionary France, to the insecurity of feudal power; and the cauldron itself, very much like the fire-chest of Plutus in the first act of *Faust II*, suggests the simmering discontent of a revolutionary situation that, should it boil over, will bring havoc and destruction to all concerned. Indeed, Mephisto's reference to his unsteady head in line 2457, though well *avant la lettre*, might be read as a prescient, but scarcely miraculous, anticipation of the eventual fate of Louis XVI in 1793.

The entry of the Witch marks the introduction of less topical material and a return to the dramatic action – for it is less certain that Mephisto's assertion of his satanic authority in lines 2475 ff. can be taken, as Arens suggests, as Goethe's comment on how the French king, by acting promptly and decisively, might have averted the catastrophe of 1789.[34] At all events, it allows for some ribald dialogue and an interesting explanation of Mephisto's physical appearance in Goethe's *Faust*: he is no longer the grotesque figure of traditional demonology, but has become secularized with the times and now moves incognito among humanity, no less dangerously or effectively for all that.[35]

The hocus-pocus that follows is generally taken as a parody of the elaborate and, for Goethe, obscurantist ceremonial of the Roman Catholic Church that he had observed with great aversion in Italy – the ritual gestures of the Witch, the music, the book, the Monkeys as acolytes bearing torches, and the drinking of the potion travesty the Eucharist. Douglas Bub goes further to argue that the reference to sweat and blood in line 2451 suggests Gethsemane and the Passion;[36] hence that the crowning of Mephisto is a blasphemous reference to the crown of thorns – surely a less satisfactory reading than the political one, since it takes no account of the broken crown.

The Witch's riddle or 'one-times table' has attracted a mass of exegetical literature, explaining it by means of arcane numerological squares, tables, or sequences, alternatively as a parody of Newtonian optics, of the trinity, of the ten commandments, or simply of any form of mystical mumbo-jumbo.[37] The most straightforward explanation of the *Hexen-Einmaleins* is that of Levedahl – namely, that the Witch reduces Faust's age not by thirty years, but by twenty-nine, thus cheating him of a year, roughly as follows: make one into ten (= 10), let two go, let three make three (= 13), ignore the four, from five and six make seven and eight (13 + 7 + 8 = 28), nine is one, and ten is none (= 29).[38]

The final exchanges of the scene emphasize the duality of Faust's situation. Even in this grotesque and chaotic milieu, he stands enthralled by the ideal vision in the mirror, while Mephisto, eager to let the potion work to stimulate his libidinous drive, hurries him away. Faust's rejuvenation is physical, not spiritual or intellectual; his idealizing urge survives the transformation, and it cannot be argued that the potion expunges from his mind all traces of his previous self or of his previous existence. Not only do Mephisto's several references to his academic career and status later in the episode (lines 2748 ff., 3040 ff., 3277, 3523, 3704, 4024), and Faust's own allusions to their pact in line 2638, to the Erdgeist in 'Wald und Höhle' and to the devil as a dog in 'Trüber Tag. Feld' indicate this; more significantly, Faust's role and behaviour throughout the Gretchen episode betray his dual nature and his dual consciousness. He is at once the lusty young lover and the renegade intellectual; he is both socially and intellectually in a *mésalliance* with Gretchen; he is torn between his twin impulses of security and restlessness; he is both the ardently sentimental youth of the garden scenes and the driven victim of his own pact with the devil that blights his relationship with Gretchen from the start. This anguished duality, already formulated graphically by Faust in the 'Vor dem Tor' scene, will find its most vivid expression in the 'Wald und Höhle' scene, in the emblematic imagery of the peaceful alpine hut and the raging mountain torrent. Here, in the 'Hexenküche', it is exemplified by the polarity of Faust's vision of sublime femininity on the one hand and the Witch's aphrodisiac potion on the other.

THE GRETCHEN TRAGEDY

One of the most notable features of the Gretchen tragedy is the extreme dramatic economy with which Goethe treats this ballad-like episode. In the *Urfaust*, indeed, it is even briefer, taking up rather less than 1,000 lines of verse plus two short scenes in prose – a masterpiece of laconic condensation in which several decisive turns of the external action (the death of Gretchen's mother and brother, Faust's desertion, her infanticide and trial) are alluded to only obliquely in the text. In the final version, which is almost doubled in length, much of the speed and economy of the sporadic structure of the *Urfaust* survives, in spite of the expansion of the Valentin scene and the interpolation of two episodes which centre largely on Faust rather than on Gretchen: the 'Wald und Höhle' and 'Walpurgisnacht' scenes.

Much critical discussion has arisen over the unity and continuity of the two major sections of *Faust I*, over whether Goethe has successfully

fused the two halves which were admittedly only tenuously linked in
the Urfaust. The main step he took in filling the 'great gap' of the Urfaust
and Fragment versions was undoubtedly Faust's abandoning, in the
second 'Studierzimmer' scene, of his whole previous career, and in
particular of his ambition to seek knowledge through conventional
scholarship or magical revelation. This explicit shift of Faust's aspirations from metaphysical speculation to a commitment to common
human experience, which was at best only implicit in the Urfaust,
provides the closest link between the university scenes and the
Gretchen episode; and this is further reinforced by Mephisto's undertaking in line 2052 that he will introduce Faust first to the narrow world
of everyday experience and subsequently to the wider world beyond
the narrow milieu of a small German town.

Goethe has further bridged the university scenes and the domestic
scenes not so much by means of the simple magic device of Faust's
rejuvenation in the 'Hexenküche' but, more fully, by showing how the
dualistic nature of Faust, already clearly present in the pre-trans-
formation scenes, remains as his salient characteristic in the Gretchen
scenes; in this sense, Faust the lover of Gretchen is not 'bracketed
out' from Faust the magus as radically as Mason, for example, has
suggested.[39] The ambivalence epitomized in the 'Hexenküche' scene
dominates and blights Faust's relationship with Gretchen; even if
he can momentarily delude himself into a domestic idyll, he is never
allowed to forget the true nature of his impossible situation or of his
own ambivalent feelings. And he is never allowed to escape the
companion to whom he has bound himself, who is constantly on hand
to shatter the self-deluding sincerity to which he pretends.

What is remarkable about Goethe's treatment of a theme that is
unremarkable in itself, a stock-in-trade of much eighteenth-century
narrative fiction and domestic drama, indeed a common feature of
eighteenth-century social life, is that he has encapsulated the human
tragedy of Gretchen not only within the supernatural framework of
Faust's pact with the devil but also within the theological framework of
the 'Prologue in Heaven' – and that he has done so without detracting
from the realism of the episode in terms of setting and psychology. The
casket of jewels, the poison administered to Gretchen's mother instead
of a sleeping potion, the manner of Valentin's death, the black horses,
and the sleep imposed on Gretchen's jailer – all these are, to be sure,
supplied by the devil; but they are not incidents that could not be
explained in naturalistic terms. Faust's own assertion in lines 2642–4
bears this out: he does not need the devil's services to seduce Gretchen –
they simply assist and expedite a process he could accomplish unaided.

Even the overt satanism and supernaturalism of the 'Walpurgisnacht', in terms of the dramatic action, stands for a long period of debauch after Faust's desertion of Gretchen. As Mason has argued, Goethe has integrated specifically magical, diabolical and supernatural elements into the Gretchen tragedy, but in such a way that they do not interfere with the natural unfolding of a genuinely human relationship.[40]

A further feature of Goethe's treatment of Gretchen is the almost brutal frankness with which he handles the tragedy of the abandoned girl. After swiftly charting the growth of love, surrender and passion, he then portrays laconically and unsentimentally her doubt, anguish and finally her distraction with great lyrical and dramatic concentration. What is also striking in Goethe's characterization of Gretchen is that he does not present her as an entirely naïve figure who is the passive object of Faust's seduction or of Mephisto's manipulation; she is not, for example, comparable with H. L. Wagner's heroine Evchen Humbrecht, who is the passive victim of near-rape, malicious intrigue and arbitrary accident. Against the extravagant idealization of earlier critics, who have often worshipped Gretchen as an angel of innocence, as a 'child of nature', or as a paragon of modest virtue, Mason has made the valuable observation that Gretchen is not without her human weaknesses, not without a degree of knowing guile, albeit under the imperative of her love for Faust. She is not immune to flattery; while she firmly rejects Faust's impertinent proposition to her in the street, she is still impressed at being approached so gallantly by a 'gentleman'. She dutifully hands over the first casket of jewels to her mother – but she shows the second gift only to Marthe. She connives, with no great resistance, at giving her mother a sleeping potion in order to sleep with Faust; and when she gives herself to him, she does so unreservedly – the monologue 'Meine Ruh' ist hin' ('My peace is gone') is a frank and physical declaration of passion.

Nor is Gretchen, on the other hand, an amoral Naturkind, but the product of a strict religious and bourgeois sexual morality, who is at once fully aware of her own sensuality and of the guilt-feelings it engenders; this is a tension that comes out in the final couplet of the 'Am Brunnen' ('At the Well') scene (lines 3585–6), and which informs much of the pathos of the three scenes 'Zwinger' ('Shrine'), 'Nacht' ('Night') and 'Dom' ('Cathedral'). Gretchen's tragedy is all the more compelling because it is presented as the result of her own and Faust's human frailties. Nevertheless, in terms of a humanitarian ethic that transcends conventional social or religious morality, the issues of the Gretchen tragedy are perfectly clear: Faust's sophisticated, but ruthless and egotistical, instincts lead him down Mephistopheles' path, while

Gretchen's ingenuous, but selfless and sincere, instincts give her increasing, if tragic, moral stature.

'Straße' I: Street I

It is by no means clear whether Faust's meeting with Gretchen is to be taken as pure accident, or as engineered by Mephistopheles. It is not conclusive to argue that, if his programme for Faust is one of trivial banalities, then he is hardly likely to have chosen for Faust someone who will fire him with feelings far beyond mere lust, since for Mephisto any such 'lofty intuition' (line 3291) is only another human delusion. Nevertheless, it is by no means certain, as many critics claim, that Mephisto's protestation in lines 2621 ff. that he has no power over Gretchen is simply feigned reluctance in order to whet Faust's appetite; just as likely is the possibility that, while he may have had easier conquests in mind for Faust, he swiftly calculates that by involving an innocent girl in his schemes he might deprave two lives rather than one. But whatever Mephisto's motives, he is contractually obliged to serve Faust's whims; his servant role here and elsewhere is in a long comic tradition of servants who contrive at once to further and to frustrate their masters' commands and wishes.

'Abend': Evening

The ambivalence of Gretchen's feelings is signalled from the very beginning. As her mind dwells on the incident in the street, her reaction is far from censorious: by his very forwardness, Faust revealed himself as a 'gentleman'. And in his subsequent monologue in her bedroom Faust acknowledges his own duality, his conflicting impulses of lechery and emotion (lines 2722–4). Faust's sentimentalized vision of Gretchen's humble and ordered existence is in stark contrast to her own more sober account of the household in lines 3109 ff.; it is also the vivid expression of what attracts him so fatally to the idyll that he projects on to her milieu – what Goethe described in a draft scheme for the Gretchen episode as 'das anmutig Beschränkte des bürgerlichen Zustands' ('The charming confines of the domestic state').[41] It is the attraction of the circumscribed but socially integrated circle of banal and unpretentious domesticity for the rootless and driven outsider, the tension between peace and restlessness, security and adventure, confinement and freedom, that runs as a leitmotif through much of Goethe's early work, and which is expressed emblematically, in Werther and in so many of his early poems, in terms of the imagery of hut and traveller or 'Wanderer'. Here, in line 2708 and again in line 3353, the image of the hut stands for the confined idyll of Gretchen's existence that is already threatened by Faust's restless impulses. The 'prison' of her milieu, furnished with the inherited possessions that Faust found so irksome in his own 'dungeon', is here invested with a glamour very much like Werther's idealized and illusory 'patriarchal' perception of humble domesticity.

The ballad of 'The King of Thule' (lines 2759 ff.) is the first of a series of lyrical monologues by Gretchen that are of central importance to the psychological action of the episode. Here, again in the scene at the spinning-wheel, in her prayer to the Mother of Sorrows in the 'Zwinger' scene, and finally in her madsong in prison Gretchen betrays her most personal feelings and state of mind. Of course, these are not her only monologues; but these lyrical set-pieces, whether sung or not, have an intensity or subtlety beyond the others. 'Der König in Thule', oblique and allusive though its reference is, fits so perfectly into the dramatic situation that it is scarcely believable that the ballad was, as is apparently the case, originally written by Goethe without any view to the Gretchen tragedy. Certainly, it is a folksong that, we must assume, Gretchen has long since known. But it is a song sung involuntarily by her as she undresses in her room shortly after an incident in the street that has made a sharp impression on her, a song that revolves around the theme of love and fidelity, symbolized in the central image of the goblet, doubtless derived by Goethe from the erotic imagery of the Song of Songs. It is a song, moreover, of the lifelong fidelity of a high-born king to the memory of his mistress; and Gretchen's awareness of the social discrepancy between herself and Faust has already been clearly expressed in the opening words in this scene. The song suggests with the utmost delicacy the wish-fulfilment of a simple girl whose thoughts are still with the stranger who accosted her shortly before – as she herself will confirm later in lines 3175 ff. To be sure, the relationship of king and mistress in the ballad is a morganatic one – in this legendary context, the realities of social convention do not impinge; but Gretchen will also defy conventional social morality in her love for Faust. It is at this point that she discovers the casket of jewels; and once again, the insistent theme of social and economic discrepancy, already touched on in 'Auerbachs Keller' and 'Hexenküche', is here reiterated in terms that seem to prefigure Büchner's *Woyzeck* – as indeed lines 2398–9 have already done.

'Spaziergang': A Walk
Mephisto's comic fury at being out-manoeuvred by the church is a fine actor's set-piece that combines sharp satire with two telling observations of Gretchen's response to the casket: far from sharing her

mother's fearful and suspicious reaction to the jewels, she is intrigued by both the present and the donor (lines 2827–30 and 2851–2). Certainly, these lines may represent Mephisto's version of her response; but they are not inconsistent with Gretchen's obvious, if guarded, delight at the second casket (2873 ff.).

'Der Nachbarin Haus': The Neighbour's House

The action moves forward one further step with the introduction of Frau Marthe, and the greater part of the scene belongs to Mephistopheles and his comic manipulation of his counterpart. The ironic discrepancy between sentimental young love and the disabused scepticism of middle-aged experience – or, in Mephisto's case, the weary wisdom of millennia – is a theme that will be continued in the coming and going of the two pairs in the first garden scene.

'Straße' II: Street II

'Sancta Simplicitas!' – with withering sarcasm, Mephisto uses the reported words of Jan Hus at the stake to expose the hypocrisy of Faust's nice scruples at committing perjury. It is a measure both of the devil's skill in sophistry and of Faust's ambivalence that he can here manoeuvre Faust into a position where his only defence is impotent abuse (line 3050), bald assertion (3055). rhetorical evasion (3059 ff.) and capitulation as he is forced to admit that he is a slave to his own sexual imperative (3072).

'Garten'/'Ein Gartenhäuschen': Garden/a Summerhouse

The first garden scene is a masterpiece of ironic stage counterpoint. Not only is the alternating flirtation of Mephisto and Marthe, based on a series of comic evasions by the devil, a parody of the earnest wooing of Faust and Gretchen; the dialogue of the young lovers itself also reveals the ominous discrepancy between Faust's specious sublimation of his lust and Gretchen's girlish awkwardness, between his idealized perception of her domesticity and her own unsentimental account of the household, between his gallant rhetoric and her artless responses. Her anxieties about Faust, about his sincerity and about the social and intellectual gulf between them, which have been so subtly stylized in the 'König in Thule' ballad, are here articulated with simple directness. Her insistence that the family is moderately well-off (3117–18), confirming what the spectator already knows from lines 2786 ff., suggests an attempt to reassure herself, if not Faust, that she is, financially at least, a reasonable match for him.

The lovers' game with which Gretchen provokes Faust's overt

declaration of love has been the subject of onomastic and symbolic
speculation. The 'Sternblume' she picks is generally assumed to be a
Margaretenblume (moon-daisy), and its dismemberment an ominous
prefiguration of her own defloration, even of her destruction. Requadt
has also associated line 3187 with Goethe's translation of the Song of
Songs: 'Da reichte mein Freund mit der Hand durchs Schalter und mich
überlief's'[42] – a counterpart, perhaps, to Mephisto's prurient allusion to
the same text in lines 3336–7. The devil as spy and voyeur is a role that
will be developed in subsequent scenes; here, in the 'Gartenhäuschen',
he cuts short the first phase of the Gretchen episode at the point where
the lovers declare their feelings – with the kiss, with Gretchen's
use of the 'du' form in line 3206, and with the promise to meet again
soon.

'Wald und Höhle': Forest and Cavern

The involved genesis of this scene, and in particular its transposition
from a point after Gretchen's seduction in the *Fragment* to the critical
moment before her seduction in the final version, raise certain problems of detail. Lines 3249–50, which in the *Fragment* clearly indicated
Faust's ambivalent post-coital state of mind, can no longer be taken in
this sense; Mephisto's lewd comment of lines 3336–7, and Faust's more
idealized image of lines 3345–7, no longer seem wholly appropriate;
nor is the violent and destructive imagery of Faust's tirade of self-hatred
in lines 3348 ff. entirely consistent with the present state of his
relationship with Gretchen. On the other hand, these are not intractable
contradictions, and structurally the new position of the scene reinforces
the architecture of the Gretchen tragedy. It balances the later 'Walpurgisnacht' episode; the reference to Gretchen's disturbed peace of mind
in line 3360 provides a satisfactory link with her refrain 'Meine Ruh' ist
hin' ('My peace is gone') in the following scene; and, more importantly,
in its new situation the scene assumes a central position as the
watershed of the relationship. It marks the end of courtship and the
beginnings of passion and suffering, the point at which Faust can no
longer delude even himself that his feelings for Gretchen represent, as
he has only just asserted, 'a bliss . . . that must be for ever' (lines 3191–2),
the point from which the episode takes a rapid downward plunge
towards tragedy.

The opening monologue is one of the great Faustian set-pieces, one
of several passages in the work where Faust draws back from the
hurly-burly of the dramatic action to take stock of his career. Between
his opening monologue and his final vision before death, the monologues of 'Wald und Höhle' (lines 3217 ff.), 'Anmutige Gegend' (4679 ff.)

and 'Hochgebirg' (10039 ff.), and his confession to Sorge in lines 11433–52 chart Faust's spiritual progress as he accepts, and increasingly affirms, the limits of human striving, as he moves from the despairing frustration of his early perception of the irreconcilable polarity of real and ideal towards an acceptance of finite experience as the fulfilment of his destiny.

The 'Wald und Höhle' monologue is, however, an early stage in this process, marking not the resolution of Faust's dualistic tensions but only a temporary refuge in nature. It is in some ways the realization of his dream in lines 386–97 of rejuvenation in a moonlit landscape of spirits. Moreover, Faust clearly acknowledges this empathetic vision as the gift of the Erdgeist; it is only an apparent contradiction that Faust, who was rejected by the Earth Spirit and granted no more than a glimpse of its personified form, should now thank the spirit for his communion with nature. While the spirit resisted his extravagant and titanic ambition to confront it in its essence, it did not appear 'in vain' to him; he is here still able to acknowledge and identify himself with natural phenomena, with the 'ranks of living creatures' (line 3225). As the Erdgeist encompassed positive and negative, creation and destruction, birth and death, so here Faust evokes both storm and calm, the elemental violence and the organic formative processes of nature.

More germane to the dramatic action, however, is Faust's recognition of his own duality, of the limitations imposed on his vision and experience, in the final section of the monologue. In Faust's perception, it is the Erdgeist who has sent him the 'companion' who tempts and goads him out of the passive pleasure of detached contemplation into restless distraction; and this perception matches the spectator's or reader's awareness of the Lord's definition of the 'companion' whose creative function is to goad and entice men into activity (lines 342–3). Indeed, in 'Trüber Tag. Feld', Faust will himself refer to the 'companion in shame' to whom he has been fettered. Mephisto's function here, in the 'Wald und Höhle' scene, is not only that prescribed by the Lord but is also consistent with his own programme: far from attempting to reduce Faust to a state of passivity on the terms of Faust's wager, he now arrives to rouse him brutally from a state of self-absorbed meditation and plunge him back into the world of Gretchen.

In the central dialogue of this scene, as in the previous scenes, Faust has no effective defence against Mephisto's persuasive arguments, which play on and expose his own ambivalence and irresolution. Mephisto mocks the anguished speculations of the 'son of earth', parodies his nature-worship, derides his moral hypocrisy, and taunts him with the image of his beloved. Paradoxically, Mephisto's description of Gretchen, sardonic travesty though it may be, is a romantic, even folkloric image of love and pathos, of a lonely maiden sighing by her window (lines 3316 ff.). It is Faust who returns obsessively to her 'sweet body', who envies the very body of Christ on the crucifix when she kisses it – a remark that provokes Mephisto's allusion to the breasts of the beloved from the Song of Songs (lines 3336–7), which he backs up with a further piece of biblical lore: God himself, who created man and woman for procreation, was the first matchmaker.

The result of Mephisto's provocation is the speech in which all Faust's self-hatred and bad conscience finds expression in the emblematic image of the destruction of the peaceful alpine hut by the raging torrent – a powerful extension of Mephisto's imagery of lines 3307 ff. Faust elaborates the 'Wanderer' motif, casting himself as an Ahasuerus figure in a rootless, aimless existence, as the destroyer of precisely what had attracted him in Gretchen: the security, simplicity and integrity of ordered domesticity. It is entirely characteristic that Faust should perceive his impetus as an irresistible force of nature; in attributing the failure of his own will to a fatalistic necessity, he indulges in a piece of Faustian self-deception that is at odds with his pretension to self-knowledge earlier in the scene. The tragic irony of lines 3363–5 is that Gretchen's fate will not be visited on him, he will not drag her down to destruction with him; she will go to her death alone, rejecting Faust and the devil. This irony was all the more striking in the *Urfaust* version because of the proximity of these lines to the final 'Kerker' scene.

'Gretchens Stube': Gretchen's Room

The new juxtaposition of this scene and the previous one created by the shift of 'Wald und Höhle' throws the relationship between them into relief; they can now be imagined as the simultaneous expressions of Faust's and Gretchen's states of mind, confessions of tortured ambivalence on the one hand and of frank passion on the other. Strictly speaking, this is not a song that Gretchen sings at the spinning-wheel but a spoken strophic monologue; it is not an oblique and allusive, vaguely legendary folksong like 'Der König in Thule' but an outspoken articulation of personal emotion. Nevertheless, it is not unreasonably (and not solely as a result of Schubert's splendid setting) referred to and treated as a song; its strophic form, refrain and lyrical intensity justify its being regarded as a poem, if not as a *Lied* – and as such it has structural significance as a high point of the psychological action comparable to 'Der König in Thule', the prayer in 'Zwinger' and the madsong in 'Kerker'.

Except that the refrain is not repeated after the emotional climax of the tenth stanza, the poem is symmetrically constructed in groups of two, three and two strophes divided by the refrain. The insistently recurrent pattern of sentence structure and refrain, corresponding to the repetitive rhythm of the spinning-wheel, are countered by the mounting emotional intensity as Gretchen articulates her feelings for Faust: her confusion and longing, his physical appearance, and her own fierce physical response – which was rather more explicit in the *Urfaust* version 'Mein Schoos! Gott! drängt sich . . .' ('Ah God, my loins strain for him!'). The reticence and diffidence of the earlier scenes give way to a full assertion and acceptance of sensuality; Gretchen is prepared to reciprocate Faust's passion and give herself unreservedly. The broad parallels between her enumeration of the beloved's features and the Song of Songs, first drawn by Otto Pniower, are entirely appropriate – though it is uncertain whether they are to be taken as the involuntary recollection of Gretchen's reading of the Bible or, as Requadt suggests, as her conscious projection of Faust as the 'bridegroom' of the poem.[43]

'Marthens Garten': Marthe's Garden
While she may privately be ready to override social, moral and religious inhibitions, however, Gretchen is unable to free herself completely from the reflexes of her upbringing. The rapid exchanges of lines 3421 ff. betoken both the uncertain tensions that still linger in her mind and the defensiveness of Faust's reactions. And the fact that Faust's lyrical and eloquent 'credo' reads like a faithful reflection of Goethe's own *Sturm und Drang* emotional mysticism, or of much eighteenth-century pietistic enthusiasm, indeed that it draws on a long tradition of theological controversy on the naming of the deity,[44] does not alter the fact that in this dramatic context it appears as specious and evasive, as the rhetorical smokescreen of a subtle and complex mind against a forthright if literal-minded challenge. The ecstatic vocabulary that Faust draws on to express his intuition of an ineffable deity has markedly sensual overtones. It is, as Arens perceptively notes, no accident that 'He who embraces and who keeps us all' (3438–9) distinctly echoes Gretchen's impassioned words in lines 3408–9 of the previous scene; and lines 3446–54 subtly associate profane and divine love, erotic and religious bliss, until finally God is equated with 'Bliss! Heart! Love!'.[45] Small wonder that Gretchen cannot quite reconcile Faust's enthusiastic religiosity with the words of her priest.

Her probing questions on Faust's relationship with Mephisto are also informed by her lingering doubts; and Faust can here no more than previously give her any frank explanation or reassurance, since she has instinctively sensed the gulf that separates them, the falseness of Faust's position and the dualism that undermines their relationship. Here Faust cannot evade her questions with brilliant sophistry; the initiative of the dialogue is now with her, and Faust can only counter with embarrassed one-line responses.

The motif of the sleeping potion is quickly dealt with – so quickly, indeed, that it remains unclear whether it is in fact poison supplied by Mephisto, whether Faust is aware of its lethal potential, or whether Gretchen herself inadvertently administers a lethal dose to her mother. Mephisto, whose constant eavesdropping satisfies both his wish to manipulate events and a voyeuristic delight, offers a more sceptical explanation of Gretchen's anxious questionings (lines 3525–7) than that of Faust (3528–33); the truth, no doubt, lies somewhere between the two.

Of the next four scenes, the first two chart Gretchen's private sense of shame and guilt, the following two her public disgrace. By alternating between social and religious contexts, they illustrate cumulatively and brutally the extreme pressures that bear in on Gretchen and drive her to infanticide: the merciless judgement of her peers and of her own family, the deaths of her mother and brother, her reawakened sense of sin and retribution, and not least her emotional confusion and misery.

'Am Brunnen': At the Well

In an ironically indirect manner, Gretchen is confronted with the self-righteous Schadenfreude that she might herself expect from her own peers, the barbarous rituals visited on 'fallen women' by the church (lines 3568–9) and by the malice of erstwhile friends (3575–6). And even if the censorious hypocrisy of social mores is clear enough in the spiteful figure of Lieschen, it is notable that Gretchen makes no attempt to resist or defy her own social or religious conditioning at this point. The ironic pathos of this scene lies in the broad analogies to her own situation; even if lines 3551 ff. are not an exact parallel to her affair with Faust – which was, indeed, a covert and furtive affair compared with that of Bärbelchen – they are close enough to force from Gretchen a horrified sympathy with the victim and an involuntary expression of her own confused hopes and anxieties vis-à-vis Faust. In the last two lines of the scene she is still able, just, to affirm her experience; but, distilled into the particle 'doch' ('yet') of line 3585 is her final, poignant attempt to reconcile hope and doubt, love and guilt.

'Zwinger': a Shrine

At a shrine symbolically situated just within the city walls, but outside the civic community itself, Gretchen is exposed to her private misery. The gestic symbolism of the scene is also striking, as Gretchen implores the Mother of Sorrows, who is herself gazing upwards at the cross, to look down on her suffering. Her lyrical prayer, unlike the regular strophic forms of 'Der König in Thule' and her spinning-wheel monologue, might initially appear to be in free rhythms appropriate to her emotional confusion; but closer reading shows that it bears clear traces of the church liturgy that would be familiar to her. The aabccb rhyme-scheme of lines 3590–607, the wording of lines 3590–2 and the metre of lines 3599–601 are directly derived from the best-known Easter sequence, the *Stabat Mater*. Moreover, when Gretchen, in the final scene in heaven, echoes this prayer in her supplication to the Mater Gloriosa (lines 12069–75), she also echoes the rhyme-scheme of the medieval sequence.[46]

The cumulative repetitions of Gretchen's prayer give way to two stanzas of more conventional strophic form (3608–15), after which her emotional stress breaks out in an anguished single-line plea for deliverance from shame and death; and this stark appeal then modulates into the three submissive lines of the opening, concluding on the ominous rhyme of 'Tod' and 'Not'.

'Nacht': Night

The Valentin episode pushes the Gretchen tragedy decisively towards its catastrophe, with Faust's flight, the death of her brother and her public disgrace. The attribution of blame in this incident is by no means straightforward. It bears all the marks of Mephisto's initiative – we might even assume that he has stage-managed the confrontation in order to contrive a drastic end to the affair of Faust and Gretchen, and it is his cynical song that provokes Valentin's attack. Yet Valentin's aggressive instincts require no provocation; lines 3648–9 indicate his murderous intentions from the start, and it is quite arguable that Faust, at least, acted in legitimate self-defence. It is by taking flight that he stands condemned by circumstantial evidence as a murderer. But no legal niceties can exculpate Faust; quite apart from the ultimate responsibility he bears as a result of his contract with the devil, his 'murder' of Valentin is only the external imperative for his desertion of Gretchen. His own responses, ambivalent from the start, have prepared the ground for his lack of any resistance to Mephisto's devices, and he has no answer to the devil's terrible question in the later scene 'Trüber Tag. Feld', when he challenges Faust to say which of them was responsible for Gretchen's destruction: 'Wer war's, der sie ins Verderben stürzte? Ich oder du?'[47]

The pathetic alternation of Gretchen's reactions between hope and doubt is mirrored by the gloomy ambivalence of Faust's feelings, expressed in his emblematic simile of lines 3650–4: his conscience, the 'Urquell' from which Mephisto has undertaken to seduce him, glows dimly like the altar-light, threatened by an encompassing darkness. But, even at this moment of self-knowledge, Faust is easily distracted by Mephisto's feline anticipation of orgiastic pleasures on the Brocken. The allusion to treasure in lines 3664 ff., evidently to the church coffers that Mephisto intends to pillage, might well also prefigure the twin leitmotifs of Mammon and sexuality, greed and lust, in the 'Walpurgis-nacht'; but Faust appears to overlook or ignore Mephisto's dark reference to the folkloric association of pearls and tears in line 3673.

Mephisto's song, which has general rather than literal relevance to the dramatic situation, is clearly, if loosely, based on Ophelia's St Valentine's song in Hamlet IV. v; it is possible, but not entirely certain, that Goethe, by playing on the St Valentine allusion, was obliquely parodying the association of Gretchen's brother with the soldier who became the patron saint of lovers. Critics have taken sides on the figure of Valentin, seeing him as a sturdy defender of family honour and of his sister's reputation or, alternatively, as a brutal and self-righteous representative of the intransigent bigotry and hypocrisy of his caste. Such discrepancies are no doubt a function of varying moral perspectives and changing social attitudes; but, to an audience that has already witnessed the private anguish of Gretchen, his censorious tirade must appear callous and indeed blasphemous, as Frau Marthe protests (lines 3764–5), even when allowance is made for the fact that he is dying at the hands of his sister's lover. Whatever our judgement of Valentin, his brief but telling appearance has fulfilled a twofold dramatic function. The first, the devastation of Gretchen, is harrowingly illustrated in the following 'Dom' scene; the second, Faust's flight to other adventures, is spectacu-larly illustrated in the 'Walpurgisnacht'.

'Dom': Cathedral

If the Valentin scene was operatic in its somewhat contrived theatricality (expository monologue, nocturnal serenade, ambush, swift assembly of crowd, loquacious and protracted death of 'hero'), the cathedral scene exploits operatic effects for intense pathos. The architecture and atmosphere of a Gothic cathedral, the solemn ritual of the mass, the organ music, the intercalation of the most awesome passages of the Requiem,[48] and the insidious voice of the Evil Spirit – all these devices intensify the claustrophobic panic as Gretchen seeks to come to terms with her terrified conscience. Since no indication is given, it is pointless to speculate whether the Requiem Mass is being sung for Gretchen's mother, as it was in the Urfaust, for her brother, or for neither.

The exact nature of the Evil Spirit which, we are told, stands behind Gretchen, is open to debate. Does it represent, as Atkins suggests, the combined force of public condemnation and her own conscience? Are we to accept it as the voice of the Evil One who denies her the solace of the Christian message of grace, as Arens argues? Or is it, as Mason believes, 'only her own troubled conscience'?[49] At least we may reasonably assume that the spirit is not Mephistopheles, since Goethe would have had no reason not to indicate this in the text. To secularize this demon as the voice of Gretchen's conscience in a drama that teems with spirits of one sort or another might seem unnecessary; on the other hand, as we have noted, it is one of the features of the Gretchen episode that there is no element of supernaturalism or diabolism that is not consistent with human behaviour or psychology. And in the words of the 'spirit' there is nothing that cannot be understood as the prompting of Gretchen's memory or conscience – including the first seven lines, which, it has been argued, could not represent her own thoughts. Indeed, where Gretchen's own voice does set in, it is to articulate not her inner thoughts or conscience but rather her responses to the inner voice represented by the 'spirit' – responses that express either her attempts to suppress that inner voice or, in the latter part of the scene, the psychological and indeed physical effects of her inner state. The voice of the Evil Spirit represents an indirect inner monologue of Gretchen; it is, as it were, a form of dramatic erlebte Rede; the confused tensions of Gretchen's mind are those of someone on the verge of mental collapse, and even those lines that appear to be spoken by an outside agency (lines 3823–4, 3828–32) indicate an almost schizophrenic alienation, presaging the approaching insanity that will be so harrowingly developed in the 'Kerker' scene.

'Walpurgisnacht': Walpurgis Night
The dramatic function of the witches' sabbath on the Brocken Mountain, or Blocksberg, is to represent a long period of distraction, debauch and adventure during which Gretchen's pregnancy, infanticide and trial run their course, and during which Faust's memory and conscience are virtually dormant. It is also Goethe's final involvement with the nordic phantom-world of Faust I, his valedictory working-out of the Christian sub-culture of superstition, evil and primitive instincts, after which, as he remarked to Eckermann, he was glad to have 'consumed his nordic inheritance', and turned to feast at the table of the Greeks.[50]

A somewhat tiresome, and indeed ultimately otiose, critical problem concerning the 'Walpurgisnacht' is its place in the chronology of the Gretchen tragedy. On a naturalistic time-scale, we can reasonably assume that the whole human action of Faust I up to and including the Valentin scene takes place between Easter and 28 April; for in lines 3660 ff. Mephisto announces the Walpurgisnacht, which takes place on the night of 30 April, for 'the day after tomorrow'. This is a perfectly adequate time-scale – some four or five weeks – for the events between Faust's Easter Day walk and the death of Gretchen's brother. If, however, the Walpurgisnacht does indeed take place two days after Valentin's death, then the 'Dom' scene is problematic, since lines 3790–3 seem to refer clearly enough to the 'quickening' of the child in Gretchen's womb – which can hardly occur until some months after conception. So we must assume either that these lines refer not to the quickening but to Gretchen's fearful intuition of the child she is carrying, or that the 'Dom' scene is to be imagined as taking place at some indeterminate time well after 30 April – perhaps, if the Walpurgisnacht is seen symbolically as representing a lapse of time, simultaneously with that episode. Alternatively, if we assume, like Arens, for example, that one year has elapsed before the Walpurgisnacht,[51] then this removes the problem of the 'Dom' scene, and also fits smoothly into the chronology of the final three scenes of Faust I. It would, however, make nonsense of lines 3660 ff. – which, it should be noted, were only written by Goethe into the final version along with the 'Walpurgisnacht' itself; and he would hardly have gone out of his way to draw attention to the exact date if he were referring to a Walpurgisnacht that we do not actually witness in the drama. There is no satisfactory solution, in naturalistic terms, to this inconsistent chronology, and we are forced to accept poetic licence in that the whole 'Walpurgisnacht' scene represents some twelve months of distraction for Faust.

The 'Walpurgisnacht' is, in a different sense again from the two previous scenes, operatic in character, if only by virtue of the musical element that is implicitly and explicitly prescribed; Arens has calculated that out of 388 lines, 235 are to be sung.[52] It is by definition a demonic nocturnal scene, lit dimly or luridly by a red moon, will-o'-the-wisps, glow-worms, sparks, fires, flames and the subterranean fire of Mammon's palace – the incandescent seams and veins of precious metals inside the mountain (lines 3912–35). The opening passages are powerful evocations of an eerie and grotesque nocturnal landscape, especially in lines 3889–905 and 3941–55. Visual, acoustic, tactile and even olfactory sense-impressions are involved; smoke and the stink of witches and goats are oppressive elements in the scene, and lines

3906 ff. suggest the confused, dream-like progress of the climbers as they appear to float through the demonic landscape.

The lines of the Witches, Warlocks and other voices between lines 3956 and 4015 are partly self-explanatory, partly allusive and partly without any clear significance at all. Urian, as Satan the lord of witches, is enthroned on the summit (lines 3958–9); Baubo, the coarse nursemaid of Demeter, here a figure of fertility rites and shamelessness, rides astride a pig (3962–3); a repulsive passage suggests voluntary or involuntary abortion or stillbirth (3976–7); the voices of lines 3987–9 have been tenuously identified with the Roman Catholic priesthood, who 'wash away' sin, are themselves pure, but are forever barren, and those of lines 3996–9 with the Protestant Church, which was some 300 years old by Goethe's day – the implication being, presumably, that try as they might, neither Church has yet quite reached the summit of iniquity; and lines 4000–3 and 4008–11 appear to allude broadly to sexual activity. The whole scene conveys more than vividly an orgiastic, obscene, blasphemous, grotesque, filthy, seething, stinking, screaming throng – 'a real witches' element', as Mephisto describes it (line 4019).

And yet it is at this point, when only a short climb separates Faust from Satan, that Mephisto seeks persistently and urgently to distract him from the summit of the Brocken. Three times he diverts Faust (lines 4029, 4052 and 4070) from the satanic climax of the sabbath. Faust reluctantly follows him – and at this point the Walpurgisnacht loses its satanic impetus. For what Faust finds in Mephisto's 'merry club' (line 4035), in a quiet backwater away from the mainstream of the satanic revels is, first, four disenchanted figures of the ancien régime who are lamenting the military, political, social and literary upheavals of the late eighteenth century; secondly, a Fairground Witch peddling her wares of seduction and death, which appear to include motifs from the Gretchen tragedy – jewels, poison and sword; thirdly, two lewd Witches with whom he and Mephisto dance briefly, Mephisto's gross exchanges with the older one parodying Faust's exchanges with the younger one in much the same way as the alternating flirtations of the first garden scene; and fourthly, the Proktophantasmist. The 'man with the haunted backside' is Friedrich Nicolai, the verbose and dogmatic pundit and indefatigable traveller of the late German Enlightenment, with whom Goethe had some literary scores to settle. Nicolai's solemn announcement that he had cured himself of a fever in which he had seen phantoms by applying leeches to his buttocks (see lines 4172–5) had caused much hilarity among an irreverent younger generation of writers; not only Goethe but also Brentano, Tieck and Hoffmann were unable to resist ribald references to the discomfiture of the arch-rationalist.

In the midst of this extraordinary mixture of erotic and satirical horseplay, Goethe introduces a stark reminder to both Faust and the audience of the unseen tragic action: the phantom vision of Gretchen with the visible stigmata of her imminent execution. And yet, once again, Mephisto is able to distract Faust's attention by dismissing the apparition as a manifestation of the Medusa, and has little trouble in diverting him towards the insipid theatrical sideshow that forms the following scene.

The central question of the 'Walpurgisnacht' episode as it stands in *Faust I* is why, at the very moment that Faust might reach the height (or depth) of satanic experience by simply following the throng to the summit of the Brocken, Mephisto should divert him towards such innocuous and, for the reader or spectator as well as for Faust, such tedious entertainment. It has been suggested that Mephisto is unwilling to stimulate or satisfy Faust's intellectual curiosity (see line 4040) – that a momentous encounter with the Evil One himself runs counter to his programme of insignificant banality, that it would be a revelatory experience such as Faust sought in the opening scenes in his study. Against this, it has been argued that, to judge by Goethe's original plans for the episode on the summit, Mephisto might fear that Faust would simply be repelled by the tasteless obscenities of the satanic ritual. Alternatively, Mephisto might be reluctant to appear in a subordinate demonic role before Faust, as he must in a scene that revolves around Satan; it has also been pointed out that the enthronement of Satan as an absolute monarch of evil would represent a dualistic cosmology that would seriously contradict the theology of the 'Prologue in Heaven', where evil was merely a function in God's creation.

Albrecht Schöne has cut through the thicket of conflicting intrinsic explanations by frankly asserting that Goethe dropped his original plan because he was convinced that the German public of the day was not prepared for such scabrous material as he had planned. But Schöne has also attempted an imaginative reconstruction of the planned scene on the basis of draft sketches and passages from the paralipomena.[53] Up to line 4015, Schöne's version of the episode proceeds much as in the published version; but Mephisto, far from diverting Faust from the summit, actually leads him there, and acts as master of ceremonies in an obscene parody of enfeoffment and/or of papal homage, in which Satan receives from his subjects the loyal kiss on his backside. There follows an equally scurrilous travesty of the Last Judgement in which Satan,

dividing the he-goats to his right and the she-goats to his left, harangues
the respective sexes in explicit images of gold and sexual organs on the
inseparable human urges of greed and lust. After a lewd exchange be-
tween Mephisto and a young girl, there follows an orgy that incorporates
Faust's and Mephisto's dance with the witches; but the apparition of
Gretchen with the red line around her neck is followed not by the
'Walpurgisnachtstraum' but by lines 4399–403 from the scene 'Nacht.
Offen Feld', and then by a grisly and nightmarish auto-da-fé that enacts
the execution of Gretchen. This is immediately followed by the scene
'Trüber Tag. Feld'; the 'Walpurgisnachtstraum' is dropped altogether.

Schöne's reconstruction, for all that he omits and transposes textual
material and supplies stage-directions of his own, is remarkably faithful
to the published and unpublished material of Goethe's 'Walpurgisnacht'. The inference is that by omitting the scenes on the summit,
Goethe removed the central core of the 'Walpurgisnacht', the dramatic
purpose of which would have been to convey to Faust in stark terms
the horror of Gretchen's situation, and thereby to save him from
perdition by distracting him from the satanic homage that would have
sealed his doom. As it is, in the version published by Goethe, all Faust
does to imperil his soul is to dance with a young, naked witch; and,
while Schöne insists that Faust saves himself only by a hair's breadth
from damnation through intercourse with a succubus,[54] it is by no
means clear as the text stands that any such extreme peril is involved in
that incident. The phantom apparition of Gretchen certainly distracts
Faust from the Witch; but it does not appear immediately or decisively
to activate his conscience or his will to rescue her – it can at most be
understood as a dim and inconclusive intuition of her fate. The
unsatisfactory result is that the 'Trüber Tag. Feld' scene is separated
from the 'Walpurgisnacht' by the feeble intermezzo of 'Oberon and
Titania's Golden Wedding'.

'Walpurgisnachtstraum': Walpurgis Night's Dream

The divertissement witnessed by Faust and Mephisto is to be imagined as
an open-air theatre with natural scenery; the arts of the late stage-
manager of the Weimar Court Theatre, Mieding (line 4224), are not
required. It is accompanied by an insect orchestra, and is written and
produced by dilettantes, by excited amateurs. The fiction of 'Oberon
and Titania's Golden Wedding' is a sketchy framework that takes up
little more than the first seven and the last three quatrains; within this
is contained, among orchestral and choreographic interludes, a satirical
review of types and individuals.

There is only a degree of unanimity among commentators on the specific identities of individual figures, except where August von Hennings and his belletristic productions, for example, are explicitly derided in lines 4307–18. The bagpipes of lines 4255 ff. might be derived from an illustration in one of Goethe's sources for the 'Walpurgisnacht', Praetorius' *Blockes Berges Verrichtung*;[55] literary archaeology might reveal Nicolai as the Inquisitive Traveller; Graf Friedrich von Stolberg as the Orthodox; the lexicographer J. H. Campe as the Purist; the musician Reichardt, the pedagogue Böttiger, or the Stolberg brothers as the Weather-vane; Lavater as the Crane; and even, more dubiously, Goethe himself as the Weltkind. Further identifications are at best speculative.[56]

What is rather clearer is the thematic grouping of the satire. The first group (lines 4259–90) appears to reflect local and topical aesthetic controversies in literature and the visual arts, the tensions between the classical aesthetics of Weimar and its critics, the gulf between quality and mediocrity that Goethe and Schiller perceived in contemporary culture. The second group (4295–330) reflects literary and religious squabbles, the polemical *Xenienkampf*, the volley of satirical epigrams that Goethe and Schiller directed at their detractors, including some former allies like Lavater. The third group (4343–62) is a parade of caricatured philosophical systems, Christian-dogmatic, Fichtean-idealist, empirical, transcendental and sceptical, all booming like bitterns among the reeds and charmed not by Orpheus' lyre but by the monotonous wailing of the bagpipes. The final group (4367–86) parades a political spectrum of revolutionary riff-raff – the opportunists who adapt indifferently to *ancien régime* or revolutionary conditions (die Gewandten, lines 4367–70); the helpless and parasitic courtiers, beached by the historical tide and ending up as querulous *émigrés* beyond the Rhine (die Unbe-hülflichen, 4371–4); the dubious prophets that emerge from the revolu-tionary swamp (Irrlichter, 4375–8); the fallen luminaries of the *ancien régime* or of the Revolution itself (Sternschnuppe, 4379–82); and the monolithic power of the mob (die Massiven, 4383–6). Ariel summons those with natural or intellectual wings to follow him to a better place, to the 'Hill of Roses' (line 4394) – which is a puzzling reference. Arens has refuted the usual conjecture that it derives from Wieland's *Oberon*, and refers it instead to the ideal aesthetic world of Schiller's poetic vision in 'Das Ideal und das Leben';[57] the wording of lines 4391–4 might also recall the third stanza of his 'Ode to Joy' – a tribute, perhaps, to Goethe's polemical companion-in-arms, for whose *Musenalmanach* this episode was originally written.

There have been many attempts to show how Goethe strove to integrate this satirical episode into the fabric of the Brocken scene, and indeed into *Faust* as a whole. Clearly, the satirical quatrains continue those of the four earlier figures of the General, Minister, Parvenu and Author; but they, and Nicolai, were incongruous elements in the first place – those whom Goethe had, as it were, wished on to the Brocken, as Dante had wished some of his enemies into his *Inferno*. Some of the figures here are political and social types, representatives of the 'wider world' such as Goethe would introduce into *Faust II*; and Ariel also reappears as a spirit of benevolent nature in the opening scene of the second part. The Shakespearian theme of the reconciliation of Oberon and Titania after their elemental quarrel might be an ironic parallel to the 'reconciliation' of Faust and Gretchen after their long separation; but this is a very tenuous link, and in any case the 'Golden Wedding' soon gives way to the parade of bizarre and ludicrous figures across the stage, a satirical revue within the slender framework of a whimsical masque within the confused revel of the Walpurgisnacht, itself an episode in the tragedy of Gretchen that is in turn encapsulated within the further circles of Faust's pact, the 'Prologue in Heaven', the 'Prelude in the Theatre' and the introductory 'Zueignung'.[58]

The dream has been seen as a satyr play, as an entertaining relief or release after the tension of the Brocken episode, as its aesthetic foil, or as part of the deliberate and progressive weakening of the nightmarish illusion of the Walpurgisnacht, representing Faust's emergence from it and his return to the dramatic reality of the Gretchen tragedy. It might even represent the extension of the bizarre and sombre demonology of the Brocken into a trivialized and secularized context: if the creatures of the Walpurgisnacht were perverted distortions of nature, what we see in the dream are their social, cultural, intellectual and political equivalents. This gradual thinning-out of the demonic impetus, which indeed begins almost exactly half-way through the 'Walpurgisnacht' itself, reaches its final dilution at the point where the whole episode dissolves into airy nothing in the final quatrain (lines 4395–8) – to be followed, with brutal dramatic and theatrical force, by the realism of the prose scene 'Trüber Tag. Feld'. Mephisto's attempts to divert Faust with 'tasteless distractions' have finally run into the sand; but they have served their purpose – they have diverted him long enough for Gretchen's tragedy to reach its final stage.

These more or less subtle critical constructions, however, ultimately represent attempts to make the best of an alien and unnecessary element in *Faust I*. Certainly, the fact that much of the material in the 'Walpurgisnachtstraum' was not originally composed for inclusion in *Faust* at all, but for Schiller's *Musenalmanach* of 1797, is not of itself conclusive proof that the episode is superfluous or irrelevant; after all, Goethe clearly made efforts to expand the original version and adapt it to its new context. If, however, his original plan for the 'Walpurgisnacht' did bear some resemblance to Schöne's reconstruction, we can only regret that he did not see fit to stick to it.

'Trüber Tag. Feld': Dreary Day: Field

It is part of the remarkable economy of the Gretchen tragedy that it is left to the reader or spectator to infer the details of Gretchen's fate from the brief and allusive information provided in the 'Walpurgisnacht' and 'Trüber Tag. Feld' scenes. Certainly, the expansion of the Valentin episode in the final version makes Mephisto's cryptic reference to Faust's 'blood guilt' rather clearer than it is in the Urfaust; but otherwise the intervening events are only briefly, if vividly, sketched out in Faust's first speech. Mephisto's brutal rejoinder that 'she is not the first' – derived, as most commentators agree, from the interrogation of Susanna Margaretha Brandt in Frankfurt, and exploited, to Goethe's indignation, in Wagner's Die Kindermörderin – sets off a curious tirade from Faust that has no evident relation to the previous action. His description of the hell-hound that used to waylay harmless travellers is scarcely consistent with the historically later 'Vor dem Tor' scene, in which the poodle introduces itself to Faust and is very soon after metamorphosed into the devil. In this and in the following scene, Goethe appears to have been concerned to preserve the style and mood of his original Sturm und Drang material at this stage of the drama, even at the expense of strict dramatic coherence.

Faust's furious attempts to exculpate himself by shifting responsibility on to his companion, even on to the Erdgeist – who can scarcely be said truthfully to have 'fettered' him to Mephistopheles – are easily countered by Mephisto's derisive but telling ripostes; once again, grandiloquent Faustian rhetoric is no match for the devil's sarcasm as he taunts Faust with a reminder of human limitations. What is more, we are also reminded here of the limits of the devil's powers, and thus of the fundamentally realistic criteria of the Gretchen episode; Mephisto can drug the jailer, provide magic horses even – but he cannot nullify a legal judgement, nor himself rescue Gretchen. This must be done by human agency, 'mit Menschenhand'.

'Nacht. Offen Feld': Night: Open Country

This brief and obscure but powerfully atmospheric scene was, in the Urfaust, a companion piece to the short scene 'Land Strase' that prefaced the Gretchen tragedy. It is, for the reader if not for Faust, a macabre anticipation of Gretchen's execution, since it is a gallows-field that Faust and Mephisto pass on their headlong ride to Gretchen's prison. Faust sees the activity around the spot as that of a consecration ritual – though whether by spirits or by clergy is not clear; Mephisto dismisses it as a witches' coven. There has been much debate on which is the more likely, on whether Mephisto is deliberately misleading Faust, or whether each subjectively projects his own vision on to what might even be the actual preparations for Gretchen's execution on the coming morning. The dark and fitful nature of the scene allows no certainty; and Arens claims to have refuted all such speculation by pointing out that this cannot possibly be the site of Gretchen's execution, since that explicitly takes place in the market square, as lines 4588 ff. indicate clearly enough, not in a gallows-field outside the town.[59] In Schöne's reconstructed 'Walpurgisnacht', the whole scene is boldly placed immediately before the nightmarish prefiguration of Gretchen's execution on the Brocken.

'Kerker': Dungeon

While much of the laconic expressive force of the original Urfaust version of this scene was lost when Goethe extended and versified it for Faust I, it remains a deeply pathetic and harrowing conclusion to the tragedy of Gretchen. As in the early version, it is in almost all respects her scene; Faust's role is reduced to brief interjections, to his frantic urgings to flight or his helpless articulation of the pity of it. There is little real communication between the two; even where their exchanges appear lucid, the dialogue founders on Gretchen's distracted responses, or on the ironic discrepancy between their respective perceptions of freedom. Otherwise, the structure of the scene is that of a fragmented monologue, determined by the abrupt shifts of Gretchen's conscious-ness as her mind moves through a complex spectrum of past, present and future, of distraction, awareness and submission, of attraction, repulsion and rejection, of fantasy, reality and certainty. As in 'Trüber Tag. Feld', Faust expresses no sense of personal guilt or responsibility, but thinks only of the practical means of escape; Gretchen, even in her distraction, accepts the legal, social and religious morality that demands her atonement.

Faust's somewhat theatrical and rhetorical opening monologue is poignantly counterpointed by the distracted voice singing the song from the fairy tale The Juniper Tree (Von dem Machandelboom),[60] which is slightly adapted to correspond broadly, though not exactly, to the dramatic situation: it is Gretchen's projection of the voice of her dead child. Her mistaking Faust for her executioner is the first of a series of ironic misunderstandings that run through the whole scene. Her distraction is vividly conveyed in her confused references to her bridal crown, in the fantasy that her child must be fed, that the whole situation is a fiction, a tale told by others, and in her vision of hell seething beneath her feet. Even her recognition of Faust's voice, expressed in ecstatic dactyls (lines 4466–9), leads only to a fantasy-vision of freedom within the prison rather than of actual escape, to a rueful contrast of past and present rather than to any future perspective, and to a desperate and incongruous sensual fury (lines 4491–2).

Line 4493 marks the beginning of Gretchen's progressive estrangement from Faust, which culminates in her final revulsion in line 4610. In her vision of the graves, in which the family shattered by Faust is reunited in death, there is no place for him; and, as she recoils from Faust, she submits to the secular judgement of her own morality, which is not his (lines 4544–9). Even to Faust's protest that he will stay with her, she replies with a distracted fiction that seems designed for his escape, not hers (4551 ff.); her way is barred by the nightmarish figure of her mother crouched on a stone. When Faust points to the dawn as a token of urgency, she replies with a disturbed but horrifyingly precise anticipation of her own execution which, in lieu of her wedding day, will end her suffering. She sees the crowd in the square, hears the death-knell and the judge's staff as it snaps above her head, feels the steel of the sword as it bites into her neck, and even senses the oblivion that follows (line 4595). As she recoils from Mephistopheles, who emerges in her imagination from hell itself, so she also recoils from Faust in a final gesture of independence, and submits to her religious instincts by throwing herself on the mercy of her God.

The voice from above, if it is indeed from heaven, and not a dramatic projection of Gretchen's inner conviction of salvation,[61] is the only unequivocally divine intervention, not simply in the Gretchen episode but in the whole human drama of Faust I; and, as such, it has appeared incongruous, disturbing, or superfluous to commentators, who frequently see it as an unnecessary piece of theatre, or as a more or less misguided attempt by Goethe to introduce a conciliatory ray of light into the stark and sombre ending of the Gretchen tragedy. Also, it is by no means clear to whom the voice is addressed, or for whose benefit it is introduced – that of Gretchen, Faust, Mephisto, or the audience. Certainly, it serves to remind the audience of the perspective of salvation for Gretchen beyond her secular judgement, and might even cryptically prefigure her intercession for Faust in the final scene of the second part – though it is uncertain how far Goethe envisaged this at the time. It is most satisfactorily understood as the voice of Goethe's theatrical God, the Lord of the 'Prologue in Heaven', who thus indicates to Mephistopheles, and to him alone of the three figures on stage, the limits of his power for evil: here is one soul, at least, that is lost to him. Realizing this, Mephisto therefore brusquely asserts his will over Faust, and calls him away: 'Her zu mir!'. This is entirely consistent with the terms of the 'Prologue in Heaven', where the Lord decreed that the scope of the devil's power was limited to the duration of human life. Here, in the case of Gretchen, Mephisto can resist the operation of divine grace even less than he will be able to do in the case of Faust. He has engineered only the secular judgement of Gretchen, and her physical destruction; but that, as Lessing remarked in another context, is already quite sufficiently tragic in itself.

NOTES: CHAPTER 5

1 On the function of polarities (contraction and expansion, light and dark, etc.) as structural principles in *Faust* I, see Requadt, *Goethes 'Faust I'*, pp. 59 ff., 105 ff. and *passim*.

2 HA. 3. 495 ff.

3 Harold Jantz, 'Faust's Vision of the Macrocosm'.

4 GA. 5. 541 (no. 1).

5 See Herder, *Sämmtliche Werke*, ed. Bernhard Suphan, Vol. 13 (Berlin, 1887), pp. 254–5.

6 Mason, *Goethe's Faust*, p. 138.

7 ibid., p. 160; GA. 13. 29.

8 See Requadt, *Goethes 'Faust I'*, p. 73.

9 Arens, *Kommentar zu Goethes Faust I*, pp. 99 ff., 103–4.

10 GA. 5. 541 (no. 1).

11 HA. 3. 502; Arens, *Kommentar zu Goethes Faust I*, pp. 117 ff.

12 Durrani, *Faust and the Bible*, p. 48.

13 ibid., p. 47.

14 GA. 5. 172. See Peter Michelsen, 'Der Einzelne und sein Geselle. Fausts Osterspaziergang'.

15 Mason, *Goethe's Faust*, p. 293.

16 Luke, ' "Der nord-südliche Goethe" ', pp. 136 ff.

17 Durrani, *Faust and the Bible*, pp. 57 ff.

18 ibid., pp. 60 ff.

19 See Arens, *Kommentar zu Goethes Faust I*, pp. 153 ff.

20 On the derivation of Mephisto's name, see White, *Names and Nomenclature*, pp. 95–110.

21 Arens, *Kommentar zu Goethes Faust I*, pp. 158–9.

22 ibid., p. 160.

23 GA. 10. 386.

24 GA. 4. 125.

25 HA. 3. 508; Requadt, *Goethes 'Faust I'*, p. 126.

26 'Maximen und Reflexionen', no. 858 (GA. 9. 613).

27 E. E. Papst, *Goethe and the Fourth Virtue: an Inaugural Lecture*, p. 8.

28 See Géza von Molnár, 'Die Fragwürdigkeit des Fragezeichens. Einige Überlegungen zur Paktszene'; Arens, *Kommentar zu Goethes Faust I*, pp. 181–2.
29 Mason, *Goethe's Faust* p. 299.
30 ibid., p. 307.
31 ibid., p. 306.
32 Arens, *Kommentar zu Goethes Faust I*, p. 214.
33 See Douglas F. Bub, 'The "Hexenküche" and the "Mothers" in Goethe's *Faust*'.
34 Arens, *Kommentar zu Goethes Faust I*, pp. 244–5.
35 On the physical appearance of Mephistopheles on stage and its implications, see Jantz, *Form of Faust*, pp. 3 ff.
36 Douglas F. Bub, 'The Crown Incident in the *Hexenküche*: a Reinterpretation'.
37 See Arens, *Kommentar zu Goethes Faust I*, pp. 249–50.
38 Kathryn S. Levedahl, 'The Witch's One-Times-One: Sense or Nonsense?'.
39 Mason, *Goethe's Faust*, p. 208.
40 ibid., p. 194.
41 GA. 5. 548 (no. 34).
42 GA. 15. 326; Requadt, *Goethes 'Faust I'*, p. 241. See the Song of Solomon 5: 4: 'My beloved put in his hand by the hole of the door,/And my bowels were moved for him.'
43 See Requadt, pp. 273–4; Otto Pniower, 'Faust und das Hohe Lied'.
44 See Durrani, *Faust and the Bible*, pp. 105 ff.; Elizabeth M. Wilkinson, 'The Theological Basis of Faust's "Credo"'.
45 See Arens, *Kommentar zu Goethes Faust I*, p. 330.
46 See F. M. Fowler, 'Goethe's "Faust" and the Medieval Sequence'.
47 GA. 5. 281, lines 20–1.
48 These lines are translated in the Missal as follows:

> Day of wrath and terror looming,
> Heaven and earth to ash consuming. . .
> Then the Judge will sit, revealing
> Every hidden thought and feeling,
> Unto each requital dealing. . .
> What shall wretched I be crying,
> To what friend for succour flying,
> When the just in fear are sighing?
>
> (*The Missal in Latin and English*, ed. J. O'Connell and
> H. P. R. Finberg, 2nd edn [London, 1957], p. 230).

49 Atkins, *Goethe's Faust*, p. 89; Arens, *Kommentar zu Goethes Faust I*, pp. 360–1; and Mason, *Goethe's Faust*, p. 191.
50 To Eckermann, 16 Feb. 1826 (Biedermann 3. 258).
51 See Arens, *Kommentar zu Goethes Faust I*, p. 373.
52 ibid., p. 371.
53 Albrecht Schöne, *Götterzeichen, Liebeszauber, Satanskult. Neue Einblicke in alte Goethetexte*, pp. 217–30; see also GA. 5. 549–57.
54 Schöne, *Götterzeichen, Liebeszauber, Satanskult*, p. 173.
55 See *Goethes Faust*, ed. Georg Witkowski, Vol. 2, p. 479.
56 See the notes in the commentaries of Ernst Beutler, GA. 5. 768–9; Cyrus

Hamlin (ed.), Faust. A Tragedy, pp. 104 ff.; Arens, Kommentar zu Goethes Faust I, pp. 424 ff.; and others.

57 See Arens, Kommentar zu Goethes Faust I, p. 433.

58 For an analysis and justification of the 'Walpurgisnachtstraum' as 'a highly mediated epiphany of creative spirit', see Brown, Goethe's Faust, pp. 124 ff.

59 See Arens, Kommentar zu Goethes Faust I, pp. 444–5.

60 Jakob and Wilhelm Grimm, Kinder- und Hausmärchen, no. 47.

61 See Durrani, Faust and the Bible, pp. 122–3.

CHAPTER 6

Faust, Part Two

PRELUDE IN NATURE:
THE NEW LEVEL OF PERCEPTION

'Anmutige Gegend': Pleasant Landscape

In view of the horrors that had devastated Gretchen at the end of the first part, and that had also shattered Faust's spirit, Goethe confided to Eckermann, he had no choice but to 'completely paralyse' his hero, to destroy him, as it were, in order to strike new life from this semblance of death. Here, all is pity and the deepest compassion. No judgement is made, there is no question of whether it is deserved or undeserved, such as might be the case before a human tribunal; such matters are of no concern to the elves. . .[1]

The 'Anmutige Gegend' scene functions both as an epilogue to the tragic experiences of Faust I and as a prologue to the allegorical adventures of Faust II. The therapeutic sleep of oblivion expunges from Faust's consciousness the horror of the Gretchen tragedy; and, on awakening from his experience of Lethe, he is granted an insight into the nature of the relationship between ideal and real, between his imperious urge to strive for the absolute and the limited and relative perception of it in the finite empirical forms of human experience.

Faust's sleep is the gift of a benevolent nature, personified in the elemental forms of Ariel and his elves. The relaxation and restoration of Faust's spirit is achieved in four lyrical stanzas that represent the healing passage of time and the therapeutic balance of tensions, expressed symbolically in the four watches of the night sung by the Chorus of elves (lines 4634–65), in the imagery of profound peace and harmony expressed by the reflection of the night sky in the surface of a lake, in the organic processes of seasonal renewal as the seed grows towards maturity, and in the sunrise as Faust emerges from the 'husk' of sleep to face a new dawn. This process resumes a whole complex of Goethean symbolism – sleep as nature's agent of restoration and regeneration; the calm reflection of stars and moon in water as a symbol of balance and harmony between the cosmic and the human; the emergence of the imago from the pupa in the mystery of natural metamorphosis;

the 'Antaeus' experience by means of which strength and vigour are derived from contact with the earth; and the light of the sun as a symbol of absolute or divine truth.

And yet, immediately, the titanic exuberance of Faust's response to the new day is curbed by a reminder of the limitations of his perceptions. As he was unable to confront the Erdgeist in its immediate and essential form, as he was forced to acknowledge in 'Wald und Höhle' that his empathetic joy in nature was disturbed and qualified by the distractions of his own sensuality, so here Faust must concede and accept his inability to grasp truth in its direct manifestation. He turns, dazzled, from the sun towards the emblem of mediated truth, towards the veil that conceals and reveals the absolute for human perception: in the flying spray of the waterfall he glimpses the coloured rainbow, the evanescent but constant reflection of the ideal in the atomized phenomena of reality, of the permanent and infinite in the flux of finite existence, of the absolute in empirical experience.

This grandiose symbolism of light and colour is, here as elsewhere, informed by Goethe's optical theory. Mephistopheles has, in lines 1780 ff., warned Faust that an absolute totality of knowledge or experience is inaccessible to him; man's perception is neither that of pure light nor that of absolute darkness, but is limited to the relative area of interaction or alternation between absolute polarities – to the intermediate zone of colours. As Goethe remarked to Eckermann in a discussion of divine revelation and human religious systems, the unveiled light of revelation is too pure and too bright for man's faculties;[2] and in a line from *Pandora*, Epimetheus similarly defines the limits of human perception, which perceives not the light but that which is illuminated – man is 'bestimmt, Erleuchtetes zu sehen, nicht das Licht'.[3] In the introduction to his meteorological studies, Goethe had defined absolute truth and human understanding in terms of a metaphorical relationship: truth, which is identical with the divine, is never perceived directly by us; we see it only as reflection, example, or symbol.[4] And the final Chorus Mysticus of *Faust* II will again define the transient phenomena of reality as a metaphor of ultimate truth: 'All that is transient/Is but a likeness' (lines 12104–5).

Moreover, the rainbow is commonly a symbol of mediation between divine and human – the sign of the covenant between God and man after the Flood (Genesis 9: 13), and of Iris, the gods' messenger to mortals in classical myth. For Faust, the image of the sun's light reflected as colour through the opaque medium ('trübes Mittel' is the term Goethe uses in his *Farbenlehre*) of the veil of spray is an assurance of the immanence of the ideal in the confused and inadequate reality of his experience. Line 4727 – 'The colourful reflection is our life' – might stand as a motto over the second part of Faust, to be answered by the closing words of the Chorus Mysticus, which indicate a transcendental reality that is to Faust's experience as the light of the sun is to the coloured rainbow.

Faust's reaction to this check on his aspirations is remarkably positive and affirmative; it is very different from the crushing sense of inadequacy that followed his rejection by the Erdgeist, or from his uneasy resignation to his sensual urges in 'Wald und Höhle'. In the 'Vor dem Tor' scene of Part One, Faust also aspired to a sphere of constant sunlight, a vision in which he pursued the sun's course in 'god-like' flight around the earth, with day before him and behind him night (line 1087). Now he accepts that the sun will henceforth be at his back; this represents the voluntary acceptance of a change in the nature of his striving, a change that also determines the nature of his experiences in the second part. He is no longer the titanic magus figure who conjured the Macrocosm and the Erdgeist in an imperious quest for revelation, nor is he the private, subjective individual passionately caught up in a tragic web of common experience. Lethe has done more to Faust than to heal the psychic wounds of the Gretchen tragedy; it has transformed his identity from that of a 'specific' individual to a 'generic' persona. From now on, he is a more detached and dispassionate public figure who plays a series of roles in episodes that have less to do with the emotional or psychological experiences of an individual existence than with the broad historical profile of an age – that is, of the age commonly termed the 'Goethezeit'.

THE IMPERIAL SCENES:
THE CRISIS OF THE ANCIEN RÉGIME

'Kaiserliche Pfalz. Saal des Thrones': Throne Room of the Imperial Palace
By Eckermann's account, Goethe had intended to portray his Emperor as a prince

who has every possible aptitude for losing his country, which he indeed later manages to do. The welfare of his realm and of his subjects is of no concern to him; he thinks only of himself and how he can entertain himself from day to day . . . This is, then, Mephisto's true element; he quickly removes the previous fool, and is at once installed as the Emperor's new fool and adviser.[5]

The Emperor of Act I was actually identified in Goethe's scenario of 1816 as Maximilian I holding his Imperial Council in Augsburg.[6] In the final version, he is virtually unrecognizable as the historical contemporary of Faust, or even as the 'last knight' of subsequent legend; he has become a composite and stylized figure with only the barest external attributes of a late-medieval or Renaissance German ruler – imperial officers, a court jester, an astrologer, a love of spectacle and pageant in the Italianate style, and a realm on the brink of disintegration. The office-bearers catalogue in turn the critical condition of the state – the breakdown of the rule of law and the corruption of justice and the judiciary that ultimately threatens the authority of the Emperor; the breakdown of the feudal military structure, the forming of private armies, the disaffection of the professional soldiery and the decentralization of power; the unreliability of allies; the lack of revenues from internal and external sources; and the extravagant squandering of resources that characterizes an unstable society, the mortgaging of the future that is the result of a situation in which no stable future is discernible.

This is indeed a broad picture of the Holy Roman Empire at the time of Maximilian, such as Goethe had evoked in *Götz von Berlichingen*, and similar, too, to the description of anarchy he had put into the mouth of Götz in a masque he had composed for the visit of the Dowager Tsarina Maria Fyodorovna, mother of Alexander I, to Weimar in 1818.[7] But, as in his early chronicle drama the state of Maximilian's empire had been in many ways an allusive comment on the terminal condition of the Holy Roman Empire in the late eighteenth century, as in the 1818 masque Götz's words had had clear application to the social, military and political upheavals in Germany during the first fifteen years of the nineteenth century, so too the chaotic picture of the empire in the imperial scenes of Act I reflects Goethe's perception of the historical convulsions of his own lifetime. The reference to the dynastic struggles of Guelphs and Ghibellines, of papal and imperial factions in the early Middle Ages (line 4845), is not only a general heading for any kind of ideological power conflict; it is an anachronistic allusion that relativizes the specific sixteenth-century setting of the scene. A further clue here is the figure of Mephistopheles, who smuggles himself into a position in the court by usurping the roles of the Emperor's previous 'advisers', who themselves have indeed been dubious enough: the Jester and the Astrologer.

Goethe had seen the infiltration of the French court of Louis XVI by charlatans and tricksters, and the hypnotic power exercised by them over the gullible but influential members of the royal circle, as the undermining of the moral and political world of the time. In particular, the influence of Giuseppe Balsamo, 'Count' Cagliostro, whose obscurantist teachings, prophecies and purported miraculous elixirs and cures had captivated the Queen herself, and above all his involvement in the diamond necklace scandal of 1785, had shocked Goethe.[8] As early as 22 June 1781, he had written to Lavater expressing his deep mistrust of Cagliostro in outspoken terms;[9] and in retrospect he came to see such criminal gullibility and frivolity on the part of the ruling classes as the symptom of the final decadence of the *ancien régime*, indeed of imminent revolution. His early reaction to these affairs finds outright expression in the *Kampagne in Frankreich* and in the satirical comedy *Der Groß-Cophta*, in which Graf Rostro, the Domherr and the Marquise are barely disguised equivalents of Cagliostro, the Cardinal de Rohan and the Comtesse de la Motte.[10]

Mephistopheles, as the Cagliostro of this politically and economically bankrupt realm, diagnoses the crisis as a purely fiscal one (lines 4889–90). The feudal establishment, church and nobility, represented by the Chancellor-Archbishop (lines 4897–916), is powerless against his diabolical weapons – verbal dexterity and the exploitation of human greed and credulity. In fantastic terms, he dangles before the court a dream of instant riches beneath the ground: veins of precious metals, the mineral wealth of the empire, coin, plate, cups, bowls, jewels and even, in an oriental flight of fancy, wines so ancient that they are preserved in their own tartar (5025–6).

These cryptic allusions to buried treasure are not immediately clear. Obviously, they represent a means of instant and spectacular wealth, irrespective of endeavour and effort – as Mephisto himself observes in his pithy aside to the spectators at the end of the scene (5061–4). The references to treasure trove in lines 4927 ff. might allude to the possibility of extortion or expropriation – a reminder to the Emperor that wealth is still concentrated in private hands but requires almost supernatural powers to locate and collect it under the present conditions in the realm, which encourage the hoarding of wealth rather than its healthy circulation in the economy. The words of the Astrologer, prompted by Mephisto (lines 4955 ff.), appear to describe an alternative source of revenue: as many medieval alchemists, failing in the 'Great Work' of transmuting base metals into gold (Sol) or silver (Luna), would resort to false alloys of quicksilver and copper (Mercury and Venus) or of iron, tin and lead (Mars, Jupiter and Saturn), so here the arcane formulae of the astrologer suggest either the blatant forgery of imperial coinage or, at least, its debasement. The description of immense riches buried in underground vaults in lines 5018–32, of gem-studded chalices, precious plate and ancient wines, suggests the almost fabulous wealth of the church which, the devil suggests, might be ripe for disendowment and requisition by the state. This is the buried wealth that, it is later explained, can be used to back the new paper currency devised by Mephistopheles.

Many precedents have been cited for the financial fraud perpetrated by Mephisto, and perhaps also by Faust, at the court. There were innumerable cases of financial scandal during the eighteenth century based on the issue of credit or paper money, from John Law's activities as French minister of finances in 1720 to the 'South Sea Bubble' in England. Paper assignats had been issued in the American War of Independence, Goethe himself had encountered the French revolutionary assignats during the 1792 campaign in France, and he later experienced the instability of Austrian currency in the Bohemian spas. It is clear that he was profoundly uneasy about the relation between 'real' wealth and paper money; the very word for banknote, 'Geldschein', suggests an element of illusion. While Goethe perforce accepted the economic fact of paper money, he could not bring himself to approve of it unreservedly, as one of his maxims of 1829 suggests.[11] Nevertheless, the most persuasive historical reference for Mephisto's buried wealth is, as Pierre Grappin has argued, the sequestration of church assets and property in 1790 by the revolutionary government in France as backing for the issue of the paper assignats, which very quickly and spectacularly dropped in value, causing inflationary chaos, hardship and unrest.[12]

At all events, it is clear that the measures proposed by Mephisto are dubious and, at best, short-term solutions to the bankruptcy of the empire; but they are still sufficient to distract the Emperor's attention from the urgent problems of state to the carnival entertainment of his Italianate trionfo. At this point Mephisto, confident that his advice will fall on deaf ears, assumes his ironic role as purveyor of sententious wisdom (lines 5048 ff.), while he is at the same time careful to encourage the wild celebration of carnival, since this will give him the opportunity to reduce the empire to total economic chaos. His final epigram of lines 5061–4, a devastating mixture of morality and cynicism, is delivered to the audience from an empty stage.

'Weitläufiger Saal' ('Mummenschanz'): Spacious Hall (Masquerade)

Many models and antecedents for the carnival masquerade of this scene have been revealed by research into sources. The spectacular festivals of German Renaissance and Baroque courts, descriptions of the figures and songs of Florentine Renaissance trionfi, Athenaeus' descriptions of

Alexandrian triumphs, visual sources such as Dürer's *Triumph of the Emperor Maximilian* or Mantegna's *Triumph of Caesar*, Goethe's own output of allegorical masques and pageants for the Weimar court, and not least his first-hand experiences of the Roman Carnival in 1787 and again in 1788; no doubt many of these sources contributed something to this elaborate spectacle. The meaning or function of the episode within *Faust II*, however, is still controversial; indeed, few commentaries provide a wholly consistent or unified thematic interpretation of all the disparate figures and episodes of this scene, except in the very broadest sense that it presents an allegorical image of human society.

Certainly, modern interpretations have attempted to do some justice to the episode, and to integrate it into the broad development of the imperial scenes, as a corrective to Gundolf's magisterial dismissal of the masquerade as 'the deepest humiliation of Goethe's genius', as representing the nadir of Faust's career, his involvement in the trivial social frivolity of court life before the cultural apogee of his encounter with Helen.[13] Emrich has identified the central theme as that of creativity, the status and function of art in a social context, the relationship between art and nature, art and fashion, which culminates in the appearance of the Knabe Wagenlenker (Boy Charioteer) as the allegory of poetry – an interpretation which perhaps over-centralizes that figure, and depends heavily on Emrich's insistence that Plutus is less an allegory of wealth or prosperity than the figure of the poet.[14] In a polemical reaction against Emrich's interpretation, Schlaffer's recent reading sees the episode as a historical allegory of the development of a modern economy from a simple barter system to a complex industrial society based on the investment and circulation of capital; the fiscal schemes of Faust and Mephisto hasten the collapse of a decaying socio-economic structure based on military and territorial power, on the tangible wealth of coinage and land ownership, and usher in a proto-capitalist bourgeois society that, based as it is on the abstract and artificial wealth of an 'allegorical' paper currency, contains the seeds of its own destruction.[15] Höhle and Hamm to some extent reconcile these positions in seeing the masquerade as adumbrating the twin themes that dominate the first four acts of *Faust II*: art and culture – more specifically, the role and status of art in an absolutist court society – on the one hand, and on the other hand the unproductive moribundity of a feudal regime in economic, social and political terms.[16] Borcherdt has argued that the episode represents Faust's attempt to educate the Emperor; and he has also suggested that Faust and Mephisto, far from co-operating in a common purpose, are pursuing quite different ends, in that Faust's high-minded attempts to instruct the Emperor in the duties and responsibilities of government are undermined by Mephisto's efforts to distract the Emperor and by the devil's sabotaging of the economy.[17]

The dramatic function of the masquerade is clearly to contrive the entry of Faust into the court and to prepare the ground for Mephisto's introduction of paper currency into the country. Its structure is that of a typical court masquerade, which conventionally would serve a threefold purpose: not only the entertainment and prestige of the court, but also the tactfully allusive education of the ruler by means of allegory. It begins with a parade of relatively simple figures and masks, followed by more elaborate groups, and culminates with the entry of the Emperor and his entourage. As a masquerade, it does not attempt to establish any kind of conventional causal or dramatic relationship between the parts, or even between the parts and the whole. In so far as it has any consistent or coherent thematic development, it presents a microcosmic spectrum of human social, economic and political behaviour and institutions: sexual relations, trade and marketing, production and consumption, industry and leisure, life and death, marriage and adultery, patronage and art, power and government, reality and illusion. Its central theme, however, is the development of the issues raised in the previous scene: the acquisition, distribution and exploitation of wealth, the harnessing of the resources of the state, and the responsibility of the ruler to ensure the economic, and therefore the social and political, stability of the realm. The penalty for the irresponsible use of national wealth and of government is vividly demonstrated by Faust to the Emperor in the conflagration that threatens both country and ruler – the fiery spectacle, or Flammengaukelspiel, which ends the masquerade.

The balletic opening exchanges of the masquerade represent a stylized battle of the sexes, in which the alluring artifices of the Florentine Flower-girls are set against the lusty natural appetites of the young Gardeners. The antithesis of art and nature, illusion and reality, that is introduced here is a theme that will recur significantly later in the act, in the contrast between real and abstract wealth and in the phantom illusion of beauty that Faust, like Pygmalion, attempts to grasp as reality. The Flower-girls' wares, paper flowers and artfully constructed nosegays, are products of art and fashion; even the Olive-branch and Corn-wreath draw attention to their symbolic or decorative value as much as to their practical value as oil or grain. The Rosebuds, both decorative and natural, mediate between the sexes, and in an allusion to the sexual licence of the Floralia (5155–7), 'challenge' the Flower-girls to respond to the outspoken invitations of the Gardeners to 'pair up' with them. The theme of sexual matching is continued in the coarsely practical advice of Mother to Daughter to 'open her lap', and in the antics of Fishermen and Birdcatchers.

If the Gardeners and Flower-girls, even the Fishermen and Bird-catchers, represent productive commercial activities, albeit in the styl-ized and allegorized guise of masquerade, so also the Woodcutters and Charcoal-burners contribute to the prosperity of the state; charcoal was the staple source of industrial fuel before the wholesale extraction of coal powered the Industrial Revolution. The Clowns and Parasites are the unproductive entertainers and consumers, as are the asocial Drunkard and the jostling literary coterie of fashionable scribblers, whose slavish catering for public taste is derided by the Satirist.

The mythological groups that follow are burlesque allegories of social behaviour and human life in a modern context. The three Graces are the social graces of giving, receiving and thanking – a corrective to the discrepancy between exploited and exploiting, between productive labour and unproductive consumption in the previous figures. The Fates are present to define the limits of human activity and existence, but even they are in carnival mood; Klotho and Atropos, young and old, respectively the spinner and the cutter of the thread of life, have exchanged their roles for the occasion, and Klotho carries Atropos' shears shut away in their case. Nevertheless, Lachesis is a reminder of the limits of mortality, as she winds the threads into the skein that is finally taken by the 'weaver'. The Furies, avenging goddesses of mythol-ogy, here represent the socially destructive forces in marriage and family: suspicion, jealousy, gossip, dissatisfaction, scandal, adultery and retribution.

This first section of the carnival is concluded by an Elephant guided by Prudence, bearing Victory and flanked by Hope and Fear in chains. This group has been variously interpreted as symbolizing the wise government of a people (Staiger), as the state itself (Borcherdt), as the apotheosis of human social activity (Lohmeyer) or of creativity (Emrich), and as an allegory of physical labour in the service of commercial profit (Schlaffer); it could equally well be read as the symbol of the military might of the nation.

At this point, a bizarre and fantastic dimension is introduced with the entry of Faust as the god of wealth, preceded by Mephistopheles in the double mask of two debunking critics, Zoïlus, the carping critic of Homer, and Thersites, the taunter and mocker of the Greek heroes from the Iliad (ii. 212 ff.). Although the Herald, striking Mephisto as Ulysses did Thersites, 'exorcizes' the devil as snake and bat, it is evident that he neither understands nor has full control over this section of the masquerade (lines 5494 ff.). Indeed, Faust will now assume the authority and function of the Herald, taking over his staff of office and directing the course of events (see lines 5710, 5739 ff. and stage direction before line 5920).

The chariot of Plutus is guided by a mysterious Knabe Wagenlenker (Boy Charioteer), and accompanied by Avarice – which is, as Goethe confirmed, a further manifestation of Mephistophelean negation and contradiction. The relationship between the Boy Charioteer and Plutus is that of poet and patron: art, as decoration or entertainment (lines 5576 ff.), as elemental genius or commissioned work (5612–15), as the homage or celebration of a prestigious patron (5616–21), is symbiotic with wealth and power (5622–9). The fierce pride of the patron in the services of art is acknowledged by Plutus in words that recall the voice of God at Christ's baptism (line 5629), and in terms of the laurel wreath that is prized above his political or material possessions. The relationship between the Charioteer and Plutus is an idealized allegory of the relationship that Goethe had portrayed in such fraught and problematic terms in *Torquato Tasso*; indeed, lines 5574–5 recall the silkworm metaphor in which Tasso describes the consuming creative processes of poetry to his patron Alfons in Act V, scene 2 of the play.

The frivolous and hedonistic court of a bankrupt and decadent empire is no milieu for the personification of poetry; Plutus releases the Charioteer into the sphere of solitude, of artistic independence and of freedom from the burden of private and public patronage that Goethe himself had found so irksome in the years before his escape to Italy. With the departure of the Boy Charioteer, the economic and political allegory resumes, as Plutus reveals his seething treasure-chest to the throng. What he offers is not real wealth in terms of gold, treasure, or coin but an allegory of wealth, potential wealth, the promise, not the actuality, of prosperity. The impatient greed of the crowd makes no distinction between illusion and reality, allegory and meaning; even the Herald sees the meretricious nature of Faust's riches, though he is unable to decipher the import of his allegory (lines 5727 ff.). Mephisto, who may or may not grasp Faust's intentions, merely offers his own cynical commentary on the relation between gold and lust by shaping the malleable metal into a phallus (5781–2). Faust's words at this stage are cryptic, but ominous: patience and counsel are urgently required at a time when need threatens chaos and the breakdown of law (5765–6, 5797 ff.).

In the final canto of Goethe's epic *Hermann und Dorothea*, the heroine recalls the words of her former fiancé, who left for Paris to fight for the new ideals of the Revolution, only to die there in prison. His description of the new order, and of the melting-pot from which he

hopes it will arise, is remarkably similar in its imagery to the fiery and
unstable liquid gold of Plutus, to his seething cauldron of coins, crowns,
chains and rings:

> . . . denn alles bewegt sich
> Jetzt auf Erden einmal, es scheint sich alles zu trennen.
> Grundgesetze lösen sich auf der festesten Staaten,
> Und es löst der Besitz sich los vom alten Besitzer. . .
> Uns gehört der Boden nicht mehr; es wandern die Schätze;
> Gold und Silber schmilzt aus den alten heiligen Formen;
> Alles regt sich, als wollte die Welt, die gestaltete, rückwärts
> Lösen in Chaos und Nacht sich auf, und neu sich gestalten.[18]

(Suddenly all is in flux now on earth, and all is divided.
Even the binding laws of securest nations are loosened,
Those who once possessed are no longer sure of possession. . .
Now the soil is no longer our own, and wealth is unstable,
Ancient and sacred forms of gold and silver are melting;
All things move, it seems that the structured world is dissolving
Back into chaos and night, to be born in a new figuration.)

This is both the situation and the allegorical imagery of the masquerade
– a decadent regime threatened by a chaos from which a new and better
order might emerge. To be sure, Faust-Plutus' political stance is very
different from the revolutionary idealism of Dorothea's fiancé; lines
5807 ff. suggest that Faust is sympathetic to the Emperor and the order
he represents. This is the 'education' that he prepares for the Emperor
as he bursts noisily in on the carnival, surrounded by the wild throng of
his courtly entourage: a dire warning, disguised as a spectacular carnival
entertainment, of the conflagration that threatens the realm.

The Wild Hunt, oblivious of or indifferent to any threatening crisis
(lines 5813–14), characterizes the situation of an absolutist court
dancing on the edge of a volcano. Its sexual mores (lines 5815–39), its
standing armies (5864–71), the sycophantic and enervating rituals of
court life (5872–97), are described in the lines of the Fauns, Satyrs,
Giants and Nymphs. The Gnomes, the neutral and impartial miners of
mineral riches, carry the Emperor to the glowing and seething treasure-
chest of Plutus, and the result is an alarming, if illusory, Flammengaukelspiel
in which not only are the Emperor and his court burned but a general
and total conflagration is threatened (line 5965). The prophetic warning
of the Herald, prompted by Faust-Plutus, could not be clearer (lines
5968–9): imperial glory will be reduced overnight to ashes.

'Lustgarten': Pleasure Garden

The allegorical import of the Flammengaukelspiel that Faust, Prospero-like, dispelled in his final speech of the masquerade has, as this scene makes clear, failed to make its didactic mark on the Emperor. He is easily distracted by Mephisto's extravagant fantasy, which turns the fiery vision of a general conflagration into one of unlimited power and delight in an elemental playground that, as the Emperor himself remarks (lines 6031 ff.), and as the researches of Katharina Mommsen have confirmed, comes straight out of an Arabian Nights tale.[19] His temporary indignation at the unauthorized production and distribution of paper currency, and his initial incredulity that his people accept the illusory wealth as real, are quickly overridden by assurances that he himself has given it his imprimatur and that it is backed by the buried wealth of the empire, by the universal confidence in the new money reported in turn by his officers, and by Mephisto's diabolically ironic description of the sheer convenience of paper money. Faust at this point is reticent; apart from single-line statements in lines 5987 and 6053, his only contribution (lines 6111–18) appears to warn the Emperor that the wealth necessary to back the new currency and to underpin the economy of the empire still lies unexploited. But, if he has any clear advice to counter Mephisto's disastrous suggestions, he fails to give it in any but the most enigmatic and inscrutable terms (lines 6117–18). His attempts to educate the Emperor economically or politically are easily nullified by Mephisto's subversive persuasion; indeed, Faust appears in this scene strangely detached and unconcerned, as someone whose warnings and advice have gone unheeded, as someone whose mind already seems set on quite different experiences and goals. The final ironic comment is left, as usual, to Mephistopheles, as he commends the wisdom of the fool who will invest his ephemeral wealth in real estate.

After line 6172, the Emperor's demand for further entertainment in the conjuring of Paris and Helen marks the introduction of Goethe's major cultural allegory into the political action of Act I. For a short while, during the remaining scenes of the act, the political and cultural strands of allegory run side by side, and are more or less integrated; in Acts II and III they separate, and the political theme is submerged, to reappear, in a radically changed historical context, in Act IV. In purely dramatic terms, the links between these two major phases of the action are tenuous, even arbitrary. As lines 6191–2 indicate, the relationship between the court scenes and the Helen episode is merely fortuitous: Faust and Mephisto have made the Emperor rich; now they are to amuse him. The re-emergence of the political strand in Act IV is equally fortuitous in dramatic terms: Faust and Mephisto return to the scene and the action of the first act, to the disastrous results of the inflationary policies that they introduced in the first place. However, in terms of the historical allegory that determines the basic structure of *Faust II*, these events form a consistent, if only broadly discernible, development: that of the collapse of a European absolute monarchy towards the end of the eighteenth century and the subsequent pattern of war, invasion, occupation, liberation and restoration.

The political scenes of Act I present a broad historical allegory of Goethe's own times up to the beginning of his own intensive pre-occupation with classicism, which can be dated roughly to his Italian journey of 1786–8. From then until Schiller's death in 1805, Goethe was intensively concerned with the Weimar Classicism to which the Helen episode is in many ways a retrospective monument. These same years, however, also cover the period of the French Revolution, the Terror and the rise of Napoleon in France, and in Germany the subsequent – and consequent – final collapse of the Holy Roman Empire, the French occupation and the political turmoil of the German territories, tanta-mount to civil war, out of which finally grew the Wars of Liberation and the defeat of Napoleon. It is scarcely surprising that in retrospect Goethe should, in a work that allegorizes his own age, have set his own classical phase against the contemporary European political situation, even if he made little attempt to integrate the two. For it cannot be said that Faust's classical experiences grow out of the imperial scenes of Act I in any meaningful way, any more than Goethe's classicism grew out of the political background of Europe in the 1780s; they are contempor-aneous, associated by historical contiguity rather than by any clear cause and effect, other than Goethe's apolitical withdrawal from direct or active involvement in contemporary political issues.

This is not to suggest that the scenes 'Saal des Thrones' and 'Weitläu-figer Saal' present an unequivocal allegory of the *ancien régime* in France on the threshold of revolution, or alternatively of the almost equally decadent German Empire on the verge of collapse. It is neither the one nor the other, but both, in the sense that the fate of the German territories in the first two decades of the nineteenth century was determined, directly or indirectly, by the French Revolution and its aftermath. There is no clear allegory of the French Revolution itself in Acts I or IV of *Faust II*, for the simple reason that the French Revolution did not, in the event, spread directly into Germany – with the exception of the short-lived Republic of Mainz. There is an allegory of revol-ution in France in the 'Klassische Walpurgisnacht' of Act II; but it is peripheral, incidental, and does not represent a threat to Faust's pursuit of his classical ideal.

What we have in the conflagration scene of the masquerade is an exemplary warning of the possibility or even imminence of revolution, or at least of a chaotic breakdown of law and government, as a result of the careless and irresponsible rule of the empire. As lines 5807–14 appear to indicate, Faust-Plutus is by no means hostile to the *ancien régime*; he is, however, aware that it is heading swiftly towards catastrophe. Goethe's view that timely reform was far preferable to, and might even have averted, the French Revolution was perhaps politically and historically naïve and, for all his subsequent claims, a wisdom acquired largely after the event. But the admonition to the Emperor in lines 5958–61 is, as Borcherdt and Requadt have pointed out, strikingly similar to the admonitory message of the poem 'Ilmenau' of 1783, in which Goethe tactfully urged his own young ruler, Karl August of Weimar, to harness the industrial, agricultural and human resources of his state in an equitable, productive and efficient system that would ensure general prosperity and stability.[20] The message of the masquerade is the equivalent of the message of 'Ilmenau' on a European scale, informed by the hindsight of the historical vantage-point of the late 1820s.

'Finstere Galerie': Dark Gallery

The myth of the Mothers that Goethe creates in this scene to prepare Faust's encounter with the phantom of Helen has generated as much critical speculation as anything else in *Faust II*. The almost insoluble problem has been to determine (a) whether this awesome and arcane mystery is to be taken seriously, either as a creation of Goethe's own myth-making imagination or as his reworking of traditional classical mysteries; (b) whether it is to be seen as a spurious piece of higher mumbo-jumbo devised and staged by Mephistopheles to meet the Emperor's demands for spectacle; or (c) whether we have here a further example of the discrepancy between Faust's spiritual idealism and Mephisto's meretricious trickery, of the process whereby Faust's imagination rises above Mephisto's illusory offerings and finds in them more than the devil had intended or anticipated – a parallel to the duality noted above in the 'Hexenküche' scene, between the Witch's hocus-pocus and the figure of beauty in the mirror, both of which, indeed, Faust here recalls in lines 6228–30 and 6495–7.

Goethe himself was even less helpful than usual to commentators on this question; he claimed that the name of the Mothers only was derived from Plutarch, and that the elaborate myth itself was of his own devising. Research has identified a passing reference to a group of female deities in Sicily from Chapter 20 of Plutarch's *Life of Marcellus*, and has discovered a further passage, in Chapters 21 and 22 of *The Obsolescence of Oracles*, that describes an eccentric soothsayer's account of a mysterious 'Plain of Truth, in which the accounts, the forms and the patterns of all things that have come to pass and of all that shall come to pass rest undisturbed . . . round about them lies Eternity, whence Time, like an ever-flowing stream, is conveyed to the worlds'.[21] Goethe's only other remark on the nature of the Mothers, in response to Eckermann's persistent questionings, was to quote Faust's words of line 6217 – which suggests a rather ironic attitude towards his own inscrutable myth.[22]

Criticism has interpreted the Mothers as archaic tellurian myths, as Goethean *Urphänomene* ('primal phenomena'), or as Jungian archetypes; in terms of a Platonic realm of ideas, of Leibnitzian monadology, and of a bewildering variety of other philosophical and mystical systems. They are seen as *Urbilder* ('primal forms'), as archetypes of creation and transformation, as symbols of natural metamorphosis, as the very archives of time, as a repository of mythical, historical and cultural forms that Faust must draw on to retrieve Helen. The sheer vagueness and obscurantism of Mephisto's account of the Mothers has allowed the critical imagination free rein – in addition to which, as Cyrus Hamlin remarks, 'critics and scholars have been struck with a ponderous awe' in response to the name and nature of these figures.[23] If Goethe did indeed conceive them as serious symbolic or mythical beings, then there is a striking incongruity between the awesome and profound ritual, the unimaginable perils and emptiness of a quest across an uncharted void, the exalted status of the heroic 'neophyte' who must endure this journey, and the end result of his quest: a shadowy dumb-show, a theatrical 'spirit farce', or 'Fratzengeisterspiel', put on before a frivolous court audience already sated with entertainment, who have no more edifying reaction to the spectacle than to comment on the respective sexual attractions of the hero and heroine.

Clearly, however, the effect of the spectacle on the audience is secondary to its effect on Faust; and it is not unreasonable to assume, as line 6256 suggests, that for all his initial scepticism towards Mephisto's exaggerated mystification, Faust finds his 'all' in the devil's 'nothing'. Nevertheless, what Faust sees in the dumb-show of the 'Rittersaal' scene is a mere shadow, an insubstantial phantom of Helen, not remotely comparable with the figure of Act III, who, while she may have no more 'reality' than the allegory she is, is far more real to Faust than the illusion he attempts to grasp bodily in Mephisto's magic theatre.

The words and actions of Mephistopheles himself in this and the two subsequent scenes recall nothing so much as those of a latter-day miracle worker, a self-styled mystagogue, who captivates the gullible and vacuous imagination of a fashionable public. In other words, he is here, as he was in the 'Saal des Thrones', a Cagliostro figure, who embodies Goethe's profound mistrust of secret societies, charlatan occultists and obscurantists who had, in his view, undermined the very foundations of moral and political life by infiltrating the court circles of eighteenth-century Europe. Goethe had already lampooned Cagliostro in his comedy Der Groß-Cophta; the Mothers episode and the 'Fratzengeisterspiel' are only a more elaborate and powerful version of the fraudulent 'mysteries' of Graf Rostro in Act III of that earlier satire. Cagliostro would insist on a period of solitary fasting for his neophytes in preparation for the arcane rites of initiation into his mysteries; he would exploit all the resources of lighting and musical effects, the paraphernalia of Masonic ceremony, magic crystal bowls and other stage properties; he would use mesmeric techniques and mediums as a means of conjuring and interpreting the spirit world to his credulous audiences; he would prescribe miracle cures and elixirs. So here, Mephisto prepares Faust for the spirit show by the ordeal of solitude; he gives him a magic talisman, the key that will lead him where there are no locks or bolts; he strikes awe into Faust by the very name 'Mothers'; he instructs him to return with a magic tripod; and he even, in a nicely ironical comment on the power of his own mystification, expresses the hope that Faust may return safely from his initiation (lines 6305–6).

'Hell erleuchtete Säle': Brightly Lit Rooms
Mephisto's behaviour in this scene is further consistent with his Cagliostro role. He heightens the expectations of his audience with a spurious allusion to Faust's quest (lines 6311 ff.), and meanwhile prescribes his magic cures to the court. A Blonde is given a bizarre alchemical recipe for freckles; the Brunette's lameness is cured by a homoeopathic kick from the devil's hoof (Goethe knew, and was sceptical of, Hahnemann's current medical doctrine of 'similia similibus curentur'); and a Lady of the court is prescribed a remedy that appears to parody Mesmer's psychosomatic practices. The problems of the Page are solved more simply by means of cynical advice. The scene is set for the performance in the dimly lit hall of the Imperial Palace – as Mephisto caustically remarks, it is a place where no magic is required to summon phantoms.

'Rittersaal': Great Hall
In the investigation of the 'prophecies' of Cagliostro to the Cardinal de

Rohan on his relations with Marie-Antoinette, his medium, the fifteen-year-old niece of the Comtesse de la Motte, testified that she had been prompted by the 'Count' as to what she purported to see in a magic crystal glass.[24] Here, it is the Astrologer who acts as the medium for Mephisto's spirit seance, and is taken through his lines by the devil, who pops up comically from the prompt-box of the stage as *souffleur*. Prompted by Mephisto, and assisted by Faust's grandiloquent invocation of the Mothers in lines 6427–38, the Astrologer creates the hypnotic illusion of the magic temple – the word 'Schein' ('illusion'), is repeated twice in the two lines 6396–7. He bids the audience not merely to suspend their disbelief but to let their very reason be spellbound by magic (line 6416); he describes Faust's appearance as mystagogue, his costume, his occult gestures and instruments – tripod, key and censer; he commands the music and describes the figures as they emerge from the clouds of incense.[25] The whole ceremony is an unmistakable parody of a pseudo-Masonic or Rosicrucian ritual staged by Cagliostro-Mephistopheles. When Faust, enthralled by the vision of Helen, fails to sustain the distinction between illusion and reality, Mephisto brusquely orders him not to step out of his role (line 6501); again he warns him not to interfere in lines 6514–15, and frantically tries to convey to him that this 'Fratzengeisterspiel' is an illusion of his, Faust's, own devising (line 6546).

This final warning to Faust suggests that up to this point he has either been conniving in or, more probably, been duped by Mephisto's extravagant but hypnotically persuasive account of the Mothers as an ideal mythical realm that contains the schematic forms of all that has ever been. For all his initial scepticism, Faust has been caught up in a magical illusion by means of which Mephisto has intended simply to meet the Emperor's request for spectacular entertainment. The court itself, as the comments of the audience testify, regards the 'show' as nothing more than a further clever piece of theatre put on by the Emperor's new advisers, and does not concern itself, any more than it would in a conventional theatre or in a spiritualist seance, with either the means of illusion or the aesthetic or poetic truth of what it witnesses. Faust, however, in spite of the fact that he is himself helping to create the spectacle, puts himself beyond Mephisto's control by stepping out of his role and, besotted with the beauty of the phantom Helen, attempts to bridge the gap between illusion and reality by intervening violently in the 'action'. The result, however, reveals the difference between one of Cagliostro's seances and one staged with the help of Mephistopheles' magic resources: not simply the exposure of fraudulent practices but an explosion that paralyses Faust.

Faust has experienced in the phantom figure of Helen something that
Mephisto has not, indeed could not have, anticipated: the personification of classical perfection. His first impatient and impulsive reaction to
this experience might reflect Goethe's own immature classicism before
his Italian journey or, in a wider sense, the initial reception of classical
culture in Renaissance Europe – more specifically, in Renaissance
Germany. A critic has interestingly observed that Faust's encomium
to Helen in lines 6487–500 reads like a clumsily executed Petrarchan
sonnet: Faust is here 'a man of the Renaissance', who expresses his
furious emotional turmoil at his first encounter with classical beauty in
this flawed poetic form.[26] The nordic 'barbarian' is overwhelmed by his
first, unprepared exposure to classicism.

Faust's violent, indeed libidinous, reaction to his first spectral and
vicarious encounter with Helen betokens a degree of immaturity and
sensual infatuation out of which he must educate himself, or be
educated, before a meaningful encounter with her, and the synthesis of
classical and romantic, Hellenic and Germanic, pagan and Christian, that
it represents, can be achieved. It is the course of Faust's education
towards Helen, of his cultural, emotional and intellectual apprenticeship to classicism, that is charted over the next two acts of Faust II.
Chaos and revolution threaten the state – as they did in France in the
years before 1789, and indeed in Germany itself shortly after; Faust
withdraws from political confusion and sets out on his quest for a
cultural ideal – as Goethe did in 1786.

In the early Weimar years before his Italian journey, Goethe had made
serious attempts to educate Karl August of Sachsen-Weimar in the duties
of a ruler. He had proposed reforms in agriculture, forestry and mining,
communications, taxation and poor relief, trade and manufacturing,
military expenditure – and even the fire services. The frustration of these
initiatives, coupled with a flagging of his own artistic output, were major
factors in his abrupt, though by no means unprepared, departure for Italy
in 1786. In the same year, Karl August allied himself with the military
adventurism of Friedrich Wilhelm II of Prussia, an ineffectual monarch
given to his mistresses and to the obscurantist order of the Rosicrucians.
Goethe disapproved of this alliance, which he saw as contributing more
to the dynastic interests of the Hohenzollerns than to the unity or stability
of the German Empire. The parallels with the first act of Faust II are more
than striking, though this is not to suggest that Acts II and III are therefore
simply an allegory of Goethe's Italian journey. They are far more than
that, in that they chart the western European response to, and absorption
of, classical culture; but they are also a retrospective summation of, and
monument to, Goethe's own long commitment to the classical ideal.

ACT II:
FAUST'S CLASSICAL EDUCATION

'Hochgewölbtes enges gotisches Zimmer': High-vaulted, Narrow Gothic Chamber
Faust's liberation from Germany, his journey from north-west to south-east, begins, oddly but appropriately enough, in the same unpromising milieu from which his quite different career in the first part began – in his vaulted Gothic study with all its apparatus of medieval alchemistic and scholastic traditions. This scene allows Goethe to reintroduce the academic satire of the early scenes of Faust I, even the very figures of the Student and Wagner and, in a rather whimsical way, to introduce the intriguing figure of Homunculus, who will diagnose Faust's illness, prescribe his cure, and play an important role in the symbolic action of Act II.

Mephisto's opening comments appear to resume the general university satire in which Goethe indulged in Faust I: the accumulated dust and moths of scholastic tradition, and the self-righteous arrogance of academic authority. But the bell that Mephisto rings after line 6619, which rings, as it were, simultaneously for the Famulus in lines 6620 ff., for the Baccalaureus in lines 6689 ff. and for Wagner in lines 6819 ff., appears to have, as Hamlin puts it, 'epochal significance'.[27] It rocks the very foundations of the scholastic edifice, shakes dust, soot and debris from the ceiling and bursts doors wide open; the reference is evidently to a liberating moment in the history of scholarship and science, a 'propitious moment' or 'Sternenstunde', as the Famulus and Wagner call it (lines 6667, 6832). The immediate inference is that this spectacular tocsin represents the 'New Learning' of the Renaissance, which, while it disturbs and alarms the pious scholasticism of the Famulus, is a propitious omen for the philosophical neodoxy of the Baccalaureus and for the experimental science of Wagner.

However, as so frequently in Faust II, the historical allegory has more than one specific reference, and there are unmistakable clues in the text that here, too, the 'Sternenstunde' represents not only the intellectual and scientific upheavals of the Renaissance but also those of Goethe's own times. The Famulus, Nicodemus, whose name associates him with the literal-minded Pharisee of St John 3: 1–21 who questioned Christ's doctrine of mystical rebirth, can be related both to the Aristotelian and monastic traditions of medieval scholasticism and to the religious orthodoxy of the eighteenth century. His submissive acceptance of authority and tradition is set against the irreverent arrogance of the Baccalaureus, whose iconoclastic idealism, while it might also derive from the spirit of the Reformation, is closer to the subjective systems of post-Kantian philosophy.

When Eckermann suggested to Goethe that the Baccalaureus might represent 'a certain class of idealist philosophers', Goethe is reported to have demurred, and to have claimed only that he personified the arrogance of youth – with particular reference to German youth after the Wars of Liberation.[28] Certainly, the allusion to his shorn 'Swedish' hair-style (line 6734) goes beyond its primary historical reference to Charles XII of Sweden: it was a style affected by the (initially) revolutionary student movement of the Burschenschaften (Student Corps) that grew out of the wars against Napoleon, and lines 6774–89 might well be an articulation of the fiery patriotism and agitation of the student movement that finally provoked the Karlsbad Decrees in 1819 after the assassination of Kotzebue. It might also, as Lohmeyer suggests, be a sartorial symbol of emancipation from the fashions and traditions of the Baroque that persisted through much of the eighteenth century.

In spite of Goethe's denial, however, many critics see in the Baccalaureus a parody of contemporary philosophy, in particular of the more extravagantly subjective dogmatism of Fichte or Schopenhauer. The airy rejection of empiricism by the speculative idealist (lines 6758 ff.), the refusal to accept transmitted knowledge (6737 ff., 6760–1), and above all the outrageous claim that the world, the cosmos and the devil himself are a projection of the subjective self or of the human will (6791 ff.) – all this reads like a caricature of Schopenhauer ('The world is my representation . . . the world is my will'),[29] or of Fichte's epistemology. For all his respect for Fichte, Goethe dubbed him 'the absolute self', remarked caustically that he regarded the world 'as his own created possession', and guyed him by facetiously referring to people and things as the 'non-selves' ('die Nicht-Ichs').[30] Given that Mephisto plants an apparent clue in line 6736, where 'absolut' is a pun on 'bald' and 'absolute', and that Fichte, through his patriotic lectures in Berlin, the Reden an die deutsche Nation, was himself closely identified with the Wars of Liberation, it is difficult not to see Goethe's disclaimer to Eckermann as a piece of disingenuous deflection.

It has been noted that, whereas in the Student scene of Faust I the satire was that of the young Goethe directed at an older generation and an ossified academic establishment, here, from the perspective of old age, it is youth and youthful arrogance that are lampooned; but this is only partly true. For, as in the earlier scene the mockery was directed not only at the faculties but also at the young 'Gelbschnabel' ('freshman') himself, so in this later scene it is not only youth but also professorial arrogance and the musty tradition of scholarship that are satirized (lines 6586–615). Mephisto, finding himself patronized and out-devilled by the rantings of this erstwhile protégé who has emerged from his youthful chrysalis in the form of an alarmingly independent butterfly, takes refuge in a series of ironic masks: benevolent donnishness (lines 6727 ff.), pedagogic scepticism (6744 ff.), sarcasm (6754 ff.), mock humility (6762 ff.), mild reprimand (6770), mock alarm (6772–3), resignation (6790), threat (6792), weary cynicism (6807 ff.) and, finally, a humorous tolerance expressed in a homely metaphor that Goethe chose to flavour with his own Rhineland accent (6814) – 'Es gibt zuletzt doch noch e' Wein' ('It'll make a decent wine in th' end').

'Laboratorium': Laboratory

Mephisto's clowning extends into this scene, especially in the richly comic opening exchanges with Wagner, who is engaged on the 'Magnum Opus' (see line 6675) of the alchemists, the creation of the 'filius philosophorum' or homunculus, that is, of living matter in vitro. The various stages of this arcane process are authentically described: the agency of fire (see lines 6677 ff.), the sequence of colour changes (6823–8), combination (6849–51), heating in a sealed vessel (6852), cohobation or distillation (6853), crystallization or 'sublimation' (6855–60), and not least the choice of a propitious moment (6832). It is unclear whether Goethe is here caricaturing the hermetic tradition itself; whether, as Hamlin suggests, it is 'a climactic parody of all scientific experiment',[31] a reflection of Goethe's anti-Newtonian distrust of laboratory experimentation; whether, as Lohmeyer believes, it is a serious allegory of the birth of modern experimental chemistry;[32] or whether Wagner is simply a comic travesty of Frankenstein, since he proves unable not only to control his own creation but even to accomplish his great work without the assistance of the devil – for, as Goethe confirmed to Eckermann, Mephistopheles evidently has some hand in the process.[33] It may be, as Hans Mayer suggests, that, while Goethe was able to ridicule Wagner's comic obsession, it is more difficult for an age that has seen the results of unbridled scientific research, of the 'eritis sicut deus' drive for knowledge, to smile at Wagner, at this caricature of modern scientific Prometheanism who looks forward to a brave new world of genetic engineering.[34]

Whatever the precise attack of Goethe's satire here, we should bear in mind that Wagner's creation, Homunculus himself, ultimately refutes his 'father's' scientific optimism; he remains an abstract, artificial product, an inorganic 'crystallization', who must, in order to become an independent viable organism, submit to the processes of creation from the very beginning. In this sense he is a striking parallel to Faust, for both he and Faust have every reason to travel to Greece: Faust to experience from its mythical and historical beginnings the civilization and culture that culminated in the perfection of Helen, Homunculus to experience from its biological origins the evolution and metamorphosis that culminated in man.

The figure and function of Homunculus has, like the Mothers, generated a huge corpus of critical speculation – much of which, it must be said, has overlooked or obscured the tongue-in-cheek comedy with which Goethe presents this physically immature yet intellectually precocious test-tube baby, who treats even his 'cousin' Mephistopheles with patronizing familiarity. Otto Höfler's claim that he represents a satire on August Wilhelm Schlegel has not found wide currency,[35] nor has Hellmut Döring's Marxist hypothesis that Homunculus symbolizes the social and educational emancipation of the German middle-class intelligentsia in the course of the seventeenth and eighteenth centuries: by his striving for the classical ideal, the educated *Bürger* aspired to turn from a 'homunculus' into a 'homo', from an unfree subject into a free citizen.[36] Höhle and Hamm also relate Homunculus not to any biological or evolutionary goal but to a social programme, albeit an unrealizable one: his plunge into the ocean represents a deliberate rejection of existing social reality such as that represented by the historical world of the Seismos episode (see p.155), and his striving for an ideał alternative in the symbolic confusion of the 'Meerfest' or 'marine pageant', that ends the 'Klassische Walpurgisnacht', reveals Goethe's inability to adumbrate such an ideal in terms of any real or existing social system.[37] For Schlaffer, Homunculus is pure knowledge or intellect; he is an indication of the abstract intellectualism of German classicism, of the 'philological' reinterpretation and reconstruction of archaic myths by modern scholarship in a historically conditioned attempt to resurrect the past.[38] Atkins sees Homunculus as the creation not of Wagner at all but of Mephistophelean magic – a bottle-imp or 'dummy', who is controlled and prompted by his creator; hence Faust's dream of Helen, the 'Klassische Walpurgisnacht' itself, are brilliant and bold Mephistophelean extemporizations, and Mephisto's professed ignorance of classical myth and demonology is only feigned.[39]

Most commentators, however, accept a report by Riemer that Eckermann informed him what Goethe had intended Homunculus to represent: pure entelechy or spirit, before any experience of life, 'die reine Entelechie . . . den Verstand, den Geist, wie er vor aller Erfahrung ins Leben tritt' – in spite of the fact that this evidence is third-hand.[40] Entelechy is a term used by Goethe as virtually synonymous with the Leibnitzian monad, as he confirmed to Eckermann; that is, as something analogous to spirit, energy, or even soul, as that part of the human personality that precedes life and survives death, and which might, as Goethe revealed in his occasional mystical pronouncements on the mystery of life and death, even become reincarnated in different existences.[41] Among the characteristics attributed by Goethe to the entelechy are restless activity; the innate gift of 'anticipation' – that is, of pre-existing knowledge or memory; and spiritual clarity – that is, the perception or awareness that attaches to such 'geistige Wesen wie der Homunkulus, die durch eine vollkommene Menschwerdung noch nicht verdüstert und beschränkt worden' ('such spirit beings as Homunculus, which are not yet darkened or confined by a complete corporeality').[42]

If Faust is the incorporation of a powerful entelechy, whose dual physical and spiritual nature, the 'single duality' of spirit and elements, as the angels define it in lines 11954–65, can only be separated after death by the force of 'ewige Liebe', of redemptive love, Homunculus is the entelechy in a pure state of pre-existence, before it is 'darkened' and 'confined' by physical existence. His progress towards a physical identity, symbolized in his erotic 'marriage' with the ocean and the triumphant fusion of the elements at the climactic finale of the 'Klassische Walpurgisnacht', is the reverse process of Faust's shedding of his elemental substance in the final scene of Faust II; the mystery of Faust's transfiguration at the end of the drama is balanced by the mystery of Homunculus' birth into corporeal existence at the end of the second act.

In the 'Laboratorium' scene, the 'spirit being' Homunculus does indeed display his active disposition (see line 6888), his impressive knowledge (6940 ff.) and his spiritual clarity – in which respect, as Goethe remarked, he is superior to his fellow-demon Mephistopheles. He is able not only to diagnose Faust's sickness but also to prescribe its cure. The dream that Homunculus reads in Faust's psyche (lines 6903 ff.) shows how completely Faust is obsessed with the vision of the 'Rittersaal'; it is a sensual dream of the conception of Helen, based, it is generally accepted, on visual sources such as Correggio's or Caravaggio's paintings of the rape of Leda by the swan Zeus. This Renaissance or neoclassical idyll, in the grotesquely incongruous setting of the Gothic surroundings (lines 6928 ff.), indicates Faust's consuming passion for the Hellenic ideal, for which the only cure can be first-hand experience of Helen's world, direct contact with the physical, mythical, historical and cultural landscape of Greece. As Goethe himself wrote from Rome, the sickness of his longing for classical Italy was one from which only the very sight and presence could cure him.[43] Faust's journey from his study to the Plain of Pharsalus marks the beginning of his classical education towards Helen, his release from the murky medieval world, the 'Nebelalter' of Christian and feudal traditions. Nevertheless, Faust will never be able to deny or to shed those traditions, he will remain, for all his Hellenism, bound to modern Western civilization; he will appear in her world as a Germanic intruder, as a crusading Frankish knight, and his union with her will be short-lived. This is, however, only a relative failure; Acts II and III represent a summit of Faustian experience, as Goethe's own classicism, even in retrospect, was for him.

'Klassische Walpurgisnacht': Classical Walpurgis Night

The 'Klassische Walpurgisnacht' is the antithetical counterpart of the modern or 'romantic' Walpurgis Night of Faust I. As the first Walpurgisnacht revealed the primitive superstitions underlying the Judaeo-Christian religious tradition, the classical episode reveals the archaic demonology of Greek religion: not the 'official' classical pantheon of Olympian deities dear to neo-classicism, who are present at the Klassische Walpurgisnacht only by proxy, as it were, but the primitive pre-Olympian cults, creatures, demigods and divinities that contemporary research was rediscovering in Goethe's day. It is a festival of light and life, of teeming natural and elemental forms, rather than an orgy of dark satanic powers; it culminates not with an obscene travesty of ritual with the appearance of Satan on the summit of the Brocken but with a celebration of wholesome beauty and life-affirming Eros with the appearance of the nymph Galatea by the shores of the sea, the source of life. Its illumination is not the dim and mournful glow of a red moon but the bright festal light of a clear, if waning, moon; it is a marine festival held under the aegis of the goddess Luna. It is a 'republican' festival, a broad thiasos or pageant of separate but equal figures, whereas the Brocken represented a 'monarchic' hierarchy of diabolism, a grotesque mass over which the devil reigned.[44] Its relationship to the first Walpurgisnacht represents Goethe's own pithily, if somewhat crassly, formulated conviction of the distinction between 'healthy' classicism and 'sick' romanticism.[45]

This broad contrast between the two episodes is largely based, however, on the marine pageant that concludes the 'Klassische Walpurgisnacht'. For even in this classical milieu there is, before the tumbling and exuberant procession of marine creatures, a 'terrestrial' journey past the more grotesque and monstrous primal forms of eastern Mediterranean myth: Sphinxes, Gryphons, Ants, Arimaspians, Stymphalides, Hydra, Lamiae, etc. The movement of the 'Klassische Walpurgisnacht' is not the spiral upward movement of the Brocken scene but a lateral movement from earth to water, from the upper reaches of the river Peneus on the Plain of Pharsalus, down the Vale of Tempe to the Aegean; it is also a movement from the flickering fires of the ghostly armies encamped on the plain to the serene moonlight of the finale. This eastward, or more strictly north-eastward, shift of the action also represents the shift from a historical to a mythical sphere; while the prologue and the scenes on the upper Peneus touch on the unending struggles of wars and revolutions, the final marine pageant is a playground of elemental mythical creatures that survive undisturbed by the transient convulsions of political and historical conflict. Underlying, and to some extent epitomizing, this transition from history to myth, from violent human conflict to elemental harmony, from unnatural revolution to natural evolution, is a scientific allegory – the conflict between the geophysical doctrines of vulcanism and neptunism.

That part of the action that concerns Faust – his experience of Helen's homeland, his education at the hands of the centaur Chiron and his entry into the underworld to petition Persephone for the release of Helen – takes up rather less than one-fifth of the whole episode. The rest is devoted, relatively briefly, to the adventures of Mephistopheles, and, at greater length, to Homunculus' search for a physical identity. The paths of the three adventurers converge only occasionally and briefly, and will therefore be dealt with separately below.

The prologue in the Pharsalian Fields ('Pharsalische Felder') is spoken, in the slow cadences of iambic trimeter, by Erichtho, one of the Thessalian witches. A ghoulish creature who feeds on the dead of battlefields, she was consulted by Pompey's son Sextus on the outcome of the Battle of Pharsalus, and is described in Lucan's *Pharsalia* in horrifyingly macabre terms – hence her tart reference of lines 7007–9.[46] She evokes the battle that in 48 BC marked the end of the Roman Republic with the defeat of Pompey by Caesar. The Battle of Pharsalus has no great significance in the episode as a historical event in itself; it is, as Erichtho makes clear in lines 7012 ff., and as Mephisto has already remarked in lines 6956 ff., only one in a series of historical power-struggles, of eternal variations on the primal conflict of gods and Titans. This theme of war and revolution will recur in Chiron's reference to the Battle of Pydna in lines 7465 ff., and in the Seismos allegory.

But Harold Jantz has pointed out that these historical references also underline the significance of Goethe's choice of Thessaly, rather than Helen's homeland of the Peloponnese, for Faust's first experience of Greece. Thessaly was 'both the cradle and the grave of classical civilization', associated with the salient names, places and events of

Hellenism: with the Argonauts, with Chiron and the heroes he tutored, with the mountains Pelion, Ossa and Olympus, and with the three decisive battles that represent crucial events in classical myth and history. The Gigantomachy marked the triumph of the Olympian deities over the 'primitively monstrous' Titans and Giants, Pydna marked the eclipse of Hellenic glory with the defeat of the Macedonian Empire by the rising Roman Republic in 168 BC, while Pharsalus and the defeat of Pompey, in a mirror-image of Pydna, put an end to that same Republic 120 years later.[47] Indeed, Lucan describes Thessaly as the birthplace of war itself, of the celebrated Thessalian cavalry, of the first sea-going ship, the Argo, and as the place where metals were first mined and forged into money and weapons.[48]

As the moon rises, the spectre of the historical battle fades and gives way to the 'hellenischer Sage Legion', to the throng of fabulous mythical creatures of the Klassische Walpurgisnacht. Faust's paralysis leaves him the moment he sets foot, Antaeus-like, in Greece; unlike Winckelmann or Goethe himself, Faust is allowed to breath the air of Greece, even if he is not yet standing on the very soil of Helen's homeland (lines 7071 ff.). The three travellers set out on their quests through the 'fabulous realm' of myth, which take them from station to station, through the hands of various guides and mentors, past temptations and distractions, to their respective goals.

FAUST'S QUEST FOR HELEN (LINES 7181–213, 7249–494)

Faust's initial reaction to the creatures he encounters (lines 7185 ff.) is that of a travelling philhellene scholar, enthusiastically identifying Sphinxes, Sirens, Ants and Gryphons from his reading of Homer, Pliny or Herodotus – or, as it were, from Goethe's own classical vade-mecum, Hederich's mythological lexicon.[49] These are the archaic primal forms of classical myth, reaching back to civilizations and religions more ancient than the Hellenic. But in these monstrous forms Faust detects the prototypical elements of Greek religious myth, in these repellent shapes he discerns 'great and valiant features' – 'im Widerwärtigen große, tüchtige Züge' (line 7182); as Mephisto perceptively remarks in lines 7191 ff., it is Faust's ruling obsession with Helen that invests these fabulous monsters with grandiose significance. A cryptic draft sketch for this scene explains the episode as a stage in Faust's quest: 'Faust (am Peneus). Noch ist ihm nicht geholfen. Alles hat nicht an sie herangereicht. Deutet auf eine wichtige Vorwelt. Sie aber tritt in ein gebildetes Zeitalter. Göttlichen Ursprungs'. ('Faust on the Peneus. Still of no help to him. None of this has reached as far as her. Indicates an important past. But she appears in a cultured age. Of divine origin.')[50]

This 'cultured age' is evidently the Heroic Age of the Siege of Thebes, of the Argonauts and the Trojan War; hence Faust must move from the archaic past, from the pre-history of Greek civilization, to the tutelage of Chiron, the mythical pedagogue who taught those very heroes.

It is Chiron who bridges the gap for Faust between the archaic and the heroic ages, between the primitive and the 'cultured'. Faust's journey takes him away from the monstrous creatures of the upper Peneus towards the Vale of Tempe on the lower reaches of the river; from here, he is carried on Chiron's back to the foot of Mount Olympus, to the very entrance of Hades. The reference in lines 7254–6 to the rumbling of a distant upheaval is an indication not only that Faust has left the confused milieu of the upper Peneus far behind him but also that the adventures of Faust, Mephisto and Homunculus are to be seen as simultaneous; for this distant rumble is the same seismic eruption that puts the Sirens to flight (before line 7503), and to which Mephisto also refers in lines 7684 ff.

In the idyllic wooded and rushy landscape of the Vale of Tempe, Faust re-experiences the vision of Helen's conception, but this time as a waking, conscious vision, not, as in the 'Laboratorium' scene, as the expression of a subliminal wish-fulfilment. Faust is not, however, permitted to remain passively absorbed in the idyll of Helen's conception, as the Nymphs tempt him to do; Chiron, the restlessly galloping centaur, takes him a further stage on his journey. Chiron has been identified as representing the dimension of historical time, as one who cannot himself bring Faust to Helen but can only refer him to the Sibyl Manto who, in her own striking phrase, exists in a still centre around which time revolves (line 7481); it is Manto who will then conduct Faust into the timeless realm of Hades from which Faust can retrieve Helen for a brief spell, beyond all time, as Achilles did (lines 7435–7). Chiron's purpose is also, as pedagogue (lines 7337 ff.), to instruct Faust in the history and background of Helen herself and, as physician (7345 ff.), to speed Faust's psychic 'cure' by bringing him to Manto.

As they pass through the Thessalian landscape, Faust coaxes from his mentor a roll-call of the Heroic Age – the Argonauts Castor and Pollux, Zetes and Calais, Jason, Orpheus, and Lynceus; the demigod Hercules; and finally Helen. Faust, riding on Chiron's back as Helen herself once did, is moving ever closer to the 'incomparable figure'; his experience of the Greek ideal is still vicarious, but as far as it is possible for a modern Western imagination to do so, he is progressing towards his goal – to defy time, to revive the past and to bring Helen to life. The precedent he invokes for this is that of Achilles, who was permitted to retrieve Helen from Hades and live with her on the island of Leuce where, as Hederich reports, he had a son by her – Euphorion.[51] Goethe, by substituting the Thessalian city of Pherae (line 7435) for Leuce, which he cited in his draft versions, is not only bringing the place closer to the present scene but also, presumably deliberately, conflating two myths: that of Helen and Achilles, and the release of Alcestis from Hades after she had voluntarily sacrificed herself for her husband Admetus, King of Pherae.

A further change made by Goethe over classical tradition, and again over his own draft versions, is that of line 7451. Manto, to whom Chiron undertakes to deliver Faust, and who will take him on the final stage of his journey, is here the daughter not of Tiresias, as she was in Goethe's draft,[52] but of Asclepius. This not only reinforces the Thessalian connection – the physician Asclepius was taught by Chiron – but also demonstrates the limits of Chiron's pedagogic powers. He can tell Faust of Helen, but cannot help him retrieve her from Hades; his sceptical diagnosis is that Faust is 'deranged', ('verrückt', line 7447), in urgent need of 'Asklepischer Kur' (7487): only the skills of the healer's daughter can cure his psychic illness.[53] Manto, however, understands and responds to Faust's quest for the impossible (line 7488); she leads him, a second Orpheus, down to Hades.

At this point, barely one-third of the way through the 'Klassische Walpurgisnacht', Faust's involvement in the scene ends, and we do not see him again until his appearance in Sparta, or Mistra, as a crusading knight in the second scene of Act III. We know that Goethe planned an elaborate scene in Hades, in which Faust, guided and protected by Manto as Aeneas was by the Cumaean Sibyl, was to petition Persephone for Helen's release. This was to be granted, and Helen was to appear as a living person in the 'imagined' house of Menelaus on the soil of her native Sparta. Why Goethe abandoned this important scene has puzzled critics ever since. Whether he felt unequal to the task, as he suggested, perhaps not entirely seriously, to Eckermann,[54] whether the audience or reader are expected to 'supply' this episode for themselves, as is at times the case in *Faust I*, or whether the final version of the 'Klassische Walpurgisnacht', and the marine pageant in particular, was substituted as an alternative, symbolic preparation for the appearance of Helen in Act III, is a question we must defer until later.

MEPHISTO'S JOURNEY TO THE PHORCYADES (lines 7080–248, 7676–850, 7951–8033)

Just as Faust retains his historical and cultural identity throughout the 'Klassische Walpurgisnacht' as a Western philhellene traveller or visitor, until he assumes a symbolic guise adapted to the eastern Mediterranean milieu in Act III – that of a Frankish crusader – so Mephistopheles also remains a recognizably modern Christian devil of northern Germanic origins, until he, too, adopts a mask appropriate to the classical context. Since sin and shame appear foreign to the demons of the 'Klassische Walpurgisnacht', his traditional powers are in abeyance; the classical equivalent of the spirit of negation, denial and contradiction is the mask of ugliness in which he confronts and challenges Helen's beauty in Act III. The mask of Phorcyas is the final stage of Mephisto's somewhat haphazard quest among the demonology of classical myth.

Mephisto's puritanical reaction to the shameless nudity of the classical bestiary (lines 7080 ff.), to the pagan 'free play of the senses' that he has already deprecated in the previous scene (lines 6970 ff.), is a comical mixture of outraged prudery and sly prurience. His unease and insecurity, covered by a defensive facetiousness, are the very reverse of Faust's enthusiastic awe of lines 7181 ff. The abstruse punning he indulges in with the Gryphons (lines 7093 ff.) is a persiflage of the playing with false etymologies that Goethe himself had enjoyed with C. P. Moritz in Italy, and which he had also parodied in the poem 'Etymologie', itself attributed to Mephistopheles.[55] His exchanges with the Sphinxes are frankly enigmatic; the cryptic comment of the Sphinx in lines 7114–15 appears to suggest that the 'spirit tones' of the myths of antiquity are embodied or reinterpreted by subsequent cultures in terms of their own values and beliefs – as indeed is illustrated by the respective reactions of Faust and Mephistopheles. Mephisto's reply is a sardonic reference to the voracious cultural appetites of eighteenth-century British travellers to Greece – whose accounts Goethe himself consulted carefully for the topography of his classical landscapes.

The following exchanges are also obscure. It is quite unclear whether Mephisto's reference to shooting stars in line 7127 has any bearing on the date of the Battle of Pharsalus (9 August, near the maximum of the Perseids meteor shower); whether line 7130 suggests that he is indifferent to the astrological or horological functions of the Sphinxes, or whether it is a lewd reference, similar to that of lines 7146–7, prompted by Mephisto's leering upwards at the breasts of the Sphinx. The following riddle (lines 7134–7) is evidently meant to characterize Mephisto himself; he is both the 'plastron' (the padded bodice of the fencing-master) against which the pious ascetic practises his resistance to temptation, and the 'companion' who tempts the impious to evil – and all for the amusement of a god. This is a broad reformulation, in classical terms, of the Lord's dispassionate view of Mephisto's dual function as tempter and 'companion' as expressed in the 'Prologue in

Heaven' (lines 336 ff.). The Sphinx's final retort to the aggression that
betrays Mephisto's insecurity is a calm reiteration of Goethe's aphoristic
distinction between 'healthy' classicism and the deformed ugliness of
the romantic imagination (lines 7148–51).

The function of the Sirens in the 'Klassische Walpurgisnacht' is
controversial. Here, on the upper Peneus among the monstrous 'terrestrial' creatures, they are in an alien element; hence they and their
alluring 'Singsang' are derided by both the Sphinxes and Mephistopheles (lines 7161–5, 7172–7). Moreover, they appear, in lines 7202–8,
to represent for Faust a seductive and distracting factor in his quest for
Helen. And yet, as creatures associated with the element of water, with
the neptunistic rather than the vulcanistic sphere, they are evidently
entirely positive mentors for Homunculus in his quest for life; indeed, it
is the Sirens who later, in the marine pageant, play a central role and
formulate the maxim which might stand as a motto over the whole
episode – that there is no salvation but through water (line 7499). While
it may be that lines 7172 ff. are a satirical expression of Mephisto's (or
Goethe's) disapproval of the superficial virtuosity of Italian opera, of
modern music, or even of the extravagant sound-symbolism of German
Romantic poetry, as commentators have suggested,[56] the role of the
Sirens can be explained not so much in that they change their function
in the course of the 'Klassische Walpurgisnacht', as Gottfried Diener
argues,[57] but rather in that their truly positive and beneficent function
only emerges as the scene and the action progress from land to sea.
While they may represent for Faust a distraction from his quest for
Helen, and while their song means nothing to Mephisto, for Homun-
culus they are essential guides who point the way downstream to the
Aegean, to his salvation in the ocean.

Mephisto's further progress through the monstrous wonderland of
classical myth reveals a series of grotesque creatures that correspond
most closely to his own Brocken demonology: the Stymphalides, the
nine-headed Lernaean Hydra and the Lamiae. The Lamiae were originally planned by Goethe to represent erotic distractions for Faust,
attempting to seduce him from his quest for Helen;[58] in the final
version, this function was transferred to the Sirens (lines 7202 ff.) and
the Nymphs (7263 ff.), and the Lamiae became part of Mephisto's
experience, not Faust's. Enticed by these vampires, Mephisto moves
on, and the Sphinxes affirm their own imperturbable permanence
(lines 7240–8) – a function they will resume in the later Seismos
episode. Mephisto reappears in line 7676, where his experiences
alternate with the two 'vulcanist' episodes, the Seismos allegory and the
Thales–Anaxagoras debate.

Confused by the shifting seismic landscape of the upper Peneus, Mephisto nostalgically recalls his own familiar northern scenery of the Harz Mountains (lines 7676 ff.) – the eruption of Seismos has cut him off from his original mentors, the Sphinxes. The metamorphoses of Empusa and the Lamiae, unlike the dynamic metamorphosis of natural forms that Homunculus will undergo in the ocean, are unnatural and sterile; they change into broomsticks, lizards, thyrsus wands and puffballs. These transformations have sexual connotations which cover four different cultures – Germanic, Italian, Greek and Eastern: the broomstick is associated with the northern witches of the Brocken; 'Lazerten' ('lizards') is the term Goethe used for the prostitutes of Venice in his *Venetian Epigrams*; the thyrsus was the phallic wand carried by Dionysus and his worshippers; and the fleshy 'Bovist' ('puffball'), as Mephisto indicates in lines 7782–3, is an allusion to the sagging beauties of the oriental harem.[59]

For all his confusion and discomfiture, however, Mephisto is beginning to find his way into Greek demonology (see lines 7740–3, 7791–800). He moves from the ephemeral distractions of Empusa and the Lamiae, away from the shifting landscape of the Pharsalian plain, to the ancient hills and woods of Thessaly. Whereas Homunculus turns eastwards away from the vulcanist milieu to the sea, Mephisto also quits the vulcanist scene, but moves west to the foothills of the Pindus range, guided first by Oreas, the nymph of its rocks (7811 ff.), then by Dryas, the nymph of its sacred oaks (7959 ff.). Here, in a cave set in this symbolic primeval landscape, he finds the ineffable ugliness that is rooted in the very soil of the homeland of beauty (7978): the ugliness of the Graiae, or Phorcyades, that he will adopt as the classical mask that corresponds to his function as the spirit of negation. Here at last he finds a true kinship; not in the shameless nudity of the Sphinxes, not in the rapacity of Gryphons or Arimaspians, not in the illusory eroticism of the Lamiae, but in the daughters of night and chaos.

For all the comic dimensions of Mephisto's exchanges with the Phorcyades, for all his outrageous flattery of the three old ladies (lines 7984 ff.), he is here taking a momentous step. He adopts the mask in which he will play a crucial role in the dramatic and symbolic action of the Helen episode of Act III. As a figure in whom a modern historical consciousness is embodied in a classical shape, it is Mephisto-Phorcyas who will direct and orchestrate the synthesis of classical and modern by mediating between Helen and Faust; his 'hermaphroditic' nature (line 8029) is not simply that of a sexual hybrid but that of a cultural one. As a figure of sublime ugliness, he will represent the negative polarity to Helen's sublime beauty; as a creature of night and chaos, he is an ever-present reminder of her own transient existence, of her origins in Hades; and, as the product of a modern morality, he is the puritanical scourge of her Trojan women. And yet at the same time it is Mephisto-Phorcyas who unreservedly acknowledges Helen's beauty, who plays her into Faust's protection, who stands guard over their nuptials in Arcadia and who, at the end, urges Faust to hold fast to Helen's dress and veil as she herself returns to the underworld.

HOMUNCULUS' SEARCH FOR LIFE (LINES 7495–675, 7825–950, 8034–487)
After the initial parting of the three travellers at line 7069, Homunculus reappears in the 'Klassische Walpurgisnacht' only at lines 7825 ff., where his path converges briefly with Mephisto's. His search for a physical form that will allow him to escape the confines of his glass bottle and become an independent viable organism has led him to attach himself to two natural philosophers, Thales and Anaxagoras, who are engaged in a polemical debate on the origins of life and of the earth's physical structure. This debate, however, is itself provoked and partly illustrated by the events of the initial episode of the scene 'Am oberen Peneios wie zuvor' – that is, by the Seismos episode of lines 7495–675.

It is generally accepted that Thales and Anaxagoras, who can only loosely be identified with their historical models, Thales of Miletus and Anaxagoras of Clazomenae, represent conflicting theories in a geophysical controversy of the late eighteenth and early nineteenth centuries. The dispute between diluvianism and plutonism, or neptunism and vulcanism, concerned the processes by which the earth's crust had been formed and modified; neptunism held that it had been formed by the gradual sedimentation of rocks in the oceans, while vulcanism saw volcanic or igneous activity as primarily responsible for the geological configuration of the earth's surface.

Goethe's own stance in this controversy has been the subject of some critical debate; while he did on occasion refer to the vulcanist school in disparaging terms, he is also recorded as deprecating the more crassly dogmatic claims of neptunism.[60] While he appeared at times to take a loftily impartial view of the dispute, and while he also expressed the opinion that such controversies were part of a productive scholarly dialectic, it is clear that by temperament and conviction he favoured the neptunist doctrine, which reflected his own gradualist instincts in other spheres, whether biological, social, or political.

In any case, the violent argument between the two comical savants Thales and Anaxagoras, the respective protagonists of neptunism and vulcanism, is presented as a *dialogue des sourds*. Not only does neither agree to concede anything to the other's point of view but they are also talking at cross purposes: Thales is intent on arguing the organic origins of life and its steady evolution in water (lines 7856, 7861–4), while Anaxagoras insists that mountains and rocks are the product of violent igneous processes (7855, 7865–8). Moreover, and more importantly, behind this scientific dispute lies a further allegory that represents, in general terms, the struggle between two broad socio-political ideologies, of reforming gradualism on the one hand and of violent revolution on the other.

For all that he acknowledged the historical necessity of the French Revolution, for all that he recognized its causes in the decadence of the *ancien régime*, for all that he conceded the vitality of the new forces it threw up, Goethe could never reconcile himself to the upheavals and excesses of the Revolution and its aftermath; and for the rest of his life he retained a deep-seated dread that a similar political earthquake would recur in France and, what was worse, that it could spread beyond the frontiers of France to the rest of Europe. Thus, in the Seismos allegory and in the scientific debate that is staged for his benefit, although Homunculus is himself forced to concede the creative potential of the seismic upheaval (lines 7942–5), it is the neptunist, gradualist doctrine that prevails. Anaxagoras is discredited as a lunatic, and, having declined the offer of sovereignty over the tiny creatures thrown up by the earthquake (lines 7873–86), Homunculus throws in his lot with the neptunist Thales, who urges him to seek his salvation in the ocean.

The earthquake that interrupts the Sirens' hymn to the element of water (lines 7503 ff.), as we have noted, impinges only peripherally on the adventures of Faust and Mephisto (7254 ff., 7686 ff.). In the Homunculus story, it is a central event; it puts the Sirens to flight down the Peneus to the shores of the Aegean, and even threatens the massive imperturbability of the Sphinxes (7523 ff.). The mountain thrown up by Seismos is immediately populated by a swarming mass of creatures: Ants, Dactyls, Gryphons and Pygmies. The aggressive Pygmies quickly enslave and exploit the smaller Ants and Dactyls, who provide them with weapons forged from the metals that the earthquake has exposed (7626–43); and with these weapons the Pygmies slaughter the arrogant Herons that roost nearby (7644–53). The slaughter of the Herons is subsequently avenged by the Cranes of Ibycus, agents of nemesis here as in Schiller's ballad of that title, who in turn massacre the Pygmies (7884–99). At this point, a cataclysm occurs; in the violent imagination of Anaxagoras, he has himself willed the moon to fall to earth, as Thessalian witches are said to have done (7900 ff.), while for Thales the whole thing is a hysterical delusion (7930 ff.). Homunculus' more sober judgement interprets it as the fall of a meteor from the moon (7936 ff.); at all events, the result is that friends and foes, Cranes and Pygmies, have been obliterated.

This extraordinary sequence of events, for all the welter of classical allusions in the speeches of the Sphinxes, Seismos and Anaxagoras, is almost universally accepted as an allegory of events in France between 1789 and 1799.[61] Indeed, in his fragmentary pseudo-Rabelaisian narrative of 1792, the *Reise der Söhne Megaprazons*, Goethe had used very similar imagery to allegorize the Revolution in unequivocal terms. A violent volcano splits the island of the 'Monarchomanes' into three parts – the monarchy, the aristocracy and the people; the class warfare of the French Revolution, and the shock-waves it sent beyond the frontiers of France, are also clearly enough allegorized in the quarrel among the sons of Megaprazon, who take passionately partisan sides in the issue of the conflict between the sybaritic Cranes and the exploited Pygmies.[62] Certainly, it seems reasonable to see the broad lines of events in France adumbrated in the Seismos allegory: the upheaval of the Revolution (lines 7519 ff.), the seizing of secular and ecclesiastical wealth by the revolutionaries (7582 ff.), the factional struggles (7626–43), and the massacre of the aristocracy (7644 ff.). It has even been suggested that the Pygmies represent the Jacobins of the Revolution, while the tiny Ants and Dactyls are the masses exploited by the bourgeois revolutionaries, and whose time has not yet come, as lines 7654–9 suggest.[63] Taking the allegory further, the fall of the meteor has been equated with the momentous arrival of Napoleon on the scene, and with the effective termination of the process of revolution on his election as First Consul in 1799.

There is, however, one major anomaly in this interpretation of the Seismos allegory in terms of the French Revolution. The avenging Cranes of Ibycus invite immediate comparison with the counter-revolutionary armies of the Austro-Prussian allies who invaded France in 1792; but as Goethe well knew, since he went as an observer with the Duke of Brunswick's army on the French campaign, this much-vaunted force failed signally to avenge the overthrow of the monarchy in France, and was decisively defeated at Valmy. I have suggested elsewhere that this striking historical inconsistency indicates that Goethe is here allegorizing not so much what happened in France between 1789 and 1799 but rather what, in his opinion, should have happened during those years – or alternatively, what ought to happen if such a revolutionary upheaval should recur, in France or anywhere else.[64] For the Seismos episode was written during the first half of 1830, a time when anyone who was remotely in touch with events in France – which Goethe was – would realize that serious political unrest was imminent.

The events of the Seismos allegory, then, are a conflation of the Revolution of 1789 and the July Revolution of 1830; and the Sphinxes, who witness the upheaval with mixed detachment and alarm, might stand for the European powers who were, or who believed themselves to be, more stable and secure from such 'vulcanist' disturbances. Indeed, the reference to the 'holy seat' of the Sphinxes in lines 7580–1 even suggests that Goethe had in mind the 'Holy Alliance' of Russia, Prussia and Austria founded by Tsar Alexander in 1815 as a bulwark against liberal or national revolutionary movements in Restoration Europe. Similarly, I have also suggested that the Thales–Anaxagoras debate not only represents the dispute between neptunism and vulcanism but is also a caricature of the bitter dispute in comparative anatomy at the French Académie des Sciences in 1830 between Baron Cuvier and Geoffroy de Saint-Hilaire – which Goethe followed with at least as much interest and commitment as he did the long-standing geological dispute between vulcanism and neptunism.

Whatever one's interpretation of the precise terms of the Seismos allegory, its function in the 'Klassische Walpurgisnacht' as a whole, and its significance for Homunculus, are clearly negative; it belongs to the 'terrestrial' or historical milieu, to the context of ever-recurring war, struggle and conflict that Erichtho evoked in the opening monologue. Whatever positive or creative processes he may discern in the eruption of the mountain and in its swarming inhabitants, Homunculus is persuaded that his future lies not in the violent convulsions of human political and social history but in the natural metamorphosis of organic forms in the fertile ocean – that is, in the marine pageant on the shores of the Aegean Sea.

Goethe no doubt drew on many sources for his marine pageant (lines 8034 ff.): on the aquatic spectacles of Baroque courts, on Calderón's *El mayor encanto Amor*, in which Galatea appears in a chariot drawn by dolphins and surrounded by sirens and tritons, on Raphael's *Triumph of Galatea* and on other marine *trionfi* by the Carraccis, Le Sueur, Feti, Poussin and other Renaissance, Mannerist and Baroque artists, as well as on representations of such scenes on sarcophagi, vases or majolicas. He also drew on his own knowledge of ancient myth, supplemented by Hederich's lexicon, and, not without a degree of sceptical irony, on the researches of contemporary mythographers who were beginning to explore and discover the roots of ancient Mediterranean cults and mysteries: Creuzer, Schelling and Görres. Karl Kerényi, in his splendid essay on this scene, has shown just how close Goethe came to touching on the primitive and irrational origins of Greek myths.[65]

The bewildering profusion of marine deities, demigods and elemental creatures, the 'festlich regen Scharen' that process across the stage, represent the 'thousand thousand forms' (line 8325), the protean metamorphoses of living organisms, the scale of creation that Homunculus must ascend after breaking the confines of his glass bottle, after his 'marriage' with the ocean. That marriage is the climax of the episode, a triumphant and hymnic celebration of creation and natural generation in the name of one primal urge: Eros. Just as Faust passed through the hands of various mentors in the stations of his quest for Helen, from Sphinxes to Chiron to Manto to Persephone, as Mephisto moved from Sphinxes to Lamiae and Empusa to Oreas and Dryas to the Phorcyades, so Homunculus is handed from Anaxagoras and Thales to Nereus and Proteus to Galatea. The whole episode is a mingling of scherzo and mystery that exemplifies as well as any other part of *Faust II* Goethe's description of the work as 'these very serious jests'.

The festal scene of the marine pageant is set by the Sirens, who hymn the moon in lines of eloquent and evocative lyricism; what they promised in lines 7509 ff. is here realized: the 'free and fluid life' of the fertile ocean. The moon they worship is not Hecate, the baleful chthonic aspect of the lunar trinity to which Anaxagoras appealed in lines 7902 ff., but her serene celestial aspect, to whom they appeal to remain at the zenith, to prolong the festive occasion (8078–81).[66] This marine festival of graceful elemental creatures, of fertility and love, of metamorphosis and growth, is held under the aegis of the beneficent Luna, who shines with doubled intensity reflected in the sea, and whose 'sacred dew' is an agent of wholesome therapy, as it was in Faust's early wish-fulfilment (line 397) and in his therapeutic sleep of oblivion (4629). The Sirens, who earlier appeared in the alien context of the historical or terrestrial milieu of the upper Peneus, now emerge as tutelary 'demons' (8057); as creatures associated with earth, air and water, they mediate between the shore-bound 'guests' and the life of the ocean, hymning the deity, describing the scene and introducing the marine creatures who are attracted by their songs. Nereids and Tritons bring treasures retrieved from the sea; the crowns, chains, gold and jewels that had such dire implications in the political and historical allegories of the previous scenes (lines 5007 ff., 5709 ff., 7582 ff.) are rendered harmless in this ahistorical, elemental and natural environment.

Homunculus' first mentor is Nereus, a cantankerous Old Man of the Sea, whose advice and warnings to mortals have, like Chiron's teachings, fallen on deaf ears. The stubborn ambitions of the heroes of the *Iliad* and the *Odyssey* (lines 8106–27) have reduced him to sour misanthropy.

Human affairs, even those of the greatest heroes immortalized in poetry
(8116), are of no consequence to him; the elemental divinities of the
marine pageant have survived both the Heroic Age of Greece and the
twilight of the Olympian pantheon; their mythical system is both more
ancient and more enduring. Nereus has eyes only for his daughters: the
Nereids, the Dorides, the 'Graces of the Sea' – and Galatea, who now
rules in Paphos as Aphrodite's successor (lines 8144–9), and whose
annual epiphany heralds the climax of the 'Klassische Walpurgisnacht'.
Nereus refers Homunculus to the penultimate stage of his quest, to
Proteus, the changer of shapes at will, the very personification of
metamorphosis, of nature in its bewildering range of manifold types,
species and forms.

   The burlesque dialogue between Thales and Proteus on the peculiar
and 'critical' nature of the test-tube product Homunculus, their snigger-
ing at his immature and androgynous characteristics, should not
obscure the serious implications of these exchanges; the artificial
'chemical mannikin', prematurely born into an incomplete existence
by 'crystallization' in Wagner's laboratory, must submit to an organic
process of birth and evolution, beginning in the ocean (lines 8257 ff.).
Homunculus, sensing the rich fecundity of the sea (8265–6), allows
himself to be taken to the last tongue of land, a narrow sand-spit, from
which the dolphin Proteus will carry him, in a whimsical caricature of
the classical motif of a boy on a dolphin's back, to his elemental
marriage with the ocean, where he will evolve according to 'eternal
laws' through a myriad forms (8321–6).

   Intercalated between the encounters with Nereus and Proteus are the
groups of creatures representing the three ancient cult centres of
Samothrace, Rhodes, and Cyprus: the Cabiri (lines 8160–224), the
Telchines (8275–302), and the Psylli and Marsi (8359–78). The mysterious
Cabiri, about whom very little is known and to whom Schelling had
devoted a study,[67] were the subject of some speculation by Goethe's
contemporaries; not only their nature and function but even their
number were matters for scholarly dispute. They were, according to
Hederich, ancient non-Hellenic deities, dwarfish but powerful (lines
8174 ff.), protective to sailors (8176, 8185), who presided over fertility
mysteries (8075 ff.); they were believed to be 'pitcher gods', ('Kruggöt-
ter', 8219 ff.), and their number was variously put at three, four, seven,
or eight (8186–99). While Goethe is here undoubtedly poking fun at
the wranglings of mythographers, and while critics still speculate wildly
on the significance of the turtle-shell of Chelone (8170–1), relating it
to the 'Urschildkröte', the 'giant tortoise' of Hindu mythology, or to
Hermes' invention of the lyre,[68] we should not therefore assume that

the Cabiri episode is pure persiflage. Their function as unconsciously self-generating forces (8076–7, 8200–5) is entirely appropriate to a festival celebrating the generation, growth and metamorphosis of natural elemental forms.

The Telchines of Rhodes, who were industrious artificers, smiths in the service of Hephaestus, and were said to have brought up the young Poseidon, promise a calm and serene ocean for the marine pageant. They are sun-worshippers, envoys, as it were, of Helios-Apollo at the festival of his sister Luna (lines 8285 ff.). Their 'terrestrial' activities and creations are derided by Proteus, who formulates a maxim which, together with the Sirens' declaration 'Ohne Wasser ist kein Heil' ('There is no salvation but through water', line 7499), might stand as motto for the whole episode: 'Dem Leben frommt die Welle besser' ('The ocean profits life far better', line 8315). The Psylli and Marsi, a priestly caste of Cyprus to whom healing powers were attributed, appear here as the guardians of the scallop-shell chariot of Aphrodite on which Galatea approaches. Undisturbed by storm or earthquake (8360–1), their cult represents the ahistorical survival of elemental nature, unaffected by the strategic power-struggles, imperial, commercial or religious, that rage on the surface of the island: Roman, Venetian, Christian and Muslim (8371–2).

The climax of the pageant is heralded by a moon-halo, a meteorological phenomenon that attracted Goethe's scientific interest and observation. Here, in the mythical festival, it is more than a mere atmospheric configuration, as Nereus explains: it is the doves of Aphrodite that accompany Galatea's chariot, the emblems of the erotic deity whose functions and attributes have been inherited by the marine nymph. The Dorides bring with them sailors rescued from the sea; but such a marriage of elemental spirits and humans, of the timeless and the transient, is not possible. Even Nereus cannot hold his daughter; Galatea passes, as Atkins aptly puts it, 'in late Renaissance theatrical splendor across the scene',[69] fading from her father's sight. Homunculus, however, borne by Proteus, smashes his glass against Galatea's shell, and in an erotic commingling of fire and water pours himself into the ocean. Whether this 'fiery miracle' is informed by Goethe's knowledge of the phosphorescence of marine micro-organisms, or derived from the fire of Circe in Calderón's drama, must remain a matter of critical controversy.[70] The Triumph of Galatea is a mystery of birth, of the fusion of spirit and elements, accomplished by the generative force of Eros, 'the source of all things' (line 8479); and the marine pageant closes with a tumultuous tutti of praise to love and to the four elements.

The critical problems concerning the integration of the 'Klassische Walpurgisnacht', and more particularly of the final marine pageant, into the dramatic and thematic structure of *Faust II* remain. Emrich contends that after such a hymnic celebration of love and beauty no further preparation, no scene in Hades, was necessary for the appearance of Helen, that her symbolic and mythical 'antecedents' are now completed and she can now appear as 'das letzte Produkt der sich immer steigernden Natur' ('the ultimate product of constantly self-perfecting nature'),[71] as a living person on the soil of Sparta.[72] Emrich's view has held currency for a considerable time, but is by no means universally accepted; Katharina Mommsen, for example, has argued persuasively that Galatea, far from heralding or preparing for Helen's appearance, represents a radically different process of creation from that of Helen. Helen is the product of an aesthetic illusion, a cultural and ephemeral ideal sought by Faust in the 'Fabelreich', the 'fabulous realm' of art, while Galatea represents the organic and natural creation that Homunculus must undergo in his search for life.[73]

Certainly, for Goethe, as the quotation from the Winckelmann essay suggests, Greek art *was* ideal nature, *was* man raised to god-like stature; and yet it is still difficult to see any very clear parallel or synthesis between the respective experiences and goals of Faust and Homunculus in the 'Klassische Walpurgisnacht', except in the sense that the one might be described as the mirror-image, or the *reverse* parallel, of the other.[74] Faust's progress is one of education, a progress that takes him ever closer to the Heroic Age of Greek history, to an encounter in Hades, and eventually to his transient union with Helen in the 'phantasmagoria' of Act III; Homunculus' progress is a search for organic life that takes him away from the monstrous forms of archaic Greek myth and away from the violent convulsions of human social and political history into an elemental world of metamorphosis, of evolving natural biological forms.

The differences between the final scene of Act II and the opening scene of Act III could scarcely be greater. The one is a Baroque polyphony, a fluid and operatic nocturnal lunar and marine pageant written, or sung, in a protean variety of rhymed verse; the other is a formal, dignified and stylized Euripidean drama played out on the sunlit *terra firma* of the Peloponnese, and delivered in the stately cadences of unrhymed trimeter, tetrameter and choric ode. For all the symbolic, mythical, or onomastic attempts to see Helen as a metamorphosis of the 'lunar' heroine Galatea, as born out of the 'mystical wedding' of Homunculus and Galatea, or as a product of the same process of creation as that of the spirit Homunculus,[75] Helen and Galatea are fundamentally different creations; Galatea is an elemental nymph, a lunar heroine, whereas the emblem of Helen's human aesthetic or cultural beauty is the sun (see lines 8909–12, 9222–45). It is quite true, as Nicholas Boyle puts it, that the abrupt transition from the teeming Aegean to the formal architecture of the following scene, from the 'All-Alle' of the chorus to the lone voice that calmly announces itself in lines 8488 ff., is 'one of Goethe's most carefully constructed and significant *coups de théâtre*';[76] but this theatrical effect itself depends on the very differences between the two scenes in theme, style and setting. The fact that Helen steps ashore still rocking with the rhythm of the waves (lines 8490–1) establishes only the most tenuous link between the two scenes.

I have suggested elsewhere that, if there is any parallel to the marine pageant scene in *Faust* II, it is the inverse parallel of the final 'Berg-schluchten' scene.[77] The one is a pagan mystery of birth and creation, of the fusion of spirit and elements, under the aegis of Eros and the female deity Luna, while the other is a Christian mystery of the separation of spirit and elemental substance ('Geisteskraft' and 'Elemente') under the aegis of divine love and the Mater Gloriosa; the one represents the progress of an entelechy towards 'geeinte Zwienatur', towards the single duality of spirit and substance, the other represents the future progress of an entelechy after its corporeal existence towards a state of grace. The many correspondences of text and motifs between the two scenes are not sufficiently explained by the fact that they were written almost at the same time; indeed, this fact suggests that Goethe might have conceived them as complementary mirror-images.

In terms of the historical allegory of *Faust* II, the 'Klassische Walpurgis-nacht' adumbrates Goethe's own education towards classicism – not simply his Italian journey, momentous as that was, but his whole cultural apprenticeship to the classical ideal that culminated in the flowering of Weimar Classicism. It may well also reflect, on a wider historical scale, the education of German or European culture towards classicism; Homunculus, at least in his early stages, does appear to be a parody of the earnest scholarship and the indefatigable travel mania of eighteenth-century philhellenes, or of the immature neo-classicism of rococo culture. Essentially, however, Acts I and II chart Goethe's own cultural mission, his withdrawal from courtly and political affairs in Weimar, from the wars and revolutions of the contemporary scene, and the beginnings of his attempt to establish, along with Schiller and others, an exemplary classical culture in the unpromising soil of Germany in the 1790s. It might also be reasonable to see, beside Faust's quest for Helen, Homunculus' quest for the metamorphosis of natural forms as representing another facet of Goethe's intellectual activity at that time, that is, the optical, anatomical, botanical and other research into natural philosophy that ran side by side with his artistic and cultural work, to which he devoted very nearly as much time and effort, and to which he at times attached at least as much importance – in a word, what he termed his 'Morphology'.

ACT III:
FAUST AND HELEN

Begun as early as 1800, the pivotal third act of *Faust II* was also the first section to be completed, in 1826; only then did Goethe turn to the task of preparing Helen's 'antecedents', to Acts I and II. The act that charts the encounter between, and the brief synthesis of, the Germanic north-west and the Hellenic south-east, of romantic and classical cultures, constitutes, as Goethe rather whimsically put it, a unity of time 'in a higher sense': the 3,000 years of Greek history from the fall of Troy to the death of Byron at Missolonghi in 1824.[78] It adumbrates, in an admittedly selective and sporadic way, the Western reception and appropriation of the classical ideal, the reflective or, in Schiller's term, 'sentimental' modern assimilation of an idealized 'naïve' or natural Greek culture.

To be sure, huge stretches of Greek history between the twelfth century BC and the nineteenth century of the Christian era are left untouched, or at most only briefly and allusively brushed over; the Hellenistic, Byzantine and Ottoman Empires are of little direct concern to Goethe's allegory of the western European reception of Hellenism, which charts instead three broad historical phases, corresponding to the three sections of the third act. The first scene in Sparta is a revival of ancient Greece, a story from the heroic age, that of Helen's return from Troy, treated in the style and manner of fifth-century Athenian tragedy. The second scene in 'Mistra' represents early pre-Renaissance encounters between the barbarian West and the eastern Mediterranean: the Germanic migrations of the *Völkerwanderung* and the medieval crusades, specifically the Frankish settlement of Achaea, or the Morea, as the Peloponnese came to be known in the post-classical age, culminating in the Renaissance itself. The third scene reflects the post-Renaissance neo-classicism of the modern age, and is in particular Goethe's elegiac retrospective review of his own classical achievement in Weimar, the passing of which he lived to see, as Faust sees Helen return to Hades at the end of the act.

'*Vor dem Palaste des Menelas zu Sparta*': *Before the Palace of Menelaus in Sparta*
Helen appears in Act III, as Goethe put it, on the soil of her native
Sparta, 'on the cothurnus of ancient tragedy'.[79] Dramatically, this scene
concerns the efforts of Mephisto-Phorcyas to manoeuvre Helen into the
protection of the barbarian invader, Faust, by means of combined threat
and enticement; allegorically, it represents a historical shift from ancient
Sparta to thirteenth-century Mistra, from the Hellenic Peloponnese to
the Christian Frankish kingdom of the Morea, from classical to medieval
culture, and eventually to the synthesis of the two at the Renaissance.

For all the apparent certainty with which Helen, stepping ashore on
the Gulf of Laconia in the southern Peloponnese and making her way
inland to Sparta, announces her arrival at her own home and firmly
states her cultural and historical identity, she is a profoundly insecure
figure, uncertain of her fate or status, unsure whether she is wife or
sacrificial victim, Queen of Sparta or a prisoner of her husband
Menelaus after the tragic reckoning of the Trojan War. Her existential
insecurity is also that of a figure revivified from Hades, uncertain as to
whether she is a phantom, an eidolon, or a living individual; she seems
herself half-aware of her mythical status and her function as a cultural
emblem of Hellenism, whose return to her own historical time and
place, to her ancestral home in Sparta, is blocked by a historical
consciousness. It is this fluid and labile uncertainty and insecurity that is
exploited by the extraordinary hybrid creature of Germanic and Greek
origins, Mephisto-Phorcyas, in order to undermine Helen's sense of
identity and to play her into Faust's hands – that is, to mediate between
the Christian Germanic context of a medieval crusade and the pagan
Hellenic heritage that she represents. For it is only in the discovery by
the Western world of the 'dead' heritage of classicism, in its continuing
response to and assimilation of that heritage, that Helen and all she
represents can survive, can live and be revivified. As we have previously
witnessed Faust's classical education towards the Hellenic ideal through
his experience of Greece and Greek culture, so here we see Helen's
absorption into centuries of modern Western civilization.

Helen's first four speeches are almost entirely expository and retrospective; she reports the ominous instructions of Menelaus, and
reflects on the contrast between a carefree childhood and girlhood
and her present state – that of a figure who is already haunted by an
ambivalent fate and reputation (lines 8531 ff.), whose individual identity
is already the stuff of tales, legends, even of fantasy (8513 ff.). Her
attempt to re-enter the palace leads to her traumatic encounter with her
own polarity, the ugliness of Phorcyas. As the issue of chaos, of Erebus
and Nux, of darkness and night, Phorcyas represents a dismal threat to

Helen's status and identity, to her very survival as a heroine whose beauty is, on several occasions, associated with sun and sunlight (lines 8695–6, 8736–9, 8909–10, 9222 ff.). Phorcyas' peremptory barring of Helen's way back to her own house represents the impossibility of her return to her own historical context, to her own age; this intimidating and repulsive figure confirms Helen's mythical status as the common property of a transmitted cultural heritage rather than as a specific historical individual.

Nevertheless, the function of Mephisto-Phorcyas as the agent of historical change is positive; it is he/she who acknowledges Helen's 'swan-like' beauty (lines 8807 ff.), who hails her, in a dramatic change of metre, as the 'sun' of the classical ideal as she emerges from her swoon (8909 ff.). It is also Phorcyas who ensures Helen's survival or revival as a mythical emblem in and through her reception by Western culture. To be sure, the tactics employed by Phorcyas are brutal; but they are totally effective in driving Helen from Menelaus to Faust, from Sparta to Mistra, from the ancient to the medieval world.

Phorcyas' initial attack is a philippic directed at the shameless sensuality of the Chorus (lines 8754 ff.). But this 'Increpatio', as a draft sketch calls it, is not exclusively directed at the 'cackling geese' (8809) of the Chorus, not simply an attack on their beauty, vanity, self-confidence, or transient youthfulness; it is clear that the trap is being laid for the mistress as well as for the women. The insistent leitmotif of Orcus (lines 8762, 8815, 8836) stresses the constant existential threat that haunts Helen herself (8838–40), and Phorcyas further confuses Helen by a recital of her legendary amours: Theseus, Patroclus, Menelaus, Paris, Deiphobus. The tirade culminates with a reference to her 'double' identity (8872–3), to the legend of the phantom Helen of Stesichorus and Euripides, and finally to her posthumous union with Achilles (8876–8).

At this point, Helen's sense of identity collapses (8879–81); and her swoon marks a critical point in both the dramatic and the allegorical development of the episode. Her existential security undermined, she experiences what a draft sketch strikingly calls 'a sense of Orcus';[80] that is, unless she loses her historical individuality, unless she is revivified as a mythical ideal, unless she is reborn and reinvigorated by assimilation into a different culture, she will be dead, a lifeless monument to a past age. Her emergence from her swoon after line 8908 marks her emergence from her historical past as the 'sun' of Western culture.

Now Phorcyas plays her decisive card – the real or imagined threat of execution by Menelaus, together with the alternative: a chance to live and survive under the 'protection' of, or assimilation into, the barbarian tribes that have invaded from the north and settled in the Peloponnese.

In terms of the allegory, this suggests that the classical heritage will not survive at the hands of the native or neo-Greeks represented by Menelaus; this was a view not uncommon in Goethe's time, and one from which even philhellenes like Byron and Hölderlin were not immune. In dramatic terms, the threat is sufficient to reduce Helen and her Chorus to phantoms, to the lifeless frozen statuary of a museum (lines 8930 ff.), and to dispose them to listen to Phorcyas' 'historical' (8984) account of the decline of Greek glory and to her plan for their survival into another era.

The tale that Phorcyas tells here (lines 8994 ff.) is a fantastic concentration of more than two millennia of Greek history into a span of some twenty years (9004). The piratical wanderings of Menelaus that themselves allowed the rape of Helen and unleashed the Trojan War (8985 ff.) are extended to represent the Greek, and the later Byzantine, neglect of the Hellenic homeland, to the point where a barbarian race from the 'Cimmerian' north has appropriated the classical regions. This account marks the beginning of the process by which the gap between Helen and Faust, between Homeric Greece and the Christian era, is bridged – a process that is symbolized by the magical dissolving of the classical milieu of the scene in Sparta into the second scene in Faust's medieval castle. And, in order to dramatize symbolically this huge historical and cultural transition, Goethe has drawn on a specific historical reference: the establishment in the heart of the Peloponnese of the medieval Frankish-Venetian fortress city of Mistra.

In the earliest plans for the Helen episode, Faust's medieval castle was to be situated in the Rhineland, a castle whose owner, we are told in the draft scenario of 1816, was crusading in the Holy Land.[81] Subsequently, and especially after an avid reading of topographical and historical accounts of the Peloponnese between April and July 1825,[82] Goethe found an infinitely more appropriate setting for the encounter between ancient Greece and medieval Germany, as well as a suitable contrast between an idyllic classical landscape and the gloomy grandeur of a Gothic fortress – a contrast that is vividly expressed by the Chorus in lines 9088–126 as the scene changes from the pleasant reedy banks of the swan-haunted Eurotas to the inner courtyard of Faust's castle. The contrast is that between the site of classical Sparta in the Vale of Eurotas and the forbidding hill site of Frankish Mistra a few miles to the south-west (or, for Goethe, symbolically to the north) of the ancient city. As Steven Runciman comments on Goethe's choice of the symbolic milieu for Faust's encounter with Helen:

There could be no better site for the meeting of the classical and the medieval world than this city, built close to the ruins of ancient Sparta, this medieval city where classical learning was so lovingly preserved and taught. From this meeting came the New Learning of the Renaissance; and in this meeting the philosophers of Mistra played a large and valued part.[83]

Phorcyas' account of lines 8994–9062 resumes in immense symbolic concentration the 'several tales', as she puts it in line 8972, of Peloponnese history after the decline of ancient Sparta. In 1204 Constantinople had fallen to the Frankish-Venetian invasion of the Fourth Crusade, and by the end of the following year William of Champlitte and Geoffrey I of Villehardouin had systematically conquered and occupied the whole of the Morea. On William's death, Geoffrey took the title of Prince of all Achaea, and by 1213 was master of the Peloponnese, which comprised twelve major fiefs. In particular, the Villehardouins 'regarded the vale of Sparta as their personal patrimony',[84] and, upon the death of Geoffrey II in 1246, his brother William set out to 'pacify' the whole peninsula. It was to impress the dissident Slavs of the Taygetus and to protect Lacedaemonia (Sparta) itself that William built a great castle on a steep conical foothill of the Taygetus range a few miles south-west of Sparta called Mistra or Myzithra. The castle was completed in 1249, but William's tenure of Mistra was brief. Ten years later he was decisively defeated by the forces of the Byzantine Emperor Michael VIII Paleologus, and the next two centuries saw the intellectual and artistic golden age of Mistra as the Byzantine capital of the Peloponnese until it fell to the Turks shortly after Constantinople itself, in 1460 – though not before it had played a seminal role in the emerging Renaissance.

Phorcyas' account to Helen hardly covers in any historical detail the complex history of Sparta or of the Peloponnese between the heroic age and the medieval settlement of the Morea. The Dorian invasions of Mycenaean Greece after the Trojan War, the decline of ancient Sparta in the post-classical period, the sack of the city by Alaric in AD 395, the loss of their ancient prestige of the classical Greek cities under Byzantine rule in the fifth century, and the rape of the Peloponnese by successive barbarian invasions – by Gauls in the third century BC, by Goths in the fourth century AD, and by Slavs in the sixth and seventh centuries AD: all this is passed over by Phorcyas as she leaps from the Trojan campaign to the Fourth Crusade in 'some twenty years'. It is, however, interesting that in a draft sketch Goethe noted the 'northern invasion of the Gauls'[85] – which suggests that he had intended to use this historical material at some stage, and that it was evidently in his mind when he was planning the historical allegory of Act III.

Certainly, we do not necessarily require any such historically, geographically or culturally specific *topos* as Mistra to explain or understand
the scenic, architectural, prosodic or dramatic symbolism of Act III.
We do not even need to adduce the settlement of the Morea by the
Champlittes or the Villehardouin dynasty to understand Faust's enfeoffment of the Germanic tribes in lines 9466 ff.; and it is doubtful that
Goethe, for all his wide reading on the history and topography of the
region in 1825, actually knew the main source for the history of the
Peloponnese, the *Chronicle of the Morea*, a French edition of which was
published in September 1825. Nevertheless, even if the symbolic
overtones of the 'medieval' episodes of Act III go far beyond their
historical prototypes, even if Faust's Gothic fortress is not a specific
reference to the *castron* of Mistra, but a composite image of the many
Frankish fortresses scattered through the Peloponnese, it is not unreasonable to use, as we shall at times, the terms 'Sparta' and 'Mistra' as a
convenient shorthand to denote the Hellenic and the Germanic, the
ancient and the medieval, the classical and the Gothic, the pagan and
the Christian – in short, the respective cultures of Helen and Faust.

The second ploy in Mephisto-Phorcyas' strategy to drive Helen and
her women from ancient Sparta to medieval Mistra and into the
protection of the 'barbarian' Faust is one of enticement rather than
threat: his/her evocation of the physical attributes of Faust and his men
(lines 9010 ff., 9045 ff.) and of the spectacular architecture of his castle
(9017 ff.). Mephisto's scathing critique of the 'plumpes Mauerwerk', of
the clumsy Cyclopian masonry of archaic Greek building (9018–21), his
eloquent praise of the soaring elegance and extravagant decoration of
the Gothic (9021–30), is a celebration of his and Faust's own native
architecture, devised both to introduce Helen and her women into a
medieval cultural milieu and to seduce them from their Hellenic
environment. To this end, Mephisto piles enticement on enticement,
not forgetting the seductive temptations of heraldry, pageantry and
romance (9030–44), or the nordic features of the barbarian invaders
(9045–6).

Helen's behaviour at this point is significant. Already she is prepared
for her new historical environment, already Phorcyas' reference to Paris
is, as she wryly remarks, an incongruous anachronism (lines 9047–8).
The final turn of the screw is given by the imminent approach of
Menelaus (9063 ff.), and Helen gives her reluctant consent (9071 ff.).
Even at this point, however, she does not give an unequivocal 'yes'; and
this veiling of Helen's innermost thoughts (9075–7), as opposed to the
jubilant eagerness of the Chorus to make the transition from Sparta to
Mistra, marks her own ultimate commitment to her classical origins. It

is a symptom that anticipates her final return to Hades, and as such it indicates Goethe's own elegiac recognition that the reality of Hellas is unattainable, an ideal or dream only partially and inadequately realizable in the modern assimilation of the classical heritage.[86]

Place becomes time; the shift from 'Sparta' to 'Mistra', the magical dissolving of the sunlit banks of the Eurotas into the gloomy grandeur of Faust's fortress, is vividly evoked in the three strophes of the Chorus (lines 9088–9121). Moreover, as lines 9049–50 and 9144 indicate, the 'journey' is accomplished without any apparent movement, as is the scenic transformation to the third section of the act after line 9573; as Goethe claimed, the unity of place in Act III is observed 'most exactly',[87] even if it is by means of magical transformation. This journey in time is not undertaken without fear; the spectre of extinction, of a return to Hades, is never far from the consciousness of the Chorus (lines 9116–21). The transition from the ancient world to the Middle Ages is a birth into a new existence, the revivification of classicism in modern culture; but it is also a threat to that existence, the threat of a renewed historical and cultural transience.

Mephisto-Phorcyas, the spirit or demon of historical change, now disappears from the scene and leaves the stage to Faust; he/she will reappear at the point where a further historical and cultural transition sets in, at the culmination of the Western European response to classicism between the medieval and modern eras – that is, at the Renaissance.

'Innerer Burghof': Inner Courtyard of the Castle

The stage direction before line 9127 confirms the historical reference of this scene: the 'fantastic' Middle Ages. Preceded by his barbarian vassals, whose nordic features are described by the Chorus in excited anapaestic and dactylic metres (lines 9152–81), Faust appears with pomp and ceremony in the courtly costume of a medieval knight, as a 'Prince of all Achaea', as it were, with a chained vassal beside him. Faust's dignity and charisma (lines 9182–91) indicate that he has mastered the sensual infatuation of the 'Rittersaal' scene, that he has matured towards Helen, and is now fit to act as the partner, protector and lover of the 'form of all forms'. As Emrich suggests, the chaining of Lynceus might itself represent Faust's mastering of the passionate impulsiveness that earlier mastered him;[88] it was Lynceus' spellbound reaction to Helen's beauty that led him to neglect his watchman's duty, and therefore caused Faust to fail in his first duty as host and protector (line 9195). Helen's freeing of Lynceus (9246 ff.) follows her recognition that her fate 'everywhere to confuse men's hearts' (9248–9) has pursued her into the new age; the prize of demigods, heroes, gods and phantoms in her earlier 'double' existence, she now brings renewed conflict, threefold and fourfold (9250 ff.). Faust's elaborate and courtly response (9258 ff.) marks the barbarian acknowledgement of Hellenic cultural supremacy; and this theme is continued in Lynceus' extended tribute to Helen in lines 9273–332.

For all the classical associations of his name, and while he might be said to mediate between Helen and Faust, between ancient and modern, Lynceus is here identified with the 'barbarian' reception of classicism. His tribute to Helen is a broad allegorical résumé of early barbarian encounters with the classical tradition; lines 9281–96 appear to refer to the rapacity and destructiveness of successive barbarian invaders of Hellas in the westward migrations of the Dark Ages. But Lynceus himself represents not simply the destructive greed of Gauls, Goths, or Slavs but rather the receptiveness of the barbarian world to the classical heritage; the ancient Western world collapsed (line 9282), but out of the chaos of the Völkerwanderung emerged a more stable and civilized order. The 'treasures' of Byzantine and medieval art, lovingly preserved (9301–28), are spread before Helen with the plea for her to invest them with new, or renewed, value and meaning – a plea for the revivification of medieval Christian culture under the impact of classicism in the Renaissance (9331–2).

Faust orders Lynceus (lines 9333 ff.) to deck out the vaults, walls and floors of his fortress with frescos, jewels and tapestries, to create 'paradises of lifeless life'. The reference here is not entirely clear; for Schlaffer, it has entirely negative connotations, denoting the lifeless 'museum' of ancient art created by Faust's 'cultural imperialism'.[89] Lohmeyer, however, associates Lynceus' treasures, and in particular the 'lifeless paradise' of Faust's palace, with Goethe's own characterization of the rich but stylized rigidity of early medieval art, with what he referred to as the 'old, rigid, mummified style', the 'dark oriental aridity' of the Byzantine tradition.[90] Lynceus' reply (9346 ff.) then characterizes the inadequacy of this static tradition against the beauty of Helen, against the burgeoning classical revival of the early Renaissance; it celebrates the 'richness of the face' (9354), the centrality of human form and physiognomy that superseded the hieratic religious icons of the Eastern tradition, as Goethe put it, between the thirteenth and fifteenth centuries. Certainly, this interpretation reflects Goethe's own account of the development of post-classical art as he records it in Kunst und Altertum am Rhein und Main. His journeys of 1814 and 1815, his reacquaintance with Rhenish architecture, the revelation of German and Flemish medieval painting through the Boisserée collection, the whole enriching

and indeed rejuvenating experience during which, as he put it in a
letter to Knebel, he had 'feasted at the table of the Nibelungs as well as
at the table of Homer'[91] – all this is acknowledged in his account of the
journeys. And the broad historical survey of a millennium of post-
classical art that Goethe records there[92] gives full recognition to the
Christian artistic tradition, serving to modify his rather better-known,
more disparaging judgements on medieval Christian culture and civilization, on what he had once called the 'eingeschränkten düstern
Pfaffenschauplatz des medii aevi' ('the dismal, constricted, priest-ridden
arena of the Middle Ages').[93]

The historical and cultural scene is now set for the union of Helen
and Faust and the symbolic synthesis of their cultures. Faust is invited to
share the throne with Helen as the partner of the 'unique figure', as
co-regent of her 'grenzunbewußten Reichs', her suprahistorical cultural
domain (line 9363). Faust's restrained courtly homage, his feudal
gesture of kissing Helen's hand, again mark the degree of maturity and
culture the 'barbarian' has gained in the course of his education towards
the Hellenic ideal. The passionate frenzy of the 'Rittersaal' scene has
been modified; he is now the 'worshipper, servant, guardian, all in one'
of the classical heritage (9364). Helen, who has already adopted Faust's
northern classicizing verse form of iambic pentameter (from line 9213),
signals her final acceptance of Faust's homage, her assimilation into
modern Western culture, by adopting the art of end-rhyme from the
verse of Lynceus.[94]

The delicate wooing of Faust and Helen, and the declaration of their
union, is expressed through the prosodic symbolism of lines 9367–84.
Goethe had already, in his West-östlicher Divan, drawn on the legend of the
invention of rhyme by the lovers Behramgur and Dilaram;[95] so here
Helen, prompted by Faust, completes his rhyming couplets. The three
strophes of the Chorus, who still retain their classical forms of strophe,
antistrophe and epistrophe (lines 9385–410), describe the physical
rapprochement of Helen and Faust, the surrender of the ancient to the
modern world; and the following exchanges between the lovers
(9411–18) mark the intensification of the bond between them by
incorporating internal rhyming into their end-rhymed couplets.

Not only is Faust here assured, dignified and serene; Helen, too, has
lost the existential insecurity, the 'Öde' and 'Schwindel' she experienced in the previous scene as her sense of identity was undermined by
Phorcyas (lines 8879–81, 8913). Even here, however, she resorts to
paradox to express herself. As the Greek ideal, she is 'so far', yet she is
'so near' to the modern age; as the symbolic emblem of a lost or 'dead'
culture, she belongs to the past, but in her union with Faust she is

'woven' into the fabric of the modern European tradition, and therefore given renewed vitality, revivified by her assimilation into a new culture.

At this point, or more particularly at line 9418, many commentators suggest, Mephisto could well step in and claim his wager – for Faust has effectively, if not literally, bid the passing moment stay; indeed, some critics, embarrassed enough by the problem, fall back on the position that in the dream-like or 'phantasmagoric' third act, the conditions of the wager cannot be strictly applied. Certainly, if Mephisto had wished Faust to lose his wager, he would scarcely have burst in on this scene with 'verwegne Störung', but would have allowed Faust to sink further into self-forgetful pleasure with Helen. But neither here nor later, in the arcadian idyll of Faust's and Helen's union, does Mephisto invoke the terms of Faust's wager; as we have argued above, Faust's wager is for him of secondary importance to his own pact. Mephisto must know that the moment of Faust's union with Helen is ephemeral; himself the agent or demon of historical change in the episode, he must know that it will end with the loss of Helen to the underworld and with Faust's departure to new spheres of activity, involving new possibilities for temptation and error.

It is as the agent of historical change that Mephisto-Phorcyas now intrudes on the scene. The attack by Menelaus, and Faust's enfeoffment of the Germanic tribes to defend his conquests, have no immediately clear specific reference within the historical allegory of the episode. In general terms, as the strophes of the Chorus in lines 9482–505 suggest, the implication is that the classical ideal, once encountered and assimilated, must be defended against attack, even if it is ultimately not to be realized as a lasting achievement; the reality of ancient Greece may be lost, but its heritage is still worthy of defence.

It is certainly possible, as Hamlin suggests, that Menelaus' attack and Faust's call to arms blend together any number of different historical periods, any number of successive barbarian invasions of Greece – Dorian, Gaulish, Gothic, Slav, or Ottoman.[96] Julius Goebel's interesting, if somewhat eccentric, suggestion that lines 9419–81 represent a call to arms to the German nation against the Napoleonic occupation has not found any general agreement, for all that it might, for those who are disturbed by such things, explain the anachronism of Faust's use of artillery to defeat Menelaus. In particular, the reference to Faust's troops in lines 9446–9 is intriguing; for Goebel, they represent 'Germans from the North and Prussians from the East' in the Wars of Liberation.[97] Alternatively, the mixture of north and east in Faust's army might, as Hauschild and others have suggested, contain a recondite allusion to the depradations of the Catalan Grand Company, which in the early fourteenth century not only attacked the Byzantine territories, including the Peloponnese, from the east through Thrace and Macedonia but also included among its Spanish mercenaries a large number of Turkish auxiliaries; the savagery of the Catalonian company was unparalleled even in a time of exceptional brutality (see lines 9446–53).[98]

The most satisfactory reading of lines 9442–81, however, is in terms of the thirteenth-century Mistra allegory, that is, as referring to the conquest of the Morea by the Frankish lords of the Fourth Crusade – which was in fact followed by its rapid reconquest by the Byzantine Greeks. The Villehardouins had originally landed at Methone in Messenia, not far south of Nestor's ancient city of Pylos; they had in fact been blown off course by a storm when trying to sail from Palestine to join the diverted crusade in Constantinople.[99] This would clearly explain lines 9454–7 (the Franks had little trouble in subduing the native Greek population), and perhaps also lines 9448–9: the nordic Franks arrived in the Peloponnese from the east, the Villehardouins inadvertently, others from conquered Constantinople, and their armies included whole regiments of Turkish mercenaries. In this context, the attack of Menelaus represents successive attempts by the Byzantine Greeks to recapture the Peloponnese after their successful recapture of Constantinople from Latin rule in 1261; as we have noted above, Mistra itself very quickly fell to the Paleologus dynasty, and the actual Frankish occupation of the city had indeed, in the perspective of the three millennia of the Helen episode, been only a moment in the history of the Peloponnese.

Goethe's allegory is clearly informed by his extensive research into the history of the Peloponnese during the writing of this episode, and Faust's enfeoffment of his vassals in lines 9466 ff. would appear to be based on the carving-up of the Morea by successive Princes of Achaea in the early thirteenth century. However, Faust distributes his fiefs not to Frankish crusaders but to the Germanic tribes of the *Völkerwanderung* – Corinth to the Germans, Achaea to the Goths, Elis to the Franks, Messenia to the Saxons, and Argolis to the seafaring Normans. Lohmeyer identifies these tribes as the five medieval crusading nations of western Europe: respectively, the Germans, the Spanish, the French, the English and the Italians (that is, the Norman kingdom of Sicily).[100] Bayard Taylor, on the other hand, reads the symbolism as literary, not historical: all the European nations shared the common classical heritage.[101] Schlaffer sees Faust's command of the Germanic tribes more polemically; the military and political conquest of south-eastern Europe is the precondition of Faust's cultural imperialism, of his possession of Helen – only after the ancient world has been destroyed as a reality can it come to represent a lost ideal.[102]

But the striving after specific historical detail, which, as Johanna Schmidt rightly warns, risks becoming an ingenious scholarly game,[103] should not be allowed to obscure the broad symbolic sweep of Goethe's 3,000-year allegory, in which space and time shift and overlap in a bewildering complex of discrete and anachronistic reference. Faust's command of the barbarian tribes, his persona as crusading knight, the struggle with Menelaus – Dark Ages, medieval crusades and Byzantine reconquest – all this, confined and condensed into a composite symbolic milieu, into the inner courtyard of Faust's Gothic castle, resumes in fantastic sequence the encounter between western European and eastern Mediterranean history, between Germanic and Hellenic cultures, in the Christian era before the Renaissance.

Defended and protected by the encircling kingdoms, Faust and Helen withdraw to their domain in the central region of the Peloponnese, to Arcadia (lines 9506 ff.). Goethe here exercises some topographical freedom in associating Arcadia so closely with Sparta and with the conception of Helen in the Vale of Eurotas (9514–21). Geographically a harsh and barren mountainous area far to the north of Sparta and the Eurotas valley, in cultural terms Arcadia is an ancient mythical and literary ideogram of the bucolic *locus amoenus*, of the Golden Age. As Horst Rüdiger has shown, Faust's panegyric of lines 9526 ff., one of the high points of Goethe's late lyric poetry, draws on centuries of European pastoral idyll – on Hesiod, Virgil, Ovid, Petrarch and Tasso, and on later generations of poets and painters who exploited the potent topos of the Golden Age.[104] The motifs of Faust's ideal landscape are classic, they are all, as Rüdiger notes, present in Virgil's tenth *Eclogue*: mountain crests, rocks, springs, meadows, fruit, trees and caves, goats and sheep, Pan, nymphs, even the reference to Apollo as shepherd.

And yet Emrich is surely correct in characterizing Faust's Arcadia not as a derivative imitation of classical models but as a product of the union of ancient and modern, of Helen's classical Sparta and Faust's Gothic Mistra.[105] It is, in other words, a celebration of the Renaissance; as Sparta dissolved into Mistra, pagan antiquity into the Christian Middle Ages, between the first and second scenes of Act III, so here the historical allegory moves in time and place through the cultural synthesis of the Renaissance into the problematic neo-classical culture of the modern world that is allegorized in the final section of the act.

'Schattiger Hain': Shady Grove

To say that Faust's Arcadia of lines 9526–73 is a timeless idyll, as so many commentators insist, is not to present the whole picture. Certainly, the landscape evoked by Faust is a timeless ideal; but in spite of his blocking out of the past (line 9563) both he and Helen are subject to history. He, and the Hellenic ideal to which he is wedded, cannot hold the present, and once again it is the abrupt entry of Mephisto-Phorcyas that heralds a historical change: time, war and death intrude into Arcadia.[106] The sleep of the Chorus indicates a lapse of time, and again Phorcyas is the midwife of the dramatic and allegorical action, as he/she appears to have been midwife to the birth of Faust's and Helen's son (9588 ff.).

Although the Faust legend relates the birth of a son, Justus Faustus, to Faust and the succubus Helen, it appears that Goethe has drawn more closely on the classical myth that Helen bore Achilles a son from her posthumous union with him on the island of Leuce: a son who bore wings, was named Euphorion ('well-favoured', after the fruitfulness of the land) and was destroyed by the thunderbolt of a jealous Zeus.[107] Not only the meaning of the name, and the identification of possible models for this curious issue of the union of classical and medieval cultures, but, inevitably, the interpretation of his allegorical and sym-bolic function in the episode has engendered a huge body of conflicting opinion. Goethe himself was, characteristically, not entirely helpful or consistent in his remarks on Euphorion. In December 1829 he declared to Eckermann that Euphorion personified poetry, which is bound to no particular time, place, or person; yet some two years earlier he had unequivocally associated his allegory of poetry with Byron, the 'greatest talent of the century', who was 'neither ancient nor romantic, but like the present day itself'.[108] Moreover, Byron is not the only contemporary of Goethe's to have been identified with Euphorion. Joseph Müller-Blattau, on the basis of Goethe's remark to Eckermann that he had conceived this episode quite differently before Byron's death in 1824, and also on the evidence of lines 9625–8, has suggested that Euphorion was originally envisaged as a tribute not to Byron but to Mozart; other critics have volunteered Hölderlin, or even Goethe's son August, as possible models.[109]

However, the stage-direction after line 9902, and more especially the threnody of the Chorus in lines 9907–30, appear to represent clearly enough the aged Goethe's tribute to a much admired younger contem-porary, a philhellene like himself. But even this evidence does not mean that we should see the Euphorion episode as a literal allegory of Byron's life or works; Euphorion is not an allegory of Byron – rather, Byron-Euphorion is an allegory of modern poetry.

Argument has also revolved around Goethe's implicit judgement of Euphorion, around whether he is presented as a positive or a negative allegory. His restless and anarchic spirit is frequently understood as Goethe's critique of modern, that is, Romantic, poetry, of its

transcendentalism, its disdain for real limitations, its idealism; these are
the dangerously wilful and impulsive tendencies inherited from his
father, the Germanic Faust, and manifested in Euphorion in an extreme
form.[110] On the other hand, there has been no lack of critical opinion
that interprets Euphorion positively, as embodying the ceaseless striving for a poetic ideal. Conversely, Marxist criticism has tended to see
Euphorion as superior to Faust, as a figure who perceives Faust's willing
self-imprisonment in Arcadia as a dangerous dalliance in sterile aesthet-
icism (whether neo-classical or romantic), which he counters by a
vigorous call to arms, an appeal to face political reality: self-fulfilment is
not possible in the illusory fairy-tale milieu of Arcadia.[111]

Lohmeyer sees in the description of the arcadian scenery in which
the conception and birth of Euphorion take place (lines 9594–7) a
symbol of the two traditions from which he springs: the 'natural'
classical culture of his mother ('Woods and meadows, brooks and
lakes') and the courtly medieval culture of his father ('Halls and
courtyards').[112] This extraordinary child, a spirit without wings, a faun
without bestiality, is endowed from birth with the urge of Icarus to fly,
but must draw his strength like the giant Antaeus from the resilience
of the earth (9603–11). His descent into the rocky chasm (9614 ff.)
is a puzzling episode which may well be paralleled and prefigured in
Goethe's Magic Flute sequel, in the underground vault from which the
child of Tamino and Pamina is resurrected.[113] Euphorion emerges from
the chasm decked out as a rococo allegory of poetry, in tassels, ribbons
and draperies, with lyre and aureole (9617 ff.); the naked, as it were
abstract, spirit of poetry has assumed the specific historical guise of a
modern culture, a neo-classical persona. The Chorus's response to
Phorcyas' account is to assert the superiority of classical myth and art
over their modern counterparts, which are only a 'sad echo' of Hellenic
glory (9637 ff.): Phorcyas' version of Euphorion's birth, growth and
attributes are for them only a feeble pastiche of the story of Hermes,
which they outline in two choric antistrophes (9645–78).

Phorcyas' reply to the Chorus is a sharp reminder of historical
transience. In the spirit of Schiller's 'Die Götter Griechenlands' or of
Byron's 'The Isles of Greece', she tells them that the polytheistic culture
of Greece is past (lines 9679 ff.); they can only live in song, can only
survive in and through a modern cultural tradition. At this point, even
the Chorus drops its unrhymed classicizing metres and responds in
modern rhymed strophes; and in this final section of Act III the Helen
episode, which began as Euripidean tragedy, modulates spectacularly
into opera – indeed, Goethe expressly related this section to The Magic
Flute, and even suggested that Helen's role should ideally be played

by two persons, initially by a tragedienne, subsequently by a singer.[114]

The Chorus responds to the emotional aural dimension of the music (9687–94); and while Faust's courtly *Minnesang* of lines 9704 ff. betrays his medieval origins, Helen at this point is a rococo heroine. This is not necessarily to be taken as a trivialization of the classical Helen into a frivolous 'Rococo courtesan', as some critics have charged; Karl Reinhardt sees in the combination of dance, counter-dance and song, of ballet and music, Goethe's tribute to the rococo culture of his youth,[115] while Lohmeyer identifies the episode as the flowering of eighteenth-century German neo-classicism, fostered by Winckelmann and Klopstock, in the music of Gluck, Haydn and Mozart.[116] Faust, however, finds such 'flightiness' unedifying (9752–4); and indeed, it becomes clear that this bucolic dalliance, which recalls the fashionable *Schäferspiele*, the pastoral games of eighteenth-century cultivated society, cannot hold the rapidly maturing Euphorion's interest for long. The elegant choreographic flirtation of lines 9745–66 gives way to the assertion of more elemental and aggressive impulses; the theme of the hunt, a metaphorical prefiguration of war, is introduced, as Euphorion's 'faunish' (or Byronic) nature asserts itself (9779–84).

No commentator has, to my knowledge, given a full or entirely satisfactory explanation of the following episode, of Euphorion's rape of the Young Girl, and in particular of her apotheosis and her enigmatic testament of lines 9808–10. Witkowski glosses these lines, without any supporting argument, as love in modern poetry, the expression of nostalgia for a lost ideal;[117] for Römer, this incident is part of the rococo allegory, of Euphorion's immature confusion of the playful hunt with serious issues;[118] Atkins sees it as the 'realistic' (*sic*) intrusion of death into Arcadia, an ominous prefiguration of Euphorion's own destruction;[119] for Lohmeyer, closely following the literary-historical allegory, this section reflects the passionate impulse of the *Sturm und Drang* and of subsequent romantic poetry.[120] It could, on the other hand, simply be a straightforward reference to Byron's mores.

What is clear is that this episode marks the transition from the childish bucolic flirtation of Euphorion to his militant manhood, the transition from the aesthetic and cultural allegory of lines 9679–766 to the political and military allegory of lines 9819–902; and here the specifically Byronic associations of the Euphorion figure become more marked. He climbs out of the arcadian idyll in which the Chorus vainly attempts to confine him (9827–34), striving for a new stimulus which he finds in the wider perspectives of the mountain heights (9811–18, 9821–2). The recognition of his geographical situation (9823–6) identifies the political and historical context of the allegory as the present day, the Greek Wars of Liberation – the final stage in the 3,000 years of encounter and confrontation between East and West.

Euphorion's call to arms (lines 9835–8, 9843–50), invoking as it does (with considerable syntactical obscurity) the heroes of ancient Greece, is an appeal to modern Greece to throw off the Ottoman yoke; at the same time, the action reflects more than a single, localized event in contemporary political history. To be sure, Byron's death, for all the squalor of his end and the military ineffectiveness of his campaign, fired the imagination of contemporary Europe, and to this day he is a Greek national hero; if he had lived, Goethe remarked somewhat extrava-gantly to Kanzler von Müller, he would have been for Greece a new Lycurgus or Solon.[121] But Euphorion-Byron, the son of Faust and Helen, is also a cultural emblem whose death allegorizes the unviability of a synthetic cultural ideal in a present historical context.

Like Icarus, Euphorion overreaches his precocious abilities, and falls dead at his parents' feet. His corporeal substance fades at once; his 'aureole' – his genius, spirit, or, in Goethean terms, his entelechy – rises like a comet, leaving behind only his exuviae, the external attributes of his garment and his lyre. After the final operatic exchanges of lines 9903–6, the lament of Helen and Faust and Euphorion's echoing reply from Hades, the Chorus recites a threnody that is at once a tribute to Byron – the 'familiar figure' of the stage-direction before line 9903 – and a final judgement on the fate of Euphorion. At this point, as Goethe himself remarked, the Chorus steps out of its historical role and betrays a modern awareness it has not hitherto displayed.[122] In particular, the two middle strophes (9915–30) delineate clearly enough Byron's chequered life: his noble birth, his self-consuming recklessness, his im-pulsive generosity of spirit, his outrageous flaunting of law and moral-ity, and his courageous but ill-fated expedition to Greece. All this is expressed at greater length in Goethe's tribute to Byron in conversation with Eckermann in 1825.[123] The final strophe (9931–8) brings a note of hope, the conviction of future heroism, and perhaps also an anticipa-tion of the liberation of the Peloponnese, which was finally accom-plished, with the help of the western European powers, some two years after the completion of the Helen episode. With the 'complete pause' after line 9938, the Euphorion episode ends, and with it Faust's union with Helen.

Criticism has for too long taken sides unilaterally for and against the figure of Euphorion. Those who have glorified him as a symbol of ever-aspiring poetic genius, as a powerful entelechy, as the glorious modern synthesis of classical and romantic, pagan and Christian, Hellenic and Germanic, have been all too easily refuted by those who have been able to point out that Euphorion is, ultimately, a failure; his death is the result of foolhardiness, a disaster rather than a tragedy. And yet those who have insisted on stressing the negative or satirical aspects of the figure, seeing him as Goethe's critique of romantic or neo-classical escapism, of subjective philosophies of the will, of militarism, nationalism, or any other form of overwrought idealism, have often chosen to ignore the more positive dimensions of one of Goethe's most imaginative, if enigmatic, creations.

Any number of more or less fanciful allegorical constructions can be, and have been, woven into this figure. He might well represent the failure of modern culture – that is, of Goethe's own age – to match the achievements of classical antiquity or of the Renaissance, the conclusion that a total renewal of the dream of Hellas is impossible; he might well reflect the fading of Goethe's and Schiller's own classical ideal in the uncongenial intellectual and cultural climate of the nineteenth century. He could be Goethe's critique of the tiresome restlessness and mis-directed enthusiasms of a younger generation. The whole Euphorion episode could reflect not only the Greek but also the German Wars of Liberation that broke in on and distracted Goethe's classical seclusion in Weimar, and Euphorion himself might even represent August von Goethe's excited attempt to join the Weimar volunteers after the Battle of Leipzig in 1813, which was frustrated by his alarmed father. But only a wilful misreading of the threnody of the Chorus, and especially of lines 9907–14, could overlook or ignore the mixture of sympathy and reservation, of admiration and deprecation, the resigned but affirmative epitaph to Euphorion – an epitaph that corresponds strikingly to Goethe's own ambivalent judgement on Byron, 'the greatest talent of the century'.

If, in the union of Faust and Helen, Goethe symbolized and cele-brated the Renaissance as the ideal artistic and cultural synthesis of classical and medieval, of south-east and north-west, as the highest achievement of modern cultural history, the subsequent development of the episode would appear to suggest that this synthesis was, historically, only a moment. Later attempts to revive the classical or neo-classical spirit, up to and including Weimar Classicism, proved very much more elusive and short-lived than the Renaissance itself. Faust loses Helen; after her valediction, in which she reverts significantly to her own idiom of classical trimeter (lines 9939–44), she returns to Hades, leaving her exuviae, her dress and veil, in Faust's arms. This 'husk' is the heritage of ancient Greece, whether in literary, plastic, or architectural form – the 'archaeological' evidence of a lost culture. This itself, as Mephisto-Phorcyas tells Faust, is divine, of inestimable value

(9949 ff.); while the reality of Hellas is lost, while the Hellenic ideal cannot be fully recreated or sustained, it should not therefore be abandoned or given over to oblivion.

The history of *Faust* criticism has not been lacking in those who have seen the Helen episode in very relative terms, as a temptation to Faust to pursue an aesthetic *ignis fatuus*, an illusory succubus as in the traditional Faust legend, as his straying from the true path of Christian or German values, or from a commitment to practical social or political activity. Temptation the Helen episode may have been for Faust, and error it may indeed have involved; but it was a temptation to fruitful error, an adventure that adumbrated the whole, to Goethe unquestionably positive and productive, interpenetration of western European and Hellenic cultures. The achievement of Greece is classical, it belongs to a past that can now only develop or progress in its various modifications and interpretations by and in Western culture; and the transformations of Helen in Act III represent the changing Western conception and adaptation of the classical heritage.

The fate of Euphorion, to be sure, appears to indicate either that the attempt to recreate the classical ideal as a present reality is doomed to failure or, alternatively, that later generations have failed to sustain the synthesis of the Renaissance. Every generation must interpret the classical heritage; the dream of Hellas should never be lost.[124] But the present age is unpromising; the conditions are not right.[125] Goethe lived to see his own and Schiller's carefully nurtured classical culture superseded, and even Byron acknowledged that it was not possible here and now to 'renovate the shattered splendour' of Greece.[126] Phorcyas' judgement on Euphorion's exuviae (lines 9955–61) is more sardonic than that on Helen's, and no doubt it echoes Goethe's own jaundiced judgement on the talents of a younger generation: an unedifying clamour of workaday talents and literary squabbles.

Helen must follow Euphorion to Hades because he was the modern historical manifestation of the ideal she stood for; with his failure, she too becomes part of a remembered tradition. But if, in the opening scene of Act IV, in Faust's final farewell to Helen, it is the 'spiritual nobility' ('Seelenschönheit') of Gretchen, the product of an exclusively Germanic and Christian spiritual and cultural tradition, that claims the 'best' of Faust's spirit and prefigures his ultimate salvation in terms of Christian theological doctrines; even if Faust turns from the cultural ideal of classicism towards an active role in political and social life – Helen's form still looms massively in the East as an inspiration and as a memory of a lost age, as the radiant reflection of the 'great meaning' of his transient encounter, 'Und spiegelt blendend flücht'ger Tage großen Sinn' (line 10054).

After the disappearance of Helen and Euphorion, there remains only the coda to the Helen episode that illustrates the fate of Panthalis and the Chorus. Panthalis, whose function has been to represent antiquity in its unchanging classical form, as opposed to Helen as the classical ideal in its transformations in modern culture, has played no active part in the 'romantic' or modern sections of the third act, and has not spoken as an individual voice since line 9191. Now she resumes her leadership of the Chorus, and, speaking in trimeter as Helen did in her valedictory speech, she summons the women back to Hades. They have, as she puts it, been delivered from the hypnotic spell of Phorcyas, from the confusing but alluring music of modernity (lines 9962–5); they are released from their historical revival in modern culture and are free to return to their ancient origins. The women, however, who have succumbed to the narcotic spell of its confused music (9964), are unwilling to resume their dismal and anonymous existence in Hades. They have no part in the immortality of Helen, even in the modest fame that Panthalis' loyalty will earn her. The heroine's mythical and historical status is assured, her symbolic and exemplary significance is established for all time; they are the anonymous substratum of the ancient world, whose only survival is not in any recorded form but in the constantly renewed cycle of elemental nature (9981–2).

I have suggested elsewhere that the fate of Helen on the one hand and of the Chorus on the other might represent a final cultural allegory in the Helen episode. In the neo-classical tradition, as Corneille argues in his Discours de la tragédie, while it is not per se necessary that kings or heroes should be the subjects of tragedy, this is in fact the rule because the action, and therefore also the characters, of tragic drama must be 'illustrious' or 'extraordinary', and must have the sanction of history, myth, or legend.[127] Helen and her handmaiden (or, in neo-classical terms, her confidante) Panthalis are assured this cultural immortality; the Chorus cannot survive as individuals ('Personen'), but only by assimilation into 'ever-living nature' (lines 9985–91), into the landscape of their native Greece as dryads (9992–8), oreads (9999–10004), naiads (10005–10) and maenads (10011–38).

The dryads evoke the rising sap of vegetation, the 'springs of life', and the maturing of fruit; the oreads echo the sounds of nature, birdsong, the fluting of shepherds' pipes and the volatile moods of nature as the voice of Pan; the naiads celebrate the eternal cycle of rainfall and evaporation; and the Bacchantes of the final section dedicate themselves to the sun-god and the fruits of the vine. The episode ends not with Faust's loss of the Hellenic ideal that he has pursued over the second and third acts, nor with Mephisto's sardonic epitaph to Euphorion, but with an ecstatic affirmation of rebirth and renewal in nature.

But even here the episode is not over; there remains the enigmatic stage-direction after line 10038, in which Mephisto lays off his classical persona, the mask of Phorcyas, steps down from his buskins, and emerges in his familiar form. It may well be that Goethe at one stage intended to encapsulate the Helen act or the Euphorion episode within a prologue and epilogue spoken by Mephistopheles; the paralipomenon that was evidently written as an introduction to the Euphorion episode was presumably part of that plan.[128] He saw fit to include neither prologue nor epilogue, but appears instead, with the phrase 'as far as it might be necessary', to have left the critics with an ironic invitation to draw their own conclusions, as he knew they would – and as they have indeed done.

ACT IV:
WAR AND RESTORATION

Act IV, in order of composition the last phase of Goethe's *Faust*, written between May and July 1831, opens with a speech that is both Faust's epilogue to the Helen episode, marking the end of his classical experience, and a prologue to the fourth act, marking his reintegration into the historical present. It preludes his 'descent' from the mountain heights into the political sphere, specifically, in terms of the allegory, his involvement in the historical and political reality of Europe in the period between the French Revolution and the Restoration of the Congress of Vienna. The form of this monologue is still classicizing; it is the trimeter of Helen, which Faust has in fact spoken on only one occasion in the whole of Act III (lines 9435–41). Faust's classical experience still clings to him briefly; with the entry of Mephisto, however, the form and style of the familiar 'Faustvers' sets in.

'Hochgebirg': High Mountain Range

The opening monologue is expressed in terms of a grandiose cloud imagery that, like so much of Goethe's late nature symbolism, is informed by his scientific studies. In 1815 Goethe's attention had been drawn to the work of the English Quaker Luke Howard, whose essay of 1803, *On the Modifications of Clouds*, had established the classification of cloud forms by altitude: nimbus, stratus, cumulus and cirrus. Goethe found Howard's studies and terminology so instructive and, what is more, they seemed to correspond so closely to his own observations that he wrote, between 1820 and 1822, a series of meteorological notes and a poem, 'Howards Ehrengedächtnis', celebrating Howard's contribution to the subject.[129] In his notes to the poem and in his *Versuch einer Witterungslehre*, Goethe explains how Howard's terminology applies to the processes of cloud formation and modification. Horizontal bands of stratus, rising through the atmosphere, densify into cumulus; at this point, according to whether the atmosphere is predominantly dry or moist, or, as Goethe also puts it, whether sky or earth is victorious in the struggle, cumulus can modify into the thinner and higher form of cirrus, or into the lower, heavy, rain-bearing nimbus. This process is exemplified in the twenty-first line of the poem, which charts the progress of atmospheric condensation through the respective stages of stratus, cumulus, cirrus and nimbus: 'Wie Streife steigt,/sich ballt,/zerflattert,/fällt' ('How vapour rises, gathers, disperses, falls').

Faust's monologue is clearly based on the scientific and symbolic structure of Goethe's theory of clouds. Not only do the paralipomena indicate that the two principal cloud forms of the speech, which we can identify as cumulus and cirrus, represent respectively Helen and Gretchen ('The cloud climbs, half as Helen to the south-east, half as Gretchen to the north-west');[130] but, in his poem to Howard, Goethe also invests his cloud forms with a spiritual, even mystical symbolism. The lowest and heaviest form, nimbus, represents the pull of earth; the highest and lightest form of cirrus represents a spiritual movement towards 'salvation':

> So fließt zuletzt, was unten leicht entstand
> Dem Vater oben still in Schoß und Hand.

> (What lightly gathered in the lower air
> Flows gently upwards to the father's care).

Helen's cloak and veil, dissolving in Faust's arms, have lifted him, as Mephisto-Phorcyas predicted, and have deposited him on a jagged and arid mountain range, presumably identifiable as the Alps, the geographical and cultural divide between Germanic north-west and Hellenic south-east. This cloud, initially stratus in form, moves eastwards 'mit geballtem Zug', and gathers into dense cumulus (in the poem to Howard, 'zum herrlichsten geballt'). Remoulding and modifying its shape, like the historical and cultural metamorphoses of the classical ideal in the modern age, it fashions itself in Faust's perception into the massive forms of classical female beauty – Juno, Leda, Helen – and finally settles as a castellated mass of cloud on the eastern horizon.

Faust's farewell to Helen is closely followed by a vision that reflects
the Christian-Germanic spiritual tradition of the north-west to which he
is returning. A light wisp of cloud rises as cirrus – the insubstantial
'Seelenschönheit' of Gretchen strives upwards towards salvation (as the
poem to Howard has it, 'Erlösung ist ein himmlisch leichter Zwang'),
drawing with it the 'best' of Faust's spirit; as line 10063 suggests, if he
had been able to hold his earlier love, it would have surpassed any
other prize, even that of Helen. The apparent 'superiority' of the vision
of Gretchen over that of Helen, of the Christian over the pagan, of the
Germanic over the Hellenic, has perhaps been overemphasized by
some critics; Faust does after all here pay full tribute to the 'great
meaning' of his transient union with Helen, as Goethe affirmed his own
commitment to Weimar Classicism. It is, however, the Germanic
tradition to which Faust belongs, and it is Gretchen who will intercede
for Faust's salvation in the final scene, where she will, moreover, appear
among the flock of penitents who cluster like clouds around the feet of
the Mater Gloriosa (lines 12013–19).

Nor does the cloud symbolism of the opening monologue end with
Gretchen's manifestation as cirrus. Implicit in the sequence stratus–
cumulus–cirrus is the fourth modification, nimbus, representing the
downward pull of earth, the world of political reality, of wars and
struggles – that is, the world to which Faust will very soon descend from
the heights of the 'Hochgebirg'.[131] The years of Goethe's withdrawal
into classical isolation in Weimar were also the years of revolution,
invasion, counter-invasion and occupation in western Europe.
If Faust left the empire at the end of Act I in a state of imminent
collapse, he finds it in Act IV in that state of collapse; and it is to its
restoration that he will, if only as a means to an end, devote himself
in this act.

The geographical, historical and cultural transition from south-east to
north-west is strikingly announced by the abrupt entry of Mephistopheles in seven-league boots; his opening line (10067) expresses his
satisfaction at the huge strides he has made in leaving the alien milieu of
the Hellenic world, even in its modern manifestations. He is here, as in
Act III, the herald and agent of historical change, and for the first time
since the 'Laboratorium' scene he is now once again in his own cultural
environment. His opening words introduce a discussion that resumes
the vulcanist–neptunist debate of the 'Klassische Walpurgisnacht';
indeed, as I have argued elsewhere, his scurrilous account of the
formation of the mountain landscape (10075 ff.) reiterates the Seismos
episode in an explicitly ribald form: the flatulent wind of the imprisoned devils generated the gas that threw up the mountain

ranges.[132] Lines 10107–21 also recapitulate, in different mythical terms, Seismos' classical account of volcanic activity in lines 7550 ff.

Moreover, as in the Seismos allegory, it soon becomes clear that the geological debate contains a political dimension (lines 10089–92). In one of his satirical epigrams, Goethe had similarly used geological terms as an analogy of political upheaval, of the topsy-turvy world of revolution in which kings are deposed, sons become fathers, omega becomes alpha.[133] Mephisto's parodic vulcanist account of the formation of the earth's crust is countered by Faust with a neptunistic or gradualist credo of natural evolution (10097–104). Even Faust's lofty vantage-point on the mountain peaks can be understood in terms of Goethe's geological doctrines: the rock on which he stands can be understood as granite, and as having all the symbolic associations of that rock form for Goethe. It is, as he argued in his well-known essay of 1784, an *Urgestein*, the neutral, primal rock that owes nothing to either igneous or sedimentary processes: it reaches from the innermost bowels of the earth to the highest mountain ridges; it does not represent, as do the fertile plains, a 'continuous grave'; it is not overlaid with the debris of subsequent geological processes, as human history is overlaid with the debris of political upheavals and struggles.[134] Faust, from the perspective of his mountain peak, can gaze down dispassionately on the struggles of men and nations.

To be sure, Faust cannot remain on such an exalted or disinterested summit, which is itself barren and sterile; he must eventually descend from this lofty perspective and involve himself in the confused 'debris' of human affairs. And this is indeed what he does in the fourth act; he commits himself to the error and confusion that is inseparable from any meaningful human activity. In so far as he does make a commitment in political terms, Faust's commitment will be 'neptunistic'; it will be for the established status quo; it will be frankly conservative and counter-revolutionary.

The 'temptation' envisaged by Mephisto in lines 10135–75 in response to Faust's challenge is cast in sufficiently general terms to have been identified as the Paris and Versailles of the *ancien régime*, as Restoration Weimar, or as a typical particularist German state of the eighteenth century. Certainly, the description of a teeming capital, spacious gardens, elaborate fountains and above all secluded hamlets built for pastorally inclined beauties (10170 ff.) is specific enough to Versailles, even if they were features shared by any number of German imitations. Faust's reaction to the vision of both the teeming township and the hedonistic luxury of the court is dismissive: the urban milieu is a breeding-ground for rebels, schooled by the educational schemes of enlightened despotism, while the life of the court reflects the sybaritic decadence of Sardanapalus. This is presumably a reference to Byron's drama of 1821, which was dedicated to Goethe; Sardanapalus was, in legend at least, the most corrupt and decadent (if, according to Byron, also courageous) in a line of Babylonian despots, whose reign was ended by a rebellion – the parallel to Louis XVI is certainly there to be drawn. But once again Mephistopheles has failed to grasp the scope of Faust's striving; against the banality of the devil's worldly temptations, Faust reveals his ambition – to conquer the sea.

Several impulses have been suggested for this motif in Faust, any or all of which might have been factors in Goethe's conception – the engineering and reclamation schemes planned by Julius Caesar, described in Plutarch's Life of Timoleon; the medieval construction of Venice; Frederick the Great's drainage and colonization projects on the Oder; or the reclamation of the German and Dutch North Sea coast. Almost certainly, the catastrophic floods that devastated the whole littoral from Belgium to Jutland in February 1825, in which 800 people died and 150 square miles of land were inundated, provided Goethe with an important impulse for Faust's final ambition.

It may seem at first sight odd that Faust, whose previous lofty and extravagant aspirations have involved the attempt to divine the secrets of the universe, to share the totality of human experience, or to be the partner of Helen of Troy should now settle for such a down-to-earth, practical activity as building dykes and reclaiming polders from the sea; but it is a not inappropriate Faustian ambition at this stage of the drama. Faust finds in this task a non-transcendental, non-speculative ideal that is entirely consistent with the direction of his energies in these last two acts. His conquest of the sea involves a titanic struggle with the elemental forces of nature; in his meteorological study of 1825, Goethe had described man's constant battle with the elements as the setting of order against chaos, of law and form against unruly formlessness, against mighty and arbitrary forces.[135] It is a battle to wrest fruitfulness from sterility; it is a productive activity (lines 10212–18); it is a struggle that demands incessant effort and vigilance, unremitting striving; and it is a gesture of defiance against the futility of eternal ebb and flow, against Mephistophelean 'pure nothing, utter monotony' (11597), a dynamic corrective to the 'pointless energy of unruly elements' (10219). It is, as Hans Rudolf Vaget puts it, 'the Faustian act par excellence'.[136] Certainly, at this point in the text, although Act V was already written, there is little trace of the utopian social and political dimension to Faust's reclamation schemes, no mention of a free community on a free soil. Here, Faust still sees the challenge in terms of a struggle between the human spirit and elemental chaos (10219–21); this is rather different from his later concern, born of his wish to be independent of the established order, to found a free society and to perpetuate his name for future ages. Before he reaches that stage, however, he will have involved himself in the defence and the restoration of the established political order.

At this point the noise of battle is heard, announcing the approach of Faust's opportunity to realize his ambition; for it is as a result of his helping to defeat the Anti-Emperor that he is invested with the fief of the tidal territories. Mephisto gives a vivid description of the anarchy unleashed by the careless frivolity of the Emperor, compounded by the chaos resulting from their financial schemes of Act I – or, more accurately perhaps, from the Emperor's failure to exploit properly and responsibly the natural resources and wealth of the empire to create a stable and prosperous political, social and economic structure.

It is tempting to read this account (lines 10261–90) in terms of the French Revolution, particularly since the prime responsibility is attributed to the weakness, irresponsibility and hedonism of the Emperor – for this is entirely consistent with Goethe's views on the Revolution; but there are factors that militate against such a reading. These are the involvement of the clergy in the rebellion – *pace* Nicholas Boyle, who sees this as a reference to the subversive role played by the secularized clergy in pre-revolutionary France;[137] and, more decisively, the support of the rebels not for a democratic or republican alternative but for a monarchistic, indeed imperial, order. The ideals, if such they are, of the rebellion described by Mephisto are far from those of liberty, equality and fraternity; they concern the establishment of peace and the rule of law in a chaotic empire. Goethe had already included a schematic allegory of the French Revolution in the Seismos episode of the 'Klassische Walpurgisnacht', as a peripheral and distant incident in Faust's quest for Helen – 'the echo of world's distant strife', as he puts it in one of his revolutionary dramas;[138] here, the conditions are rather closer to the situation in Germany in the first fifteen years of the nineteenth century, to the Napoleonic invasion and occupation, the Wars of Liberation and the restoration of a feudal regime after 1815.

It is of course true that the Anti-Emperor in this instance is not a foreign invader, but is 'elected' by the dissident estates of the realm; the situation described by Mephisto is more like civil war than attack by a foreign power. Against this, it might be remembered that Napoleon appeared to many Germans not as a foreign oppressor but as a liberator who, as the heir to the French Revolution, abolished feudal distinctions and privileges, introduced an enlightened administrative and legal system into many parts of Germany, and was to many Germans no more alien than their own rulers. Moreover, in the chaos of the subsequent Wars of Liberation, the military and political situation was more like a civil war of shifting alliances and coalitions than a concerted national movement against a foreign invader. Prussia, Austria and Russia all made, or were forced to make, their peace with Napoleon, and it was only in 1813 that the three nations came together as allies. Germans fought on both sides even in 1813; Bavaria, Baden, Würtemberg and Hesse-Darmstadt provided troops for the French, and, even at the start (though not at the conclusion) of the decisive *Völkerschlacht*, the Battle of Leipzig of October 1813, Saxony and Würtemberg were still on the French side.

Nevertheless, it must be allowed that Mephisto's description could well represent a symbolic foreshortening or conflation of the Revolution, the subsequent rise of Napoleon and the European aftermath of these events; after all, the Napoleonic occupation of the territories of the German Empire, and its formal abolition in 1806, represented the historical effects on Germany of the French Revolution. Whatever the case, the battle scenes of Act IV appear to adumbrate the Wars of Liberation against Napoleon, in which Faust intervenes decisively on the side of the feudal party, that is, for the Restoration. Act IV was written under the direct impact of the July Revolution in Paris, which had shaken Goethe profoundly.[139] He had feared above all 'a repeat of the tragedy of 1790',[140] as he put it; and, while he saw the causes of the 1830 Revolution in the weaknesses of the regime of Charles X, as a dire analogy to that of Louis XVI before 1789, he was by all his political instincts committed to Restoration Europe, even to Tsar Alexander's 'Holy Alliance' of Russia, Prussia and Austria as a bulwark against disorder or revolution in Europe after 1815.

Nevertheless, the political attitudes discernible in Act IV towards the restoration of feudal monarchy on the one hand and towards the Napoleonic figure of the Anti-Emperor on the other are, characteristically for Goethe, ambivalent. For, not only is the rival emperor defeated by dubious means – with the help of Faust, Mephistopheles and above all the three mighty thugs introduced in lines 10323–44, who intervene with supernatural violence to save a chaotic empire and a weak emperor; but also, if the figure of the Anti-Emperor is to be associated with Napoleon, then it might seem odd that Goethe, such a fervent admirer of the 'daemonic' figure of Napoleon, should present him here as such a negative figure, as a shadowy but sinister threat to the German Empire.

This has led Pierre Grappin, for example, in a somewhat Francocentric interpretation, to suggest that not the Anti-Emperor but the 'legit-imate' Emperor provides closer parallels with Napoleon. Napoleon had, after all, recreated some of the territories and titles in conquered Germany on the Carolingian model, as Goethe's Emperor does in the final scene of Act IV; Napoleon's *Blitzkrieg* victories in Europe, and the ephemeral empire he thereby established, must have appeared to those living at the time almost miraculous, if not supernatural, like the victory of Faust and Mephisto; and Napoleon's legitimacy, like that of Goethe's Emperor, was based on the force of arms.[141]

Grappin, however, undermines his own case. There is nothing re-motely daemonic or Napoleonic about Goethe's singularly uncharis-matic Emperor; it is not he but his 'allies' who fight and win his battles. Moreover, it should be noted that, while the legitimate Emperor is a weak and questionable figure (for all that he might be partially rehabili-tated in this act), the Anti-Emperor, though a shadowy background figure who never appears on stage, is not weak or irresolute. He is, indeed, by implication at least, a vigorous and potentially liberating force, who might not only restore peace, but might also 'infuse the Empire with new life ... in a freshly created world' (lines 10281–3). Napoleon saw himself in this light, as did many at the time, Germans as well as French; he saw his empire as a new order embodying enlight-ened principles to set against the old regime that embodied privilege and faded glories. For him, Francis of Austria, the German Emperor he deposed, was 'a skeleton whom the worth of his ancestors had placed on the throne'.[142]

Much of this Goethe also saw in Napoleon. He was – largely, but not wholly, as a result of his personal encounters at Erfurt and Weimar in 1808 – forever impressed by the powerful charisma exercised by the French Emperor; and all his life he took pride in the order of the Légion d'honneur presented to him that year. Napoleon was the man who had led France out of revolutionary chaos, and even during the Wars of Liberation Goethe would not countenance any criticism of 'his' Emperor. Wilhelm Mommsen, however, stresses how distinct Goethe's personal admiration of Napoleon was from his perception and judgement of his political career; and Ilse Peters also suggests that Goethe's attitude towards Napoleon was modified between 1813 and 1815.[143] By 1831, moreover, the image of Napoleon had been even further revised or 'corrected' in Goethe's perception.

It is, then, scarcely surprising that in the political allegory of Act IV the Anti-Emperor remains such a shadowy and ambivalent figure, a potentially constructive force that threatens the ramshackle structure of the old empire, but, defeated with the help of external forces, then

disappears from the German scene. Indeed, such reticent and schematic treatment of such a momentous figure in European history might
well be due to Goethe's unwillingness to represent in any more detail a
figure for whom he had such enormous personal regard, amounting
to hero-worship, yet whose historical image is qualified by despotic
ambitions and by the suffering visited on the nations of Europe – a man
who, Goethe conceded to Eckermann in 1830, 'had trampled underfoot
the lives and happiness of millions'.[144]

The dubious allies of Faust and Mephisto in the unexpected, indeed
miraculous, overthrow of the Anti-Emperor are the three 'allegorical
louts' Raufebold, Habebald and Haltefest (lines 10323–44), and, in the
following scene, the *vivandière* Eilebeute (10531 ff.). The biblical reference in the text, probably supplied by Riemer, not by Goethe himself,
casts little light on the meaning of these figures, which has been the
subject of much critical speculation. For Emrich, they are the three ages
of man, reflecting the characteristics of youth (aggression), middle age
(acquisitiveness) and old age (consolidation). Lamport extends the
analogy to Faust himself: the thugs are 'Mephistophelean caricatures of
the three tragic roles which Faust plays in the course of the drama', in
the Gretchen episode, in the Helen episode and in the fifth act.[145] In
general terms, they represent military might; they are ruthless mercenaries – for Atkins, 'the quintessence of primitive violence . . . whose
Romantic-chivalric armor only heightens the ugly fact that love of
brutality [Raufebold], lust for gain [Habebald], and the will to maintain
privilege and advantage [Haltefaest] are the basic motives of aggressive
militarism'.[146] Within the specific allegory of the Napoleonic Wars,
these dogs of war who play a decisive part in the defeat of the
Anti-Emperor might represent the three, subsequently four, allied
nations that finally subdued Napoleon: Prussia, Russia, Austria, and
'greedy' Britain, last on the scene, but always with an eye to commercial
gain – a common enough Continental perception of her role in
international affairs.

'Auf dem Vorgebirg': On the Foothills

The desertion or prevarication of the Emperor's allies (lines 10375–406)
corresponds to the hesitancy of the Rhine Confederation and other
German states in coming to the help of the allies, specifically of Prussia,
in the 1813 Wars of Liberation. At this point the Emperor, recalling his
fiery vision of power and glory in the masquerade of Act I (10417 ff.),
assumes a degree of resolution he has not displayed before. Nevertheless, this moral and political 'rehabilitation' of a previously irresponsible
ruler remains questionable. His military victory is compromised by his

reliance on the three thugs and on the supernatural forces summoned by Mephistopheles, or at least by his reluctance to inquire too closely into the extent and implications of such involvement; his subsequent claim (10857–8) that victory was gained by means of his own resources is clearly a piece of self-deception, if not fraudulent. His restored empire will itself be compromised and decentralized, in an uneasy compact with the church, vulnerable to renewed dynastic and political power-struggles between the factions he himself creates in the *Erzämter-szene*, the scene in which he confers the imperial offices. Even his belated, if courageous, challenge to meet the Anti-Emperor in single combat is an archaic feudal and chivalric gesture, contemptuously dismissed by his rival; it is, moreover, made at a point where his military position appears hopeless. His rehabilitation, if such it is, is scarcely comparable with that of Prince Hal in Shakespeare's *Henry IV/Henry V* trilogy.[147]

The Emperor's rhetorical resolve to single combat is in any case quickly overridden by Faust's arguments, which reduce him to little more than a ceremonial figurehead (lines 10473 ff.); it is not by the force of his own fist ('Faust', 10472), but with the help of Faust, that the enemy will be defeated. The curious motif of the Necromancer of Norcia, evidently an invention of Goethe's (10439 ff.), is identified by Boyle as a 'Cagliostro-like figure', and is therefore associated not with the Wars of Liberation but with the French Revolution, which seems inappropriate at this stage of the allegory.[148] However, the reference certainly serves to stress the compromising of the Emperor's alliance by dubious forces, and gives the church a later pretext to wring concessions from the restored feudal order. The derisive reply to the Emperor's challenge reported by the Herald (10489–96) also serves to emphasize the archaic and even illusory nature of an attempt to restore the old *Reich*, even in a more rationalized and less chaotic form: he is an echo of the past, an ancient fairy tale.

At this point, the Emperor relinquishes his military command; the battle is fought for him by proxy, by magical means, by his allies. Mephistopheles comically resurrects the hollow relics of medievalism from armouries and museums (lines 10554–70). This is more than a satirical reference to the early nineteenth-century craze for collecting medieval armour, or even to the medievalizing fashions of German Romantic literature, to the visions of writers such as Fouqué of a heroic and colourful but unhistorical age of chivalry, or to those writers who saw in the medieval German empire a stability and order it had scarcely ever displayed; it sums up a whole movement of romantic patriotic conservatism that contributed to the overthrow of Napoleon and the

restoration of feudal monarchy in France and Germany – the Middle
Ages revivified, 'das Mittelalter lebhaft aufgestutzt' (10562).

These quixotic figures, animated by Mephisto's imps, go clanking
into action in full medieval panoply as feudal auxiliaries in the 'new
battle' for restoration (10569–70); and the battle proceeds as a ghostly
encounter, as mirage (10584–92), as St Elmo's fire (10593–602). No
doubt Goethe is here drawing on many legendary sources for the
supernatural portents and wonders of this phantom army, which are
attributed by Mephisto to the 'master', the Norcian necromancer; [149]
the point of this episode, however, is pithily summed up by Boyle – the
Emperor, 'in attempting to defend himself against those who doubted
whether he was any longer real . . . has himself colluded with the force
of unreality'.[150] Faust traces, for the Emperor's benefit, a propitious
omen in the sky: a battle between the 'authentic' eagle and a chimerical
gryphon. As is usual with such portents, this is interpreted according to
the perceptions of the beholder; the eagle, an emblem of imperial
power associated as much with Bonaparte as with the German Empire,
is divined by Faust as the true Emperor, and the gryphon, perhaps with a
covert reference to the rapacity of Napoleonic ambition ('Dem Greifen-
den ist meist Fortuna hold', 7103), represents the Anti-Emperor. The
long-drawn-out battle is finally won by the decisive intervention of
Mephisto's supernatural illusionism, by his unleashing of elemental
spirits of water and fire to reinforce the imperial army (10711–41, 10742–
63). This puts new life into the empty armour of the medieval battalions,
who are reinvigorated by an atavistic sense of history, of generations
and centuries of feud, of dynastic and party struggles (10764–82).

It is perhaps a crude allegorical correlation to suggest that this battle
in the foothills corresponds to the decisive Battle of Leipzig in the
Continental Wars of Liberation. Topographically, there are no similarities, and the Emperor's victory – or rather, that of his allies – is no
doubt a composite representation of the allied defeats of Napoleon in
the years before 1815. Nevertheless, the Völkerschlacht of 16–19 October
1813 was a protracted affair of shifting fortunes for both sides, which
was only won by the allies by force of overwhelming superiority in
numbers and fire-power, by desertions and by apparently inexhaustible
reinforcements. It was also a battle in which murderous artillery fire
(see lines 10747 ff.) was decisive; it was a battle in which even the
element of water conspired against the enemy in an episode of black
farce – due to the premature blowing of the Elster bridges, Napoleon's
generals Macdonald and Poniatowski were forced to swim to safety.
Poniatowski and many others were drowned, and some 1500 men and
250 cannon were left in allied hands.

'Des Gegenkaisers Zelt': The Anti-Emperor's Camp

The plundering of the defeated Anti-Emperor's tent is explicitly associated by Habebald with war reparations (lines 10827–8); the ruthless
pillaging, however, is checked by the Emperor's aides, who assert,
perhaps without hypocrisy, the integrity of the imperial cause. And
indeed, the financial reparations demanded of the French by the
victorious allies in the first Peace of Paris in 1814 were remarkably
lenient; the real struggles were to come in the constitutional and
territorial settlements of the Congress of Vienna. This is the theme of
the following *Erzämterszene*: the restoration of the old order, decentralized, feudal, reactionary but, for the time being at least, peaceful.

For this scene of pomp and ceremony Goethe chooses, clearly
deliberately and no doubt with partly satirical intent, the high formal
rhetoric of alexandrines. The distribution of imperial offices is based on
the document that established the constitutional principles of the Holy
Roman Empire from the fourteenth century until its demise in 1806,
that is, on Charles IV's Golden Bull of 1356, in which the offices,
privileges, succession by primogeniture and territorial rights of
the German Electors were confirmed, but which also formalized the
decentralization of the Empire. The electoral college established in the
Bull comprised the three ecclesiastical Electors, the Archbishops of
Mainz, Cologne and Trier, with the four secular Electors, the King of
Bohemia, the Duke of Saxony, the Margrave of Brandenburg and the
Count Palatine of the Rhine. To each office ritual duties were attached –
to Saxony, Imperial Lord Marshal (*Erzmarschall*), to Brandenburg, High
Chamberlain (*Erzkämmerer*), to the Count Palatine, High Seneschal
(*Erztruchseß*), and to Bohemia, Imperial Cup-Bearer (*Erzschenk*); the
Archbishop of Mainz was also High Chancellor (*Erzkanzler*) of the Empire
in Germany. The Bull was designed, among other things, to counter
papal interference in the affairs of the Empire; it established an orderly
procedure for royal and electoral succession, but it also perpetuated,
indeed confirmed, particularism and checked the centralization of
imperial power and authority.

Except that he merges the three ecclesiastical Electors into the single
figure of the Archbishop-High Chancellor, Goethe's scene follows
closely the Golden Bull of 1356 – or, more precisely, the commentary
published by J. D. von Olenschlager in 1766, which Goethe borrowed
from the Weimar library in 1831. Indeed, as Goethe records in Book 4 of
Dichtung und Wahrheit, Olenschlager had been a family friend in Frankfurt,
he had discussed his commentary with the young Goethe and had
drawn his attention to the historically ironic opening words of the Bull:
'Omne regnum in se divisum desolabitur; nam principes ejus facti sunt

socii furum'.[151] The Congress of Vienna also represented the triumph of particularism, perpetuating the centrifugal forces of the old Empire in the new Germany. Stein, who had dreamed of welding the old *Reich* into a strong and unified nation-state (and not exclusively in the cause of Prussian hegemony), was out-manoeuvred by Metternich, who, with the support of the majority of the ruling princes in Germany, created a decentralized patchwork of states, the loose union of the German Confederation, in the interests of Austrian influence and, as he saw it, of peace, order and stability.

Behind the ritual ceremonial of the *Erzämterszene*, behind the formal homage and flattery of the princes who have been elevated dangerously close to the status of the Emperor himself (line 10950), lie the potential tensions of the 'balance of powers' of Restoration Europe; behind the faintly absurd honorific offices lie its quaint survivals and revivals from the old order; behind the conditional assurance of the Archbishop-High Chancellor's homage lies a scarcely veiled threat to the restored Emperor (10963–4). Behind the inflated nomenclature and titles lie the territorial scrambles of the Congress of Vienna. Weimar itself had furthered its interests at the Congress – it was promoted from Duchy to Grand-Duchy, and Goethe's prince became Grand-Duke Karl August of Sachsen-Weimar-Eisenach; the state was almost doubled in size, and more than doubled in population.

The Emperor of Act IV is older and sadder, but not a great deal wiser. His rehabilitation is by no means unqualified; his military victory is compromised by his involvement with scarcely trustworthy allies, and even his formal restoration has delivered him into the hands of his secular and ecclesiastical princes. The rehabilitation of Prussia after 1815 was not complete, either; certainly, the disgraces of Jena and Auerstedt had been wiped out at Leipzig, and her territories were consolidated, at least in the west of Germany. But Prussia's influence, for better or for worse, was checked by the Congress, by the alliance with Austria and Russia, and by the innate timidity and irresolution of Frederick William III, who grew steadily more conservative after 1815, and resisted any reforming initiatives on the part of his ministers Humboldt and Hardenberg.

The severest check on Goethe's Emperor is represented by the Archbishop-High Chancellor who, by virtue of his spiritual office (line 10977), calls the Emperor to account for his alliance with Faust, and wrings from him one ecclesiastical privilege after another in atonement. The church had also revived with the European Restoration, above all the Catholic Church in Austria; and Frederick William of Prussia also had his tussles with Lutherans and Calvinists in the north, when he attempted to unite them into an Evangelical Church, as well as with his Catholic subjects in the Rhineland. Indeed, the Archbishop's demand for the foundation of a mighty and richly endowed cathedral (lines 11005–32) suggests the campaign to complete the construction of Cologne Cathedral beyond its already completed medieval choir and crossing (see lines 11008–9), which gathered strength during the Restoration period. To be sure, the impulse of this campaign was not simply religious but also cultural, and for that reason its prime mover, Sulpiz Boisserée, won the growing enthusiasm of Goethe himself for the project; but Boisserée also gained the support of the Prussian king in 1816, and the project ultimately became the focus of national German aspirations.

There are scarcely sufficient correspondences to see the *Erzämterszene* as a detailed allegory, or, as Boyle has it, as a parody of the Congress of Vienna,[152] any more than Goethe's Emperor can be consistently identified as Francis of Austria or Frederick William of Prussia; if the Emperor represents anything, it is the survival of the old German *Reich* in all but name, in a politically enfeebled, if ceremonially inflated, form. The scene is, rather, a broad and schematic account of European restoration after the upheavals of the Napoleonic era, and as such the whole drift of this and the previous scene is far more than simply the dramatic means by which Faust is shown to acquire the coastal territories. Indeed, Goethe had already written part of the scene of Faust's formal enfeoffment, but evidently regarded it as superfluous or, at least for the time being, as of secondary importance to the broader historical theme.

Goethe's personal and political stance vis-à-vis Napoleon's occupation of Germany, his defeat and the Restoration was characteristically ambivalent. We have already suggested that a distinction might be drawn between his overwhelming personal admiration for Napoleon on the one hand and on the other his acknowledgement of the inevitability, even the desirability, of his political fall. Moreover, from the perspective of 1831, and particularly after the July Revolution of 1830, Goethe could affirm the Restoration as a stabilizing factor much more wholeheartedly than he had in the confusion of October 1813, when Weimar was in chaos from the aftermath of Leipzig, with Russian, Austrian and French troops still skirmishing in and around the town. Wilhelm von Humboldt wrote to his wife at the time that the liberation of Germany had not yet impressed Goethe; he was complaining that the cure was worse than the illness.[153] And, in conversation with Luden in December 1813, Goethe opined that the recent events had served Germany's liberation but not her freedom; if Germany's destiny, he explained, defending himself against charges of indifference towards German patriotism and freedom, were simply to destroy the Holy Roman Empire and to create a new order, she would long since have perished.[154]

Many critics are reluctant to see very much satirical intention towards the restoration of feudalism in Act IV;[155] and the question is fraught with critical and political ideologies. Both National Socialist and Marxist criticism, for different reasons, have chosen to stress the satirical or negative elements: it is the restoration of a moribund reactionary order, from which Faust must emancipate himself in the following act if he is to establish a free community on a free territory, under whatever ideological banner he is perceived to do so. And it is indeed difficult to ignore the manifestly satirical elements in Goethe's allegory of the Restoration: the three thugs; Mephisto's comical army of reactivated suits of armour; the derision of the Anti-Emperor; the concentration of restored power in the hands of the secular and spiritual princes; the pomp and ceremony of revived feudalism; the self-deception and impotence of the Emperor, who has indeed signed away his restored empire (line 11042).

No doubt Goethe's reservations towards the 'liberation' of Germany were based less on the reactionary and illiberal character of Metternich's Europe than on his ineradicable admiration for Napoleon, whose total defeat was the precondition of restoration. Nevertheless, from the perspective of 1831, Goethe could affirm the stability and order of post-Congress Europe, the Holy Alliance, and even the formal ritual and ceremony, which to him represented not simply meretricious pomp but the outward symbolic legitimation of authority and power. As a draft sketch for the Erzämterszene puts it, the inner significance is reinforced by the necessary outward forms: 'Sowohl das Innere als das Äußere durch die nötigen Formen zu bekräftigen'.[156] Various anecdotes from Restoration Weimar and, most strikingly, Goethe's own letters to Grand-Duke Karl August testify how punctiliously he observed the formal procedures and etiquettes of court life.

Goethe's political instincts were fundamentally gradualist or 'neptunistic'; what he feared and detested above all in his late years was the spectre of disorder and revolution, which had preoccupied him more than anything else in the twelve months preceding the writing of the final section of Faust. Overriding any political commitment to conservatism, however, was his instinct to rise above the factional hatred that is so gleefully fuelled by Mephistopheles (line 10778), and to preserve an ironic detachment that was, and has often been since, labelled with the cliché of 'Olympian' indifference. This was for Goethe, as he carefully explained in his account of the French campaign of 1792, which was written from the perspective of Restoration Europe in the early 1820s, a means of preserving his integrity and impartiality as a poet, an ironic mediation between party conflicts.[157] Goethe's Restoration allegory of Act IV preserves an ironic ambivalence which should not, however, be mistaken for indifference.

ACT V:
POWER, GUILT, DEATH AND REDEMPTION

In many ways, the dramatic interest of the fifth act reverts to the issues and themes of Part One, to the pact and wager, to the final reckoning between Faust and Mephistopheles; but this is not to say that the broad structure of the historical allegory that has informed Part Two is entirely abandoned. Certainly, as the Marxist critic Thomas Metscher rather ponderously puts it, it is very much more difficult than in the other acts of *Faust II* to reconstruct with precision 'the social and historical substratum of the aesthetic process'.[158]

Faust is in extreme old age; Goethe informally put him at a symbolic age of one hundred,[159] which has led many critics to insist that some fifty years have elapsed since the end of Act IV. On the other hand, it appears that his reclamation schemes have progressed with alarming, indeed with miraculous, speed. There is also no very clear indication of the relationship between Faust and the restored Emperor and his realm. We are told that Faust's lands were granted by imperial decree (lines 11115 ff.); but Faust appears to enjoy absolute autonomy of rule, unrestricted by any feudal obligation, and there is no mention of the tithes and taxes that the Archbishop demanded on behalf of the church (11035 ff.). Faust has wrested his own territory from the sea; this, over and above the symbolism of the Faustian struggle with the elements, would appear to indicate his political and territorial independence from the restored empire, which later allows him, at least in theory, to project a vision of a free community.[160]

If Act IV was set in the Europe of the early nineteenth century, in Act V Faust has become a man of the burgeoning Industrial Revolution, the paradigm of a mercantile entrepreneur, whose trading practices are scarcely distinguishable from piracy (lines 11187–8), whose technology is miraculous but sinister (11123 ff.), and whose 'colonization' (11274) is carried out with ruthless energy and single-mindedness. Goethe lived to see the beginnings of the spectacular expansion of trade and finance, of engineering and communications, of technology and labour, that began in the politically stable period of post-Congress European history, and his reaction was a characteristic mixture of acceptance and reservation, of affirmation and suspicion. He saw the inevitability of industrial and technological progress, of railways and steam navigation, indeed he even discussed with interest, well before their realization, the construction of canals between the Rhine and Danube, in Suez and in Panama.[161] At the same time, he was sensitive to the negative symptoms of headlong industrialization and to the potential political instability, even chaos, of a rapidly changing social and economic order, of the 'confusing doctrines for confused dealings' that ruled the world in his last years.[162]

Just as Goethe's attitude to the new age was ambivalent, so too his 'hero' Faust is here, as ever, a fundamentally ambivalent individual. His idealism is qualified by his daemonic ruthlessness, his satisfaction in achievement is limited by his obsessive covetousness, his altruism is vitiated by his impatience, his prosperity by his crimes, and even his final utopian vision is subverted by a profound irony. He is still beholden to Mephistopheles; he has still not fought himself free from magic, let alone from the accumulated guilt of a human lifetime in which that association has involved him, indeed which that association has itself symbolized.

'Offene Gegend': Open Country

Goethe is said to have claimed that his Philemon and Baucis had nothing to do with the proverbially hospitable old couple of Ovid's *Metamorphoses*, except in name.[163] Nevertheless, he preserved their traditional attributes of altruistic kindness and helpfulness, and their fate is a grimly ironic parallel to the original legend. They serve the exposition of the fifth act, and in quite specific terms may well represent a pre-industrial idyll, even a whole class of peasant smallholders forced from their land by the Agricultural and Industrial Revolutions. Their modest 'hut' is the idyllic polarity to Faust's grandiose 'palace', which is not that of a feudal sovereign but that of a nineteenth-century merchant prince or industrial baron, not the 'Sardanapalian' court of an absolute monarch but the centre of a thriving, if ruthless, productivity.

Just as importantly, however, their role is to provoke and to fall victim to Faust's last, and arguably worst, crime. Even so, their own accounts of Faust's engineering activities are not entirely consistent with each other; it is often overlooked, as Harold Jantz has forcefully pointed out, that two rather different perceptions are provided by the old couple.[164] Certainly, Philemon's submissive piety (lines 11115–6, 11139 ff.), his ambivalence and his apparent willingness to consider Faust's alternative offer (11083 ff., 11135–6) might make his almost admiring comments carry less weight than the forthright, if superstitious, instincts of Baucis; on the other hand, her view, tragically borne out by events, itself contributes ironically to the catastrophe: it is her stubborn insistence that they remain on their traditional elevated mound, or *Warf* (11137–8), that gives Mephistopheles the opportunity to exceed his instructions.

'Palast': Palace

None of this, however, can remotely exculpate Faust, who bears the ultimate responsibility for the catastrophe; as Mason remarks, the fact that he can palliate even the eviction of Philemon and Baucis as a magnanimous gesture (line 11348) is a particularly odious piece of self-deception.[165] Moreover, as this scene clearly demonstrates, his motives for their resettlement are entirely egotistic and despotic, as the reference to Naboth's vineyard confirms (11286–7). The insistent ringing of the bell is both a *memento mori* (11253–4) and a challenge to his illusion of absolute and unlimited power and territory. It is only one of the ironies of Faust's last days that the one physical affliction of old age he suffers is that which ends his ability to view his 'infinite' territories (11344–5): blindness. Faust's employment of Mephisto and the three thugs also demonstrates that his wealth, like that of more than one would-be philanthropist of the nineteenth century, is built on dubious, aggressive and exploitative practices – whether the thugs are perceived here as the military dimension of colonialism and world trade, as embodying the 'might is right' principle of imperial adventuring (line 11184), or as allegories of mechanical and technological power. The ironic discrepancy between appearance and reality is underlined by Lynceus' purely visual description of a deceptively peaceful seascape and landscape (11143–50, 11163–6).

'Tiefe Nacht': Dead of Night

Similarly, Lynceus' lyrical, but dramatically ironic, hymn to the cosmos (lines 11288 ff.), sung from the detached vantage-point of his tower, is an objective visual image that quickly gives way to a nightmarish vision of fire and destruction: the almost instant destruction of a centuries-old social and economic tradition by Faust's new order (11336–7). At this point, for the first time in the whole work (11340–1), Faust admits to something like guilt or remorse. Mephisto's brutal elaboration of Lynceus' vision (11350–69) brings home the point to Faust, and leaves him vulnerable to the attack of Sorge (Care); from the smoking ruins of the hut, four grey shapes form to hover around Faust's door.

'Mitternacht': Midnight

The four grey women, no doubt based on Aeneas' encounter with the
human ills at the entrance to Hades, are the harbingers of Faust's death.
An important critical problem here is the interpretation of the figure of
Schuld – whether she is to be understood as guilt, or simply as debt. On
the face of it, she must represent debt, related to her material sisters,
want and need; after all, the three acknowledge that none of them can
afflict a wealthy man (line 11387) – only the erosive and paralysing force
of care, which Faust evoked so powerfully in lines 644 ff., has access to
him. For some critics, Staiger, Emrich, or Mason, this is too glib or trivial
a reading of Schuld. Staiger's argument is based almost entirely on
grounds of textual genesis: there is no genetic, and therefore no
thematic, cause and effect between the previous scene and this one – an
argument that excises lines 11378–83 completely from the text.[166]
Mason understands Faust's immunity from 'Schuld' as indicating that,
while he is by no means free from guilt, he refuses to acknowledge any
guilt; this, however, ignores the evidence of lines 11340–1 and of lines
11387 and 11393.[167] And Emrich's contention that Faust is immune
from guilt is consistent only with his disturbing claim that Faust's
destruction of Philemon and Baucis does not represent any kind of
moral guilt but is part of a universal destiny attendant on all forms of
rule or work.[168] Erich Trunz is surely right here to insist on the reading
of 'Schuld' as 'debt'.[169]

If there is any rehabilitation of Faust in the drama, then it must lie in
this episode, where Faust, just before his death, first expresses his wish
to be free of magic (lines 11403 ff.) and then actually wills himself to face
Sorge without recourse to magic spells (11423). To be sure, this gesture,
or indeed any other form of reparation, can scarcely diminish a
lifetime's accumulated hubris or guilt for Faust; but his resolve to face
Sorge independently, and his confessional review of his own life in lines
11433–52, represent a degree of self-awareness, a shedding of self-
deception and illusion, that Faust has not shown before. The renunciation of magic, which leads, more or less directly, to Faust's death, is, as
Mason puts it, 'the nearest that he can come to a religious conversion',
given his atheistic and titanic nature.[170] And Durrani has demonstrated
how Faust's encounter with Sorge, his 'confession', his assertion of an
'inner light', and even line 11502, which is a profession of faith in
human powers that refuses to acknowledge any divine or transcendental authority, themselves present an ironic counterpoint to Christian or
biblical precepts; they are Faust's secular equivalent of a religious
confession of sin and the acknowledgement of a guiding spiritual
truth.[171]

Faust's confession to Sorge is far more than a simple declaration of atheism, nor does it mark his capitulation to her. This dramatic dialogue represents a tense struggle between the paralysing power of care and Faust's defiant resistance to its attack, vividly articulated in the insistent trochaic rhythms of Sorge's dismal litany and Faust's iambic responses. The outcome of this struggle is not decisive either way: Faust is physically blinded by Sorge, his determination not to have recourse to magic has left him vulnerable to the infirmities of old age, but she has not destroyed his spirit or his will. Indeed, his defiance of her results in the reversal of her own description of her victims in lines 11457–8: Faust's external vision is paralysed, but the darkness is without, not within. The fact that his blindness causes an ironic confusion on Faust's part between the continuation of his reclamation schemes and the digging of his own grave need not vitiate either his confession or his assertion of intention in lines 11499 ff. His renunciation of magic and of Mephistopheles is quite genuine; in the following scene, Mephisto must appear incognito, as it were, to Faust in the role of overseer, and his derision of Faust's schemes is spoken in an aside, *sotto voce* (11544 ff., 11557–8), not directly to Faust.

The confession of lines 11433–52 is an important part of Faust's final testament, arguably at least as important as his final vision of lines 11559 ff., which has received far more critical attention. The curve of Faustian ambition in the drama has consisted in a progressive limiting of the scope of that ambition. From his initial defiance of the limitations of humanity, his titanic and speculative attempts to fathom the mysteries of nature and of the macrocosm, his imperious urge for supernatural revelation, he has by stages accepted, more or less voluntarily, more or less as the result of experience, that such knowledge or revelation is not given to man. The early checks on his urge for revelation resulted in despair, and to his pact with the devil; in the 'Wald und Höhle' monologue, he accepted human duality and the imperfection of human existence; in the 'Anmutige Gegend' scene, he acknowledged the validity of empirical perception and experience as the reflection of the ideal.

This progressive acceptance of limitation has not involved any lessening of Faustian effort or striving. Faust's final ambition to conquer the sea cannot be seen as a diminution of his striving, nor as a reluctant compromise, the settling for a *pis aller*; it is entirely consistent with his own summation of his life's activity. Certainly, we should not over-estimate his defiance of Sorge, as many earlier critics have done, as a heroic or triumphant assertion of Faustian titanism; Faust here comes as near to genuine humility as he ever will do. Lines 11433–40 are an ironic and critical retrospect of his career, followed in lines 11441–52 by his profession of a new-found, but not abrupt or wholly unprepared, acceptance of a non-speculative ambition which turns away from the transcendental and the supernatural, which renounces Promethean attempts to wrestle with an authority 'above the clouds' projected by man in his own image, which applies itself to this world and which, most importantly, still involves an unremitting onward momentum ('Weiterschreiten') that is fuelled by constant dissatisfaction – not by the empty frustration that characterized Faust's immature titanism.

Faust's renunciation of titanism suggests not a state of rest, satisfaction, or torpor but an ideal tension between the acceptance of finite limitations and a dynamic dissatisfaction, which he will imagine he has found, or rather might find, in his vision of a free community on a free soil that must earn its freedom by a ceaseless, indeed daily, struggle with the sea. This vision clearly remains unrealized in the dramatic action of Faust – in this respect, at least, we must acknowledge the Marxist view that Goethe was evidently unable to envisage Faust's ideal community in any specific sense or within any existing social or political context. The fact that this vision of a free people is articulated by a man who is himself unfree, that this society is imagined by a man who has never felt himself part of, or been part of, a human social community, that this work ethic is formulated by a man who, at least since the beginnings of the drama, has always had recourse to magic rather than toil, is ironic; but it does not therefore invalidate the terms of his vision.

'Großer Vorhof des Palasts': Great Courtyard before the Palace

This scene immediately qualifies Faust's exalted sense of resolve and enthusiasm. The 'workers' he summons are Lemures, living skeletons, who are digging not his ditch ('Graben') but his grave ('Grab'). His conviction of a guiding vision that controls a thousand hands (lines 11509–10) is subverted by Mephisto's role as overseer; his urge to 'finish' his great work (11501) is mocked by Mephisto's quotation of Christ's last words, 'It is finished' (11594); his triumph over the sea (11539 ff.) is contradicted by Mephisto's anticipation of the destruction of his defences. The crucial critical question here is: how far can a vision accompanied by such ironies be taken seriously? Does Faust's 'highest moment' represent an exemplary vision, or a tragic satire on that vision, indeed on any such vision?

In so far as there is a consensus view of this question among Marxist critics, it is in broad terms that Faust's vision is exemplary, but clearly unrealizable from Faust's (or Goethe's) historical perspective. Faust has admittedly emancipated himself from his tactical pact with feudalism in Act IV; he has progressed as far as a bourgeois-capitalist social and economic activity in Act V, with all the accompanying symptoms of that system: exploitation, colonialism, oppression, eviction, piracy, and technological, agricultural and industrial revolution. His vision, however, remains conditioned by his own age; if it is a socialist vision at all, it is only a nineteenth-century phase in the dialectical process; it is at best the vision of the 'utopian socialists' of the early nineteenth century, of Robert Owen, Charles Fourier, or Saint-Simon, who were thus dismissively labelled by Marx and Engels because they lacked any scientific insight into the economic structure of bourgeois society, any awareness of dialectical materialism or of the problem of the proletariat. Any such views could therefore be only fictitious, fanciful and utopian. Some Marxist criticism has actually identified the Lemures as the proletariat, who in digging Faust's grave are, as it were, burying capitalism or the bourgeois society – though this is by no means universally accepted by Marxist critics.[172] The idea that Faust's vision anticipates but cannot articulate a classless society is, however, common to most Marxist criticism, which therefore sees his final speech as exemplary, if only provisionally so; as Boyle somewhat brutally summarizes Lukács's view, 'Faust dies in disappointment because he dies before the era of Marxism'.[173]

Boyle himself neatly turns the tables on 'perfectibilist' Marxist interpretation by arguing, as G. C. L. Schuchard did in 1936, that Faust's final speech, far from being an exemplary vision, is a satire on the proto-communist visions of the Saint-Simonistes, a utopian quasi-religious sect that flourished in France precisely around the time of the 1830 Revolution, with whose doctrines Goethe was quite familiar, and which he deplored.[174] Oddly enough, in the same year as Boyle, the Marxist Heinz Hamm also drew attention to traces of Saint-Simonian thinking in Act V – but without Boyle's emphasis on the satirical treatment of those elements.[175] Hans Rudolf Vaget has attacked Marxist and perfectibilist assumptions from a different angle; he argues that Faust's schemes in Act V are neither Marxist-progressive nor bourgeois-utopian, but are based on neo-feudal values of 'Herrschaft' and 'Eigentum' – 'power' and 'territory'.[176]

It is surely fanciful to regard Faust's utopian community as Goethe's anticipation of Marxist systems; and it is clearly outrageous to see his activities as a prefiguration of, or to use them as an apology for, Wilhelmine expansionist policies or National Socialist 'resettlement' projects. It is by no means unreasonable, indeed it is historically plausible, to see this vision as a satire on Saint-Simonian doctrines; but this argument firmly defines the 'final conclusion' of Faust's wisdom

(line 11574) as a tragic illusion, and also raises the question of why
Goethe should have incorporated into his life's work at such a crucial
stage a social and political doctrine that he detested.

Certainly, any utopian programme formulated, satirically or not, at
that time could scarcely fail to include some traces of contemporary
visionary doctrines. Schuchard and Boyle have also indicated, as a
positive counterweight to Saint-Simonian elements, the possible influence of the agricultural, social and economic ideas of Sir John
Sinclair, whose memoirs Goethe read at the same time as the doctrines
of Saint-Simon, in May 1831; he was also aware of the reforming ideas of
Bentham and Sismondi. And, although there is no evidence that Goethe
interested himself in the projects and achievements of other utopian
socialists at the time, it is unlikely that he was ignorant of the ideal
communities projected by the visionary Charles Fourier, whose Le
Nouveau Monde was published in 1829, or of the more practical, and
indeed partly realized, industrial co-operative communities of Robert
Owen, whose exemplary settlement at New Lanark had enjoyed
international interest and esteem from 1813, even if his later 'New
Harmony' experiment in Indiana proved disastrous.

We may safely say that, in general terms, Faust's vision shares many
of the features of typical philanthropic or utopian projects of the early
nineteenth century; it may well also, by implication, suggest Goethe's
scepticism towards the practical viability of such utopias. But, for all the
ironic discrepancy between what Faust imagines and what is actually
going on around him, he does not make the mistake of believing that he
has realized his utopia; his vision is hypothetical, provisional and
conditional. The reward he claims is the nineteenth-century sceptical
materialist's equivalent of immortality: the perpetuation of his memory
(lines 11583-4).

It is possible to detect a certain shift in Faust's ambitions between his
initial urge to conquer the sea in Act IV as a titanic or egotistic challenge
(10198 ff.) and the practical social application of this ambition later in
Act V; indeed, as Mason argues, there is even a degree of progress
discernible within Act V itself. Faust's ruthless and autocratic will to
enjoy sole possession of his territories as far as he can survey them from
his belvedere (11344-5) develops into a future vision of a free, if not
equal, society of people, in which 'communal effort' ('Gemeindrang',
11572) and co-operation ensure the security and integrity of the
community. A significant change made by Goethe to a previous draft
of Faust's speech would appear to indicate his intention to make the
vision more altruistic, less proprietorial; an early version of line 11580
reads 'to stand on land that is truly my own' – 'Auf wahrhaft eignem

Grund und Boden stehn'.[177] In the final version of his vision, Faust is
concerned not solely with power and territory, nor solely with his
titanic struggle against the sea; he is concerned with the draining of a
pestilential swamp, with the contentment, wellbeing and freedom of an
active people. Moreover, as Mason points out, this moral shift in Faust's
intentions has been accompanied by his resolve to renounce magic and
accomplish his task by human agency. Mason is, however, careful not to
over-glamorize either Faust's vision itself or his eleventh-hour 'change
of heart'; and he firmly rejects Emrich's metaphysical argument that
Goethe is not concerned with Faust's moral guilt or with social ethical
issues.[178]

There is in the final analysis not sufficient intrinsic textual evidence to
refute the optimistic or 'perfectibilist' interpretation of Faust's vision,
for all that many such interpretations have outrageously exaggerated the
implications of that vision. To see it as a tragic illusion, as Faust's last and
greatest error, is to share the nihilistic judgement of Mephistopheles: 'It
is as if it had never been' (line 11601). And while, as Schuchard claims,
Mephisto by no means always speaks untruth, it is difficult to accept that
Goethe would give the devil the final word on Faust's career on earth,
any more than he allows him the last word on the fate of Faust's soul. It
is also odd that so many anti-perfectibilists should so readily accept
Mephisto's opinion of the futility and ephemeral nature of Faust's civil
engineering in lines 11544–50, when Goethe himself was perfectly well
aware of the successful reclamation of land from the sea along the
Dutch and German coasts – in spite of, and in defiance of, the periodic
devastation of storms and floods. But just as pessimistic, tragic, or
satirical interpretations of Faust's final vision are forced to adduce
extrinsic evidence to throw light on Goethe's judgement of Faust's
achievements on earth, as indeed are Marxist 'perfectibilists', so, too,
optimistic interpretations are forced to depend heavily on Goethe's
own reported characterization of Faust as 'a man who out of grave
confusion constantly strives for the better', who pursues 'an ever higher
and purer activity to the end'.[179]

The terms of Faust's wager with Mephisto have only been conditionally fulfilled; he has not explicitly bid the passing moment stay, he
has not fallen into a state of passive self-satisfaction or been deluded
by pleasure. He has, however, acknowledged a 'highest moment', not
conditionally as an anticipation of the future, as in lines 11581–2, but now
(line 11586). At this point, as he foresaw in the wager scene (lines
1703–6), the clock will stop, he will have lived his time and be ready to
die. The terms of the wager are broadly, though not literally, reiterated
by Mephistopheles and the Chorus in lines 11592–5; but, just as Faust,

in his wager could scarcely have the final word on the fate of his soul, neither does Mephisto here have any such authority, whether by virtue of the pact, of his wager with Faust, or of his wager with the Lord. Moreover, he appears to realize this: the battle for Faust's soul is still to be fought. In the following 'Grablegung' scene, we see an uncharacteristically defensive devil, one who is no longer confident of the 'triumph' he anticipated in lines 332–3; indeed, already in lines 11595 ff. he is deeply disturbed by the word 'vorbei' of the Chorus. The suggestion that Faust's life is 'past' implies that something has been, something that might indeed leave some 'trace' in the future; and that is anathema to his nihilistic convictions.

'Grablegung': Burial

The following action is for the most part a comic, even ribald, burlesque concerned with the outwitting of Mephistopheles and his infernal legions. From the very beginning of the scene, the devil is on the defensive, defiant, certainly, but unconfident of his powers and even unsure of his theological status, under attack from the scepticism of modern secular thought, regretting the 'old days' of doctrinal certainties, and relying on the sensationally gruesome aspect of traditional, Dantesque hell-fire to shore up the crumbling superstitions of modern sinners. His self-parodying antics are those of a 'fugleman' – strictly, a term denoting a soldier who signals the sequence of military drills by means of exaggerated gestures. Here, it serves to cast Mephisto as the stage-manager of a theatrical hell that is wheeled on to the stage by his raffish team of assistants like the scenery of a medieval morality play; this is, in admittedly more overtly burlesque and comic form, the counterpart of the theatrical heaven of the 'Prolog im Himmel'.

Mephisto's crudely anatomical views on the location of the soul and its egress at death – whether it leaves the body above as eructation or below as flatulence – are a persiflage of popular superstition, and perhaps also of doctrinal wranglings on the subject. The angels who enter theatrically 'above right' (after line 11675) are themselves not free from the burlesque of this scene. They are pious choirboys, epicene and seductive, for Mephisto devils in disguise (11696); and no doubt his derision of their 'ghastly jingling' (11685) reflects some of Goethe's own mistrust of sanctimonious religiosity, whether expressed in sentimental piety, in the neo-Catholicism of much Romantic literature, in music, or in Nazarene painting. Some critics even see in lines 11691–2 a reference to the practice, not unknown even in Goethe's day, of castrati choirs – though it is usually understood simply as sexual lust. The whole is based on an ironic and theatrical contrast between the grotesquely humorous and the piously sentimental, between absurd devils and rococo rose-strewing angels.

Mephisto finally loses control through the incompetence of his own troops (lines 11719–20), whose fiery breath turns the roses into flames that send them arse-over-tip back down to hell, whereupon Mephisto's own rout is hilariously accomplished by his pederastic lust. Smitten by the subtly 'kittenish' appeal of the young angels, his reaction (11794 ff.) is a comic reversal of his earlier prurient indignation at the shameless nakedness of the creatures of ancient myth (7086–9). This distraction is, however, only a tactic in the angels' strategy to snatch Faust's soul; Mephisto's quasi-medical diagnosis of his 'illness' diverts his attention from the trick that is being played on him. The plague of love that has afflicted his inner self now takes a turn for the better as it breaks out on his skin (11814). As Harold Jantz has explained, the boils with which Mephisto, like Job, has been afflicted are not the disease itself, but a sign that he is throwing off the disease as it works itself out of his system.[180] Hence he can triumphantly establish, in a line that is a 'blasphemously witty anticipatory parody' of the later line 11934, in which the angels celebrate the salvation of Faust's 'noble part', that the devil's 'noble parts' are safe and that he can once again rely on his 'staff' (lines 11811–13).

This is Goethe at his most ribald, and Mephisto at his most comical. His indignant fury at his deception is qualified by rueful self-parody and self-reproach; his huge investment of diabolical resources in the cause of Faust's perdition has been squandered, a foolish infatuation has frustrated the schemes of someone who ought to have known better (11836–43). There is no court, no higher authority, to whom he can appeal, since those who filched Faust's soul are envoys of that authority. Certainly, Goethe was careful not to introduce any appeal scene in heaven with the Lord or Christ presiding, as he had evidently at one stage intended, and as the 'Prologue in Heaven' has led us to expect;[181] the issues are altogether too finely-balanced for such a scene, and the legal, even the moral, implications of Faust's salvation are overridden by a transcendental and mystical judgement. The victory of the angels in the 'Grablegung' scene may be a victory of love over hate, of grace over malice, but it is achieved by a form of theological sleight-of-hand; it is, as Durrani notes, 'a triumph of one kind of deceit over another'.[182] Goethe was clearly unwilling to conclude his work on such a burlesque tactical victory of the forces of light over those of darkness; but he was, equally, evidently unable to present Faust's salvation uniquely in terms of the solemnly transcendental religious mystery that follows.

'*Bergschluchten*': *Mountain Gorges*

This scene, often referred to as the 'Scene in Heaven', which is a
debatable description, is based on an identifiable visual source – a fresco
in the Campo Santo in Pisa of hermits in the Theban desert;[183] the later
vision of the Mater Gloriosa is also no doubt derived from one or a
number of representations of the Assumption of the Virgin Mary.
Visually and structurally, the parallels are close: lions, rocks, gorges,
caves, trees and even a river feature in the *Thébaïde*. More strikingly still,
the anchorites' cells are layered upwards, corresponding to the vertical
progression of Goethe's scene, to the ascending stations of the Patres
Profundus, Ecstaticus and Seraphicus and Doctor Marianus. The fathers
stand in varying stages of proximity to the deity; this vertical structure
also corresponds to the steady ascension of Faust's spirit as it is pulled
upwards by the attractive power of love and by the progressive
lightening of its earthly integuments, here expressed as the wispy shreds
of the pupa from which it emerges (lines 11981 ff.). The vertical
structure of the scene also corresponds to Goethe's theory of clouds; as
Gretchen's image climbed as cirrus into the ether (10065), so here
Faust's spirit rises towards the penitents who are gathered like clouds
around the feet of the Mater Gloriosa (12013 ff.). The Blessed Boys
(Selige Knaben) are also perceived as a 'morning cloud' (11890); as in
the poem 'Howards Ehrengedächtnis', the upward movement and
modification of clouds is analogous to the spirit's ascent towards
salvation: 'Erlösung ist ein himmlisch leichter Zwang'.[184]

If it is arguable that the later part of the scene is set in heaven, as the
editions of Witkowski and Trunz have it, there is no point at which this
scene comes to rest; we do not see Faust's soul, his immortal self or his
entelechy, in a final state of grace, only its ascension and its progressive
purification as it rises through successive stages towards 'higher spheres'
(lines 12094–5). Moreover, in the first part of the scene it is a natural
landscape of woods, roots, echoing rocks and mountain streams that is
described; this is no longer the theatrical morality-play theology of the
'Prologue in Heaven' or the 'Grablegung' scene, but the landscape of a
natural theology. The mystical contemplation of Pater Profundus, even
the ascetic ecstasy of Pater Ecstaticus, are expressed in terms of streams
and growth, of lightning, and of the 'constant star' of eternal love, as
well as in the sharply erotic imagery of mysticism: of fire and pain, of
arrows, spears and clubs, of 'chasm' and 'tree' (11854–61, 11866–73).
Faust's transfiguration is represented as a process of nature, as the
organic metamorphosis of chrysalis into imago; and the cloud imagery
of the upper regions also suggests a natural process of ascent from lower
to higher. In this symbolic scenery where earth and heaven meet, the

natural landscape and the figures inhabiting it are manifestations of the love 'that forms and cherishes all' (11873).

The Angels who carry Faust's spirit recite the lines which, Goethe confided to Eckermann, contain the 'key' to Faust's salvation (11934–41): unremitting effort towards a higher and purer activity, answered by eternal love from above. Moreover, he added, this is entirely consistent with our religious assumptions, whereby we are redeemed not by our efforts alone but by grace also.[185] The stage-direction before line 11934 read, in a manuscript version, 'Angels . . . bearing Faust's entelechy';[186] why Goethe made the change from 'Faust's entelechy' to 'Faust's immortal part' is not clear; at all events, while he does not completely exclude the term 'soul' in this final scene (see lines 11946 and 12065), he appears reluctant to use it in this context – as against the previous scene, where Mephisto refers frequently and specifically to Faust's soul in the traditional Christian terminology.

The Younger Angels rejoice at the defeat of hell by means of the roses from the hands of the penitents (11942–53); and the More Perfected Angels adumbrate the mystery of corporeal life (11954–65). Faust's spirit is still weighed down by the traces of his earthly existence; 'geeinte Zwienatur', the single duality of spirit and elemental substance that constitutes physical life, can only be separated out by divine love. Here and elsewhere, as we have noted above,[187] the transfiguration mystery of the 'Bergschluchten' scene represents a reverse parallel to that of the finale of the 'Klassische Walpurgisnacht': the spirit Homunculus under-goes the natural mystery of birth by the fusion of spirit and elements under the generative force of Eros, while Faust's spirit emerges from that duality by a process of separation that is accomplished by 'die ewige Liebe', by redemptive love.

The scene moves upwards to a higher level, where the clouds give way to the radiance of heaven (lines 11970 ff.). The Blessed Boys, who have accumulated no 'earthly remnant' in their brief existences, bear Faust's spirit upwards as it sheds the wraps of its cocoon, the last vestiges of physical substance. Even here, the process is dynamic and reciprocal, a giving and receiving; the children buoy up Faust's spirit, but they in turn will be instructed by him (12082–3). From this perspec-tive Doctor Marianus, whose 'highest, purest cell' brings him closest to the mystical union with the Queen of Heaven, hymns her as the ideal paradigm of femininity: 'Virgin, Mother, Queen' (12009–12), pleading for the penitents who have suffered in love. Placed higher than the mystics of the earlier, lower regions, the penitents themselves intercede for Gretchen in the name of their love, citing their own secular experi-ences of human frailty, of suffering and penance, from the biblical and legendary accounts: the washing and anointing of Christ's feet, the encounter at the well in Samaria, and the forty-year penance of Maria Aegyptiaca in the desert. Gretchen's prayer (12069–75) similarly recalls her own tragic experience of profane love, as she echoes the words from the prayer of the 'Zwinger' scene; all these examples represent the transfiguration of 'inadequate' human experience into the 'Ereignis', the actuality of a transcendental reality (12106–7) into which Gretchen will induct Faust (12092–3).

The Mater Gloriosa points the way onwards and upwards, Doctor Marianus echoes both his own earlier lines (12009–12) and the Sirens' hymn to Luna (8042–3), hailing the Madonna as Virgin, Mother, Queen and Goddess; and the Chorus Mysticus declares the higher reality of which the transient phenomena of human experience are but a simile. Faust's acknowledgement and acceptance of these 'inadequate' phenomena at the beginning of Faust II is answered at the end by the intimation of a sphere where truth is reality, where the relative and imperfect becomes absolute and perfect, where what is beyond human imagination to describe or comprehend is done. The final image of the drama expresses the dynamic and attractive power of the eternally feminine ideal, 'das Ewig-Weibliche' – the mystical, and indeed still metaphorical, summation of the force of which this scene is the ultimate celebration: love.

The final scene of Faust, with its emotional and mystical extravagance, its sentimental religiosity and its open-ended perspective, has offended the instincts and the perceptions of many critics – not so much because it unequivocally demonstrates Faust's salvation, but because in doing so in this manner Goethe has evaded, or at the very least has glossed over, the ethical and moral ambiguities of Faust's career on earth by means of the deus, or dea, ex machina, of a transcendental solution. Alternatively, this extravagant flourish tacked on to the end of the 'real' theme of Faust is often regarded as a piece of higher irony, as the theological equivalent of the tragic irony that Schuchard and Boyle, for example, see in Faust's final vision on earth.

Mason distinguishes three fundamental critical attitudes towards the issue of Faust's salvation: the 'Christian' view – that he is a sinner saved by the agency of a grace that he has done little or nothing to merit; the 'Faustian' view – that Faust is beyond conventional criteria of sin or guilt; and the 'Pelagian' view – that, while Faust has earned the possibility of salvation by his unremitting striving, his salvation is only achieved by virtue of a grace, mercy, or forgiving love that reciprocates that striving.[188] Support for and objections to all these views can be derived from the work itself and from Goethe's own observations – always assuming that the latter are authentic and accurately reported. The one thing that can be said with near certainty is that Faust is not saved by his own efforts alone, because of what he has achieved, or even because he was conscious of the 'right way'; that, as Goethe said, would be practical, enlightened rationalism, 'Aufklärung'.[189] It would, in any case, be dubiously dependent on a fundamentally positive evaluation of his treatment of Gretchen, of his activities in Act V, and indeed of his pact with Mephistopheles and all its implications.

Faust is not saved or justified by good works, nor is he saved or justified through faith. If he is saved by grace alone, then Goethe must have had more time for the Catholic theology of redemption and the doctrine of intercession than he ever displayed in his works or his life. Durrani, indeed, argues persuasively that Goethe is, at the end of Faust, 'provocatively employing a Christian motif which helps to draw attention to the fundamental discrepancy' between his treatment of Faust's development and either the Protestant justification through faith or the Roman Catholic doctrine of salvation through grace.[190]

The Faustian, or even 'Nietzschean', view of Faust's justification, that he is an amoral superman beyond good or evil, might appear to be consistent at least with the younger Goethe's titanism, with the attitudes of the early Urfaust version, and with Goethe's 'Shakespearian' dictum that what we call evil is only the obverse of good. But this view is not only repugnant to an age that has seen the practical excesses of amoral cults of the will; it also renders the last two scenes of the drama superfluous or absurd, and must ignore the evidence of Faust's confession to Sorge, indeed of any development on Faust's part from his early ruthless titanism. A further critical category that Mason does not consider, the Marxist view, is also embarrassed by the superfluous and mystical nature of the final scene: Faust's justification lies in his commitment to practical social activity in Act V.

There may be, as Mason remarks, something dissatisfying about a 'fifty-fifty' solution;[191] but it remains the stance for which there is the most compelling evidence in the text and in Goethe's own pronouncements – unless, that is, we admit quite frankly that Goethe painted himself into a corner and fudged the issues. Faust remains to the end a profoundly flawed and ambivalent individual, in whom activity and guilt, striving and error, are inseparable. Goethe wrote to Carl Ernst Schubarth in 1820 that Mephisto can only 'half' win his bet, while 'half the guilt' remains with Faust; but 'the old gentleman's prerogative of mercy intervenes and brings the whole to a most cheerful conclusion'.[192] This remark, to be sure, must be treated with some

caution – it was made some years before the final phase of work on
Faust II; its tone is not entirely serious; it was made in response to
a somewhat tortuous interpretation of Mephisto's two wagers by
Schubarth; and it is not entirely clear which of the two wagers Goethe
is referring to, the wager in heaven or Faust's wager with Mephisto.
However, in 1831 Goethe did insist that lines 11934–41 contain the key
to Faust's salvation, thereby indicating clearly enough his own 'fifty-fifty'
view of the question: 'in Faust selber eine immer höhere und reinere
Tätigkeit bis ans Ende, und von oben die ihm zu Hilfe kommende
ewige Liebe' ('in Faust himself an ever higher and purer activity to the
end, and from above eternal love coming to his aid').[193]

There are three distinct, but scarcely separable, issues involved in
Faust's salvation – the wager, or more properly the arrangement or
agreement, between the Lord and Mephisto in the 'Prologue in
Heaven'; Faust's wager with, or more properly his challenge to,
Mephisto; and Faust's pact or contract with the devil. In terms of the
first issue, Mephisto has not succeeded in seducing Faust's spirit from
its 'Urquell'; he has not dragged Faust down his path by corrupting him
beyond redemption. In terms of the second, he has not reduced him to
a state of torpid self-satisfaction, deluded him with pleasures, or made
him, in so many words, bid the passing moment stay. He has certainly
brought Faust to his 'highest moment', at which point Faust is ready to
die; but Faust is now in any case in extreme old age, and he remains
indifferent, as he was at the very start of his career with Mephisto, to the
fate of his soul – Faust has lived his life without any implicit or explicit
reference on his part to the 'beyond'. This is not to say that Faust's
career on earth has no bearing on his salvation; only that Faust's
perspective is not that of the Lord, of the dramatist, or of the spectator –
it is not Faust who has the final judgement on the matter.

By resisting the devil's nihilism to the end, by refusing to capitulate to
his sterile cynicism, by his commitment to dynamic and restless effort,
Faust has left himself open to salvation, which is given irrespective of
the real or illusory, the lasting or ephemeral, nature of his achievements. His constant and tireless commitment to effort does not
expunge, but it qualifies, the ethical debits of his career; even then,
however, the issue is still in the balance. The angels' words are 'Wer
immer strebend sich bemüht,/Den können wir erlösen': 'Whoever
strives with ceaseless effort, him we *can* redeem' – not 'him we *will*
redeem', or 'he will be redeemed'. The loving grace that is the final and
crucial factor in Faust's salvation is also the force that cancels Faust's
pact with the devil and renders Mephisto's document null and void. It is
certainly difficult to share unreservedly Goethe's reported description

of Faust's career as 'an ever higher and purer activity to the end', when one of his last acts is to be implicated in the murder of Philemon and Baucis; but Faust is not to be perpetually damned because of this crime, any more than he is to be saved because he renounced magic or devoted himself to good works. Goethe's affirmation of Faust's life is based on a very much broader view of his imperfect striving and his flawed humanity.

Goethe evidently sought to reconcile his secular humanist instincts and his emotional, even mystical, instincts in the issue of Faust's salvation; whether he successfully or satisfactorily synthesized the two will remain a matter of critical debate. He clearly felt that Faust's life on earth was to be affirmed in spite of everything; but he also felt that this affirmation was beyond human legal or ethical judgements. This is why he used the Christian iconography and imagery, the doctrine of intercession and the terminology of love and grace as poetic vehicles or metaphors for a higher sanction, and also why he claimed that this understanding of Faust's salvation was 'in accord' with our religious ideas; that is not to say, however, that it is identical with them. For his affirmation of grace through love, through 'das Ewig-Weibliche', the figure of Mary was more suited to his purpose than the ironic 'old gentleman' of the 'Prologue in Heaven' or than the figure of Christ; Goethe had always taken a very wary view not so much of Christ himself but of the crucifixion symbolism that is inseparable from the doctrine of redemption through Christ's blood.

Goethe's Faust does not represent all humanity, he is not Everyman; he represents an exceptional individual who shares, and rages against, human limitations. He does not represent Goethe; but he is a representative, even emblematic, figure of the age of Goethe, whose career has broad but distinct parallels to Goethe's own first-hand and vicarious experience. He is neither an exemplary ideal figure nor an exemplary warning figure; Goethe has exploited the ironies and ambivalences inherent in the figure and the legend of Faust, which even the Lutheran authors of the Volksbuch versions, for all their strident orthodoxy, could not entirely suppress, and he has used them as a structural principle underlying his work. Faust's salvation, as Goethe insisted, is not an idea that informs the whole work, or each particular scene of the work; it is only the final and most striking of the ironies and paradoxes of the figure and theme of Faust.

NOTES: CHAPTER 6

1 To Eckermann, date uncertain (Biedermann 4. 305–6).
2 Conversation of 11 Mar. 1832 (Biedermann 4. 441).

3   'Pandora', line 957 (GA. 6. 439).

4   'Versuch einer Witterungslehre' (GA. 17. 639).

5   To Eckermann, 1 Oct. 1827 (Biedermann 3. 460).

6   GA. 5. 558.

7   GA. 3. 737–8.

8   For a lucid account of the scandal, see Stefan Zweig, *Marie Antoinette*, pp. 195–250.

9   *Briefe*, HA. 1. 365.

10 See Dieter Borchmeyer, *Höfische Gesellschaft und französische Revolution bei Goethe. Adliges und bürgerliches Wertsystem im Urteil der Weimarer Klassik*, pp. 311 ff.; Marlis Mehra, 'Goethes Groß-Cophta und das zeitgenössische Lustspiel um 1790'.

11 'Maximen und Reflexionen', no. 480 (GA. 9. 560).

12 Pierre Grappin, 'Zur Gestalt des Kaisers in "Faust II"', p. 112.

13 Friedrich Gundolf, *Goethe*, p. 763.

14 Emrich, *Die Symbolik von Faust II*, pp. 176 ff. See also Ulrich Maché, 'Goethes Faust als Plutus und Dichter'. Against this interpretation, see Mommsen, *Natur- und Fabelreich in Faust II*, p. 244; Boyle, '"Du ahnungsloser Engel du!"', pp. 137, 147.

15 Schlaffer, *Faust Zweiter Teil* pp. 79–98.

16 Thomas Höhle and Heinz Hamm, 'Faust. Der Tragödie zweiter Teil', pp. 58 ff.

17 H. H. Borcherdt, 'Die Mummenschanz im zweiten Teil des "Faust". Versuch einer Deutung', pp. 303 ff. See also Paul Requadt, 'Die Figur des Kaisers im "Faust II"'.

18 'Hermann und Dorothea', 9th canto, lines 262–5, 271–4 (GA. 3. 241–2).

19 See Katharina Mommsen, *Goethe und 1001 Nacht*, pp. 222 ff.

20 Borcherdt, 'Die Mummenschanz im zweiten Teil des "Faust"', pp. 303–4; Requadt, 'Die Figur des Kaisers im "Faust II"', p. 171.

21 'The Obsolescence of Oracles', in *Plutarch's Moralia*, Vol. 5, trans. Frank Cole Babbitt (London 1936), p. 417.

22 To Eckermann, 10 Jan. 1830 (Biedermann 4. 188).

23 *Faust. A Tragedy*, ed. Hamlin, p. 328.

24 See E. M. Butler, 'Goethe and Cagliostro', p. 25.

25 Many of the motifs of this ceremony are also found in the 'Egyptian Lodge' ritual of Graf Rostro in Act III, scene 9, of *Der Groß-Cophta*: the temple, music, incense, a tripod that rises out of the floor, even the 'imperious gesture' of Faust after line 6293 (see GA. 6. 630 ff.).

26 See M. G. Druian, 'A Note on Faust II, ll. 6487–6500'.

27 *Faust. A Tragedy*, ed. Hamlin, p. 331.

28 To Eckermann, 6 Dec. 1829 (Biedermann 4. 178).

29 Arthur Schopenhauer, *The World as Will and Representation*, trans. E. F. J. Payne (New York, 1969), Vol. 1, pp. 3–4 and *passim*.

30 Letters to Jacobi of 23 May 1794 and to Voigt of 10 Apr. 1795 (*Briefe*, HA. 2. 177, 195). See also 'Fichtes Wissenschaftslehre' (GA. 2. 517); 'Tag- und Jahreshefte 1794' (GA. 11. 636).

31 *Faust. A Tragedy*, ed. Hamlin, p. 331.

32 Lohmeyer, *Faust und die Welt*, pp. 174 ff.

33 To Eckermann, 16 Dec. 1829 (Biedermann 4. 180).

34 Hans Mayer, 'Der Famulus Wagner und die moderne Wissenschaft', p. 200.
35 Otto Höfler, Homunculus – eine Satire auf A. W. Schlegel. Goethe und die Romantik.
36 Hellmut Döring, 'Homunculus', p. 194.
37 Höhle and Hamm, 'Faust. Der Tragödie zweiter Teil', p. 67.
38 Schlaffer, Faust Zweiter Teil, pp. 108–9, 113 and passim.
39 Atkins, Goethe's Faust, pp. 149 ff.
40 First published in Goethes Faust, ed. Heinrich Düntzer (Leipzig, 1857), p. 525.
41 See conversations with Falk of 25 Jan. 1813 (Biedermann 2. 169 ff.); with Eckermann of 11 Mar. 1828 (Biedermann 3. 495–6), 1 Sept. 1829 (Biedermann 4. 163) and 3 Mar. 1830 (Biedermann 4. 221–2); letter to Zelter of 19 Mar. 1827 (Briefe, HA. 4. 219).
42 To Eckermann, 16 Dec. 1829 (Biedermann 4. 180).
43 Letter to Karl August, 3 Nov. 1786 (Briefe, HA. 2. 16).
44 To Eckermann, 21 Feb. 1831 (Biedermann 4. 334–5).
45 To Eckermann, 2 Apr. 1829 (Biedermann 4. 81).
46 Lucan, Pharsalia, vi. 507 ff.
47 Jantz, The Form of Faust, pp. 157 ff.
48 Lucan, Pharsalia, vi. 395 ff.
49 Benjamin Hederich, Gründliches mythologisches Lexikon.
50 GA. 5. 581 (no. 89).
51 Hederich, Gründliches mythologisches Lexikon, s.v. Helena, col. 1222.
52 GA. 5. 571.
53 See Mommsen, Natur- und Fabelreich in Faust II, pp. 134 ff.
54 To Eckermann, 15 Jan. 1827 (Biedermann 3. 319).
55 See GA. 11. 507 ff.; GA. 2. 82.
56 See e.g. Goethes Faust, ed. Witkowski, Vol. 2, p. 340; Diener, Fausts Weg zu Helena, pp. 322 ff.; Lohmeyer, Faust und die Welt, p. 222; Emrich, Die Symbolik von Faust II, pp. 269 ff.
57 Diener, Fausts Weg zu Helena, pp. 490 ff.
58 GA. 5. 570–1.
59 See Momme Mommsen, 'Zu Vers 7782 f. der "Klassischen Walpurgisnacht"'.
60 For discussion of Goethe's attitudes to vulcanism and neptunism, see Diener, Fausts Weg zu Helena, pp. 411 ff. and 440 ff.; Mommsen, Natur- und Fabelreich in Faust II, pp. 190 ff.
61 For an interpretation of the Seismos allegory in terms of Greek political history, see Eva A. Meyer, Politische Symbolik bei Goethe, pp. 75–83.
62 GA. 9. 472 ff.
63 See Diener, Fausts Weg zu Helena, p. 422; Schlaffer, Faust Zweiter Teil, p. 88.
64 See John R. Williams, 'Die Rache der Kraniche. Goethe, Faust II und die Julirevolution'.
65 Karl Kerényi, Das ägäische Fest. Erläuterungen zur Szene 'Felsbuchten des ägäischen Meers' in Goethes Faust II.
66 On the lunar symbolism of this scene, see John R. Williams, 'The Festival of Luna: a Study of the Lunar Symbolism in Goethe's Klassische Walpurgisnacht'.
67 F. W. Schelling, 'Über die Gottheiten von Samothrake' (1815), in Schellings Werke, ed. Manfred Schröter (Munich, 1927), Vol. 4, pp. 721–45.

68 See Kerényi, *Das ägäische Fest*, p. 54; Diener, *Fausts Weg zu Helena*, pp. 511–12; Katharina Mommsen, *Natur- und Fabelreich in Faust II*, pp. 210–11.

69 Atkins, *Goethe's Faust*, p. 189.

70 See Wilhelm Hertz, 'Der Schluß der "Klassischen Walpurgisnacht"', p. 296; Atkins, 'Goethe, Calderón and *Faust II*', p. 96; Swana L. Hardy, *Goethe, Calderón und die romantische Theorie des Dramas*, p. 184.

71 'Winckelmann und sein Jahrhundert' (GA. 13. 421).

72 Emrich, *Die Symbolik von Faust II*, p. 301.

73 Mommsen, *Natur- und Fabelreich in Faust II*, pp. 183 ff. and *passim*.

74 See Hilda M. Brown, 'Goethe in the Underworld: Proserpina/Persephone', p. 154.

75 See Von Wiese, *Die deutsche Tragödie von Lessing bis Hebbel*, Vol. 1, p. 183; Kerényi, *Das ägäische Fest*, p. 69; Diener, *Fausts Weg zu Helena*, p. 601; White, *Names and Nomenclature in Goethe's 'Faust'*, pp. 113 ff.

76 Boyle, '"Du ahnungsloser Engel du!"', p. 119.

77 Williams, 'Festival of Luna', pp. 659 ff. See also Durrani, *Faust and the Bible*, pp. 140, 147, 172.

78 Letters to Wilhelm von Humboldt and Sulpiz Boisserée of 22 Oct. 1826 (*Briefe*, HA. 4. 205, 207).

79 GA. 5. 574.

80 GA. 5. 583 (no. 93).

81 GA. 5. 559–60.

82 See Johanna Schmidt, 'Sparta-Mistra. Forschungen über Goethes Faustburg', pp. 147 ff.; Richard Hauschild, 'Mistra, die Faustburg Goethes'.

83 Steven Runciman, *Mistra: Byzantine Capital of the Peloponnese*, p. 148.

84 ibid., p. 27.

85 GA. 5. 583 (no. 95).

86 See Emrich, *Die Symbolik von Faust II*, pp. 333–4; Lohmeyer, *Faust und die Welt*, p. 311.

87 Letter to von Humboldt of 22 Oct. 1826 (*Briefe*, HA. 4. 205).

88 Wilhelm Emrich, 'Das Rätsel der Faust-II-Dichtung', p. 218. For a differing interpretation, see Walter Müller-Seidel, 'Lynkeus. Lyrik und Tragik in Goethes Faust', pp. 87 ff.

89 Schlaffer, *Faust Zweiter Teil*, pp. 121–3.

90 Lohmeyer, *Faust und die Welt*, pp. 319 ff.

91 Letter of 9 Nov. 1814 (*Briefe*, HA. 3. 281).

92 GA. 12. 572 ff.

93 'Von deutscher Baukunst' (GA. 13. 25).

94 For a fuller analysis of the prosody of this scene, see below, pp. 226 ff.

95 'Behramgur, sagt man, hat den Reim erfunden' (GA. 3. 360–1).

96 *Faust. A Tragedy*, ed. Hamlin, p. 239.

97 Julius Goebel, 'Traces of the Wars of Liberation in the Second Part of Faust', pp. 202 ff.

98 See Hauschild, 'Mistra, die Faustburg Goethes', p. 15. Lohmeyer sees a reference to the Catalonian company not in lines 9446–9 but in lines 9468–9 (*Faust und die Welt*, pp. 332–3).

99 See Runciman, *Mistra*, pp. 17 ff.; Hauschild, 'Mistra, die Faustburg Goethes', pp. 11 ff.

100 Lohmeyer, *Faust und die Welt*, p. 333.
101 *Faust. A Tragedy*, ed. Bayard Taylor, p. 601.
102 Schlaffer, *Faust Zweiter Teil*, p. 111.
103 Schmidt, 'Sparta-Mistra', p. 154.
104 Horst Rüdiger, 'Weltliteratur in Goethes "Helena"', pp. 187 ff.
105 Emrich, *Die Symbolik von Faust II*, p. 347.
106 See M. Kay Flavell, '"Arkadisch frei sei unser Glück": the Myth of the Golden Age in Eighteenth-century Germany', pp. 18–19.
107 See Hederich, *Gründliches mythologisches Lexikon*, s.v. Euphorion, col. 1073.
108 To Eckermann, 20 Dec. 1829 (Biedermann 4. 184) and 5 July 1827 (Biedermann 3. 407–8).
109 See Joseph Müller-Blattau, 'Der Zauberflöte Zweiter Teil. Ein Beitrag zum Thema Goethe und Mozart', p. 178; Erich W. Skwara, 'Homunculus und Euphorion'; Wilhelm Resenhöfft, 'Goethes Euphorion: August von Goethe'.
110 For a particularly negative assessment of Euphorion, see Jantz, *Form of Faust*, pp. 35 ff.; and Hellmut Döring, '"Der Schöngestalt bedenkliche Begleiter". Betrachtungen zu *Faust II*. 3'.
111 See e.g. Höhle and Hamm, 'Faust. Der Tragödie zweiter Teil', pp. 74–5; Karl-Heinz Hahn, 'Faust und Helena oder die Aufhebung des Zwiespalts zwischen Klassikern und Romantikern', p. 132.
112 Lohmeyer, *Faust und die Welt*, p. 342.
113 See Emrich, *Die Symbolik von Faust II*, pp. 350 ff.; Oskar Seidlin, 'Goethes Zauberflöte', pp. 51 ff.
114 To Eckermann, 29 Jan. 1827 (Biedermann 3. 334).
115 Karl Reinhardt, 'Goethe and Antiquity', pp. 278–9.
116 Lohmeyer, *Faust und die Welt*, pp. 352–3.
117 *Goethes Faust*, ed. Witkowski, Vol. 2, p. 374.
118 Horst Römer, 'Idylle und Idyllik in Goethes *Faust II*', p. 144.
119 Atkins, *Goethe's Faust*, p. 224.
120 Lohmeyer, *Faust und die Welt*, p. 355. For a recent Freudian interpretation of this section, see Scholz, *Die beschädigte Seele des großen Mannes*, p. 160.
121 Conversation of 20 Nov. 1824 (Biedermann 3. 142).
122 To Eckermann, 5 July 1827 (Biedermann 3. 408).
123 Conversation of 24 Feb. 1825 (Biedermann 3. 161–5).
124 See Mommsen, *Natur- und Fabelreich in Faust II*, p. 247.
125 See T. J. Reed, *The Classical Centre: Goethe and Weimar 1775–1832*, pp. 255 ff.
126 Byron, *Childe Harold's Pilgrimage*, canto 2, 84.
127 See John R. Williams, 'Faust's Classical Education: Goethe's Allegorical Treatment of Faust and Helen of Troy', p. 38.
128 GA. 5. 610 (no. 196).
129 GA. 17. 639 ff. On Goethe's cloud-symbolism, see Karl Lohmeyer, 'Das Meer und die Wolken in den beiden letzten, Akten des "Faust"'; Joachim Müller, '"Meiner Wolke Tragewerk". Fausts Abscheid von Helena'; Albrecht Schöne, 'Über Goethes Wolkenlehre'.
130 GA. 5. 588 (no. 106).
131 See 'Howards Ehrengedächtnis', lines 45–52 (Nimbus).
132 See John R. Williams, 'The Flatulence of Seismos: Goethe, Rabelais and the "Geranomachia"', p. 107.

133 'Wie man die Könige verletzt' (GA. 1. 665).

134 'Über den Granit' (GA. 17. 480–1).

135 'Versuch einer Witterungslehre' (GA. 17. 642–3).

136 Hans Rudolf Vaget, 'Faust, der Feudalismus und die Restauration', p. 348.

137 Boyle, 'The Politics of *Faust II*': Another Look at the Stratum of 1831', p. 32.

138 'Die natürliche Tochter', line 32 (GA. 6. 316).

139 See Schuchard, 'Julirevolution, St. Simonismus und die Faustpartien von 1831'; Boyle, 'Politics of *Faust II*'; Williams, 'Die Rache der Kraniche'.

140 Letter to Knebel, 12 Sept. 1830 (Briefe, HA. 4. 394).

141 Grappin, 'Zur Gestalt des Kaisers in "Faust II"', pp. 113 ff.

142 See Vincent Cronin, *Napoleon*, p. 342.

143 Wilhelm Mommsen, *Die politischen Anschauungen Goethes*, pp. 135 ff.; Ilse Peters, 'Das Napoleonbild Goethes in seiner Spätzeit (1813–1832)', pp. 144–5.

144 Conversation of 10 Feb. 1830 (Biedermann 4. 207).

145 Emrich, *Die Symbolik von Faust II*, p. 379; Lamport, 'Synchrony and Diachrony in *Faust*', p. 128.

146 Atkins, *Goethe's Faust*, p. 240.

147 As argued e.g. by Requadt, 'Die Figur des Kaisers im "Faust II"', p. 171. For an opposing view, see Deirdre Vincent, '"Die Tat ist alles": A Reconsideration of the Significance of *Faust II*, Act Four'.

148 Boyle, 'Politics of *Faust II*', p. 29.

149 See Beutler in GA. 5. 816.

150 Boyle, 'Politics of *Faust II*', p. 34.

151 'Every kingdom divided against itself will be brought to desolation; for its princes have become the companions of thieves' (Luke 11: 17; Isaiah 1: 23). See GA. 10. 175.

152 Boyle, 'Politics of *Faust II*', p. 36.

153 Regine Otto and Paul-Gerhard Wenzlaff (eds), *Goethe in vertraulichen Briefen seiner Zeitgenossen* (Berlin, 1979), Vol. 2, pp. 592–3.

154 Conversation of 13 Dec. 1813 (Biedermann 2. 214–5).

155 See e.g. Emrich, *Die Symbolik von Faust II*, pp. 386–7.

156 GA. 5. 591 (no. 110).

157 'Kampagne in Frankreich' (GA. 12. 423–4).

158 Thomas Metscher, 'Faust und die Ökonomie. Ein literarhistorischer Essay', p. 85.

159 To Eckermann, 6 June 1831 (Biedermann 4. 374).

160 See Schlaffer, *Faust Zweiter Teil*, p. 129. Vaget, however, stresses Faust's continuing commitment to restored feudalism ('Faust, der Feudalismus und die Restauration', p. 349).

161 See letter to Zelter of 6 June 1825 (Briefe, HA. 4. 146); conversation with Eckermann of 21 Feb. 1827 (Biedermann 3. 349–50).

162 Letter to von Humboldt of 17 Mar. 1832 (Briefe, HA. 4. 481).

163 To Eckermann, 6 June 1831 (Biedermann 4. 374); see Ovid, *Metamorphoses* viii. 628–720.

164 Jantz, Form of Faust, pp. 49 ff.

165 See Mason, *Goethe's Faust*, p. 334.

166 Staiger, *Goethe*, Vol. 3, pp. 434–5.

167 Mason, *Goethe's Faust*, pp. 335–6.

168 Emrich, *Die Symbolik von Faust II*, p. 400.

169 HA. 3. 618 (8th edn, 1967).

170 Mason, *Goethe's Faust* p. 338.

171 Durrani, *Faust and the Bible*, pp. 163–4.

172 See Hamm, *Goethes Faust*, pp. 227–8.

173 Boyle, 'Politics of *Faust II*', p. 5.

174 See Schuchard, 'Julirevolution, St. Simonismus und die Faustpartien von 1831'.

175 Heinz Hamm, 'Julirevolution, Saint-Simonismus und Goethes abschließende Arbeit am "Faust"'.

176 Vaget, 'Faust, der Feudalismus und die Restauration'.

177 WA. I. 15, ii. 157.

178 See Mason, *Goethe's Faust*, pp. 345 ff.; Emrich, *Die Symbolik von Faust II*, pp. 399–400.

179 To Eckermann, 6 May 1827 (Biedermann 3. 394) and 6 June 1831 (Biedermann 4. 374).

180 Jantz, *Form of Faust*, pp. 27–8.

181 GA. 5. 592 (no. 112).

182 Durrani, *Faust and the Bible*, p. 168.

183 See *Goethes Faust*, ed. Witkowski, Vol. 2, p. 512.

184 See Lohmeyer, 'Das Meer und die Wolken in den beiden letzten Akten des "Faust"', pp. 114 ff.; Schöne, 'Über Goethes Wolkenlehre', pp. 36 ff.

185 Conversation of 6 June 1831 (Biedermann 4. 374).

186 WA. I. 15, ii. 165.

187 See above, pp. 145, 162.

188 Mason, *Goethe's Faust*, pp. 365 ff.

189 Conversation with Friedrich Förster of 1828 (Biedermann 3. 516).

190 Durrani, *Faust and the Bible*, pp. 172–3.

191 Mason, *Goethe's Faust*, p. 370.

192 Letter of 3 Nov. 1820 (*Briefe*, HA. 3. 493–4).

193 To Eckermann, 6 June 1831 (Biedermann 4. 374).

CHAPTER 7

A Note on the Metre and Verse Forms of Goethe's *Faust*

The prosodic scope and variety of Goethe's *Faust* is at least as great as its thematic scope and variety; there can scarcely be another work with a greater profusion of metrical forms. Goethe, the most metrically versatile of German poets, used verse forms with highly conscious artistry, and a full understanding of *Faust* is hardly possible without an awareness of that artistry; above all in the central classical sections of *Faust* II, the symbolic use of verse is crucial to its understanding. Space allows here little more than a descriptive survey of the principal verse forms of the work.[1]

In so far as there is a standard or basic verse form in *Faust*, it is often assumed to be *Knittelvers*, which translates rather loosely as doggerel.[2] For the *Urfaust*, Goethe adapted this unfashionable, indeed widely despised, form (though not, oddly enough, by Gottsched) from Hans Sachs – no doubt equally for its sixteenth-century and for its popular cultural associations. However, not only does Goethe take considerable licence with his *Knittelvers* compared with the Hans Sachs model; he also mixes it with a less 'rough-hewn', extremely versatile, form known as *Madrigalvers*. The strict *Knittelvers* of Hans Sachs consists of four-beat lines of eight or nine syllables, rhymed in pairs; but Goethe and Schiller, in *Faust* and *Wallensteins Lager*, draw on a freer *Knittelvers* tradition, which allows any number of unstressed syllables (*Senkungen*) from none to five between the four stressed syllables (*Hebungen*), and thus varies the syllabic length of the line. *Madrigalvers* was a sung Italian form that became popular in Germany during the late seventeenth and early eighteenth centuries. It is primarily iambic (consistently so as used by Goethe), but is variable in length, including two-, three-, four-, five-, or even six-beat lines; it is also very free with its rhyme-scheme, rhyming aabb, abab, abba, etc., and even incorporating single unrhymed lines (*Waisen*).

Both forms, Knittelvers and Madrigalvers, go to make up the basic verse form of Faust. Faust's opening monologue, for example, is in Knittelvers as far as line 401, at which point the rhyme-scheme varies, though regular four-beat lines continue up to line 429. At this point, Madrigalvers takes over with a mixture of four-beat lines, iambic pentameters and an occasional six-beat alexandrine. Heusler, who coined the term Faustvers for Goethe's iambic Madrigalvers, claims that even in the Urfaust true Knittelvers accounts for only one-third of the text; in Faust I, it takes up only about one-tenth. And in Faust II, Heusler allows only the Satyr's lines 5829–39 as strict Knittelvers[3] – though Kurt May also counts in the previous six lines of the Fauns.[4] It is not always easy in practice to detect just where the one form gives way to the other; in the scene 'Spazier-gang', for example, lines 2815–55 are classifiable as Knittelvers, but the opening lines 2805–14 have the varied metre and rhymes of Madrigalvers. Indeed, Goethe himself, in Dichtung und Wahrheit, mentioned writing occasional poetry in a metre 'that hovered between Knittelvers and Madrigal'.[5] Nor is it any easier when Madrigalvers gives way to free verse, as for example at lines 468 and 3432. The general perception of the difference between Knittelvers on the one hand and Madrigalvers or Faustvers on the other is that the former is bumpy, jerky and short-winded, due to the irregular 'filling' of unstressed syllables, while the latter is smoother in cadence, even if it is less regular in rhyme or in the number of stressed syllables, and therefore considerably more flexible in length.

If scarcely one-third of the Urfaust is in true Knittelvers, in the Fragment and Faust I, Madrigalvers or Faustvers predominates still further, and there is a marked tendency in the new material towards longer lines of pentameter, and even towards sporadic groups of six-beat alexandrines. Regular passages of rhymed iambic pentameter occur occasionally in more formal or sententious passages of Faust I – though as blank verse only in lines 3217–50, in the 'Wald und Höhle' monologue composed in Italy concurrently with Iphigenie and Torquato Tasso. In rhymed form, it occurs as ottava rima in the 'Zueignung' (and in the unpublished 'Abschied'); this stanza form was generally reserved by Goethe for solemn or elegiac material. It is also notable that the sententious first speech of the Writer in the 'Prelude in the Theatre' (lines 59–74) forms two stanzas of ottava rima, no doubt for ironical effect. Iambic penta-meter also occurs as terza rima in the opening scene of Faust II (lines 4679–4727).

Only one of the prose scenes of the Urfaust survives in that form into the final version, as 'Trüber Tag. Feld'; the following scene 'Nacht. Offen Feld' is generally regarded as free verse, though it is a marginal judgement. 'Auerbachs Keller' and 'Kerker' were recast into Faustvers with intercalated songs and, in the latter, free verse forms. Both the scenes in prose and the songs of the Urfaust are undoubtedly devices derived from Shakespeare, and Gretchen's distracted folksong in 'Kerker' very probably specifically from Ophelia's songs. Some of Gretchen's important monologues are written as songs, or at least in lyrical form. Her prayer in the 'Zwinger' scene is metrically more sophisticated than the simple strophic forms of 'Der König in Thule' and 'Meine Ruh' ist hin'; it combines folksong metre in lines 3608–15 with lines that echo the motifs, rhyme and metre of the medieval Stabat Mater sequence – an anticipation of the use of the Dies Irae sequence in the 'Dom' scene.

In Faust I, the lyrical intercalations are even more frequent than in the Urfaust. The Easter hymns of lines 737 ff.; the Beggar's and Soldiers' songs and the Peasants' ballad of 'Vor dem Tor'; the Spirit Choruses of the 'Studierzimmer' scenes; the satirical drinking songs of 'Auerbachs Keller'; the magic incantations, snatches and jingles of 'Hexenküche'; Mephisto's sardonic serenade of lines 3682–97, loosely adapted from Ophelia's St Valentine's Day song in Hamlet; the eerie antiphonal chanting and the Witches' quatrains of the 'Walpurgisnacht' and the satirical quatrains of the 'Walpurgisnachtstraum' – all these forms elaborate the already highly figured and lyrical text of the drama.

As striking as anything else in Faust I are, however, the points at which the verse breaks down into free forms: Faust's conjuration of the Erdgeist (lines 468–81), the Erdgeist's own lines (501–9), the conjuration of Mephistopheles (1271 ff.), the Spirit Chorus and Mephisto in lines 1607–34, Faust's 'catechism' to Gretchen (3431 ff.), and Gretchen's disjointed and distracted verse in the 'Kerker' scene. Most vivid and most theatrical of all is undoubtedly the operatic 'Dom' scene, with its alternation of three different lyrical registers: the rising panic of Gretchen's voice against the insistent insinuations of the Evil Spirit, both in free rhythms, counterpointed by the eschatology of the Dies Irae sequence.

Something should be said here about Goethe's use of short metrical lines in Faust. A distinction should be made between the lines of the Spirit Chorus of the first 'Studierzimmer' scene (1447–1505), which are very regular adonics (dactyl + trochee, -vv -v), and the Easter hymns of the earlier 'Nacht' scene (lines 737 ff.). The latter are also dactylic; but they are rather unconventional dactyls. In particular, Goethe tends on occasion to stress an unexpected final syllable, as in lines 789, 791, 794, 798 and 806; moreover, he reinforces this eccentric stress by rhyming a more conventionally stressed syllable – 'zurück' and 'Glück' (lines 794 and 796), 'Schoß' and 'los' (798 and 800), 'nah' and 'da' (806 and 807).

This flexible use of dactylic metre has been dubbed 'false dactyls' by Heusler;[6] and, while the Easter hymns are the only instance of such metre in *Faust* I, Goethe uses false dactyls with increasing frequency in *Faust* II – and with increasing flexibility and subtlety: in the Euphorion episode (9745 ff., 9811 ff., 9863 ff., etc.), and above all in the heavenly choruses of the 'Grablegung' (lines 11745 ff.) and 'Bergschluchten' scenes (11844 ff., 11926 ff., 11954 ff., etc.). In the final scene, above all, these passages cannot possibly be scanned or spoken as two-beat dactylic lines, as most of the lines of the Easter hymns of *Faust* I might be; the tendency is even more towards an eccentric third stress on the final syllable: 'Waldung, sie schwankt heran' (11844), 'Höhle, die tiefste, schützt' (11849), 'Siedender Schmerz der Brust' (11856), 'Uns bleibt ein Erdenrest' (11954), 'Und wär' er von Asbest' (11956), 'Löset die Flocken los' (11985), 'Schon ist er schön und groß' (11987), etc. Ultimately, however, it must be admitted that these lines defy regular scansion, and that they frequently allow secondary stresses at different points in the line – even if it is difficult to accept Heusler's definition of them as four-beat lines.[7]

If *Faust* I contained a broad variety of metrical and verse forms, *Faust* II is, in Wagenknecht's phrase, even more of a 'metrical pandemonium'.[8] The second part is also characterized in Act III by the striking use of classicizing metrical and strophic forms. In the opening scene, 'Anmutige Gegend', the elves, led by Ariel, sing in four-beat trochaic strophes (identified by Atkins as the metre of Calderón and Golden Age Spanish drama)[9] – except for Ariel's instructions of lines 4621–33, which are predominantly iambic pentameter, with occasional four-beat lines. The four stanzas of lines 4634–65, almost a complete lyric poem in themselves, are based on the four vigils of the night; and it is commonly believed, though there is no certain evidence, that Goethe originally indicated this in his manuscript by heading the stanzas respectively, in musical terms, 'Serenade', 'Notturno', 'Matutino' and 'Reveille'.[10]

Faust's awakening speech is, by contrast, in iambic pentameter with *terza rima* – the only instance of this verse form in *Faust*; and Kayser suggests that Goethe chose this repetitive yet fluid form as an appropriate vehicle for Faust's imagery of stability and flux, sun and waterfall, for the synthesis of polarities in the 'changing permanence' of the rainbow.[11] But with the shift of the action to the political milieu of the Imperial Palace, *Faustvers* takes over as a mixture of four- and five-beat lines. This is sustained in the Herald's opening speech of the 'Mummenschanz', or masquerade, but we are then pitched into the bewildering metrical variety of the carnival masquerade. The sung choruses of the Flower-girls, Gardeners and their wares are four-beat trochaics, and the Herald adapts his speech to their forms (lines 5108–15). The strophes of the Mother (5178–98) are mixed four- and three-beat trochaics; and these give way to the iambic two-beat lines of the Woodcutters, Pulcinelle and Parasites – each group with its own distinctive rhythmic character. Trochaic metre resumes with the Drunkard, and continues with the Graces and the Fates, briefly broken by the quatrain of the Satirist, which has the informal metrical style of some of Goethe's 'gentle polemics', the *Zahme Xenien*. The Herald, again adapting his metre to that of the allegorical figures, introduces the Furies in quatrains of iambic pentameter; the Furies speak in the same metre, with the stark exception of Tisiphone, whose lines are more laconic four-beat trochaics. After a brief switch to the Herald's iambics (5393–406), trochaics are sustained by Fear, Hope and Prudence until the entry of Mephistopheles as Zoilo-Thersites, who reintroduces the *Faustvers*. This is broken by the trochaic forms introduced by the crowd at line 5484, which are continued by the Herald and the Boy Charioteer until line 5537, where the *Faustvers* resumes and now, with some exceptions, dominates the rest of the scene. In other words, the trochaic metres are, with the exception of the Gnomes' quatrains (5898–913) and Faust-Plutus' concluding lines (5970–86), largely confined to the early allegorical masks of the carnival, culminating with the entry of the Boy Charioteer.

Otherwise notable in the rest of the scene is the regularizing of the *Faustvers* into iambic pentameter at Faust's solemn farewell to the Boy Charioteer (lines 5689–714). From now on, four-beat lines dominate, with occasional sections of pentameter, until the verse breaks into two-beat rhythms with the entry of the Fauns, after which *Knittelvers* takes over with the entry of the Wild Hunt, broken by the pentameters of Plutus (5807–10, 5914–19), by the two-beat lines of Fauns and Nymphs (5819–22, 5872–5), and by the trochees of the Gnomes (5898–913). Finally, Faust-Plutus' concluding incantation is, appropriately enough, stylized in heavy trochaics.

The remaining scenes of Act I are, in contrast, predominantly in iambic pentameters, with only occasional 'lapses' into the more informal four-beat form of *Faustvers* – which May characterizes as the 'parlando' dialogue style of much of Act I. At the same time, May suggests, four-beat lines are used here to express a state of agitation, of growing excitement or tension – as in lines 6045–51, 6189–92 and 6247–8, and most strikingly of all in lines 6496–7 and 6499. The stichomythia of lines 6145–72 is notable, though whether it is, as May suggests, an anticipation of later classicizing devices in Act III is

uncertain.[12] It has also been interestingly claimed that Faust's encomium to Helen (lines 6487–500) is a clumsily executed Petrarchan
sonnet, indicating Faust's excitement at his first encounter with classical
beauty.[13]

The two opening scenes of Act II are metrically relatively unremarkable. *Faustvers*, appropriately enough for the return to Faust's Gothic
study, predominates, broken by the restless anapaests of the Insects'
Chorus (6592–603), and by the trochaic opening lines of the Famulus
(6620–33) and the Baccalaureus (6689–720). Again, there is a broad
tendency to use longer lines of pentameter for more serious or
mock-serious passages (6793–6806, 6903–17), as opposed to the more
informal use of four-beat lines; but this distinction is not consistently
maintained.

With the 'Klassische Walpurgisnacht' a quite new metre is introduced
for Erichtho's opening monologue: the heavy cadences of unrhymed,
end-stopped, iambic six-beat lines that are the modern version of
trimeter, the metre of Greek tragedy that will later dominate the
opening scene of Act III. With the disappearance of Erichtho, however,
the classical metre also disappears, and after the alternate trochaic
chanting of Homunculus and Mephistopheles (lines 7040–55), *Faustvers*
takes over from the moment Faust emerges from his swoon, predominantly as pentameter. The songs and strophes of Sirens and Sphinxes
are distinguished by trochaic four-beat lines – though in their conver-
sational dialogue with Faust and Mephisto the Sphinxes also use the
'nordic' *Faustvers* form, as do the other mythological creatures. The scene
'Am unteren Peneios' is marked by shifting metrical patterns; the
opening four-beat trochaics of Peneios and Faust are followed by the
rocking short lines of the Nymphs tempting Faust to rest and dream.
Most critics would scan these lines (7263–70) as anapaests, but they are
better described as perfectly regular amphibrachs (v-v) – a form that will
recur towards the end of the 'Klassische Walpurgisnacht'. Faust's vision
of Helen's conception is clearly divided into a first section of four-beat
iambics describing Leda and her maids bathing, which changes at line
7295, with the arrival of Jupiter and his swans, to agitated trochaics. With
the entry of Chiron, *Faustvers* resumes for the rest of the scene.

The following scene, 'Am oberen Peneios wie zuvor', has even less
uniformity of metre. Trochaic metres dominate the first section up to
line 7675, broken by the *Faustvers* of Seismos in lines 7550–73, of the
Sphinxes in lines 7578–81, and of the Gryphons in lines 7602–5, while
the tiny creatures swarming in the wake of the earthquake speak in
short lines of restless dactyls. The second section, from line 7676, is
almost exclusively in *Faustvers*, except for the shorter dactylic lines of the

Lamiae (7696–709), and the breaking of the metre in Anaxagoras' apostrophe to the moon (7910–13).

The final scene of Act II, 'Felsbuchten des ägäischen Meers', is characterized not only by enormous metrical and rhythmic variety but also by a progressively freer use of metre; the verse form is an integral factor in the fluid and operatic marine thiasos that is itself a celebration of protean natural forms and metamorphosis. Especially towards the end of the scene, the *Faustvers* of the dialogue becomes swamped by the hymnic choruses and paeans of praise to Luna, to Galatea, to the sea and finally to the elements. The opening choruses are in the now familiar four-beat trochaics; after the *Faustvers* dialogue of lines 8082–159, the sea-creatures hymn the Cabiri in a fluid mixture of two- and three-beat iambic and trochaic forms that culminate in the operatic 'Allgesang' of lines 8217–18. The *Faustvers* dialogue resumes until the entry of the Telchines, whose four-beat amphibrachs (8275–84, 8289–302) give their hymns a rocking and flowing rhythm that recalls the shorter forms of the Nymphs in lines 7263 ff. The Sirens' trochees alternate with the *Faustvers* of the dialogue, until Nereus and Thales also take up the trochaic form (8347–58); and the Psylli and Marsi sing in a free and complex metrical pattern which May describes comprehensively as 'mixed iambic-dactyloanapaestic lines with a varying number of stresses'.[14]

The marine pageant moves towards its tumultuous climax in a rapidly changing medley of forms. The Dorides initially continue the Sirens' trochees, alternating with Nereus' iambics until lines 8416–23, when their exchanges with the sailors assume an iambic strophic form of four and three beats. Nereus' lines become more ecstatic at the approach of Galatea; two dactylic lines mark her appearance (8424–5), followed by freer mixed metres, which are taken up by Thales, three more dactylic lines (8442–4), and further mixed metres in lines 8445–57. After the *Singspiel* duet of Homunculus and Proteus, the 'marriage' of Homunculus with the ocean at the foot of Galatea's chariot is celebrated in emphatic, strongly dactylic lines with ecstatically sexual rhythms, which give way to the triumphant trochaic shouts of the eight-line finale.

The metrical contrast between the chaotic and jubilant polyphony of the marine pageant and the stately, regular cadences of the opening lines of Act III could not be greater. Helen, as Goethe indicated in his draft scenario, was to appear 'auf antik-tragischem Kothurn' ('on the cothurnus of ancient tragedy');[15] and accordingly she speaks in the 'lofty cothurnus style' of classical trimeter, in the language of Euripidean tragedy. This remains the basic metre of the dialogue of the first scene; but it is interrupted and varied by two further classicizing forms. The

Chorus of Panthalis and the Trojan women chant in choriambic odes, usually arranged in the form of strophe and antistrophe, which are metrically identical, followed by an epode in a different metrical pattern. Thus the opening speeches of the Chorus, alternating with Helen's trimeter, are structured as strophe (lines 8516–23), antistrophe (8560–7) and epode (8591–603). This pattern is repeated in lines 8610–37; and in lines 8697–753 the Chorus also recites a remarkably symmetrical series of responses which can be tabulated as: strophe 1 (8697–701), antistrophe 1 (8702–6); strophe 2 (8707–12), antistrophe 2 (8713–18); epode (8719–27); strophe 3 (8728–35), antistrophe 3 (8736–43); strophe 4 (8744–8), antistrophe 4 (8749–53). The third classicizing form used in this scene is a restless tetrameter, which from line 8909 alternates with the steady trimeter, and recurs sporadically throughout the scene (8909–29, 8957–61, 8966–70, 9067–70, 9122–6) – notably at moments of excitement or tension. The tensions of the dialogue are also reinforced by the devices of stichomythia (8810–25), by double or triple stichomythia (8850–81), and by line-splitting (8923–7).

The trimeter and the choriambic responses of the Chorus survive into the opening sections of the medieval 'Innerer Burghof' scene; but with the entry of Faust in his persona as a Frankish crusader, unrhymed iambic pentameter takes over. Oddly but appropriately, this strictly non-classical, indeed Shakespearian, form, which is nevertheless associated with the drama of Weimar Classicism, is here the classicizing verse form of the nordic barbarian Faust. It represents, as it were, the classical refinement of the Faustvers, which has throughout the first two acts in any case tended increasingly towards pentameter; it is the language of the modern philhellene Faust, mid-way between archaic trimeter, tetrameter and choriambic ode on the one hand and the free operatic rhymes and rhythms of the Euphorion episode on the other. Astonishingly, Helen at once replies in Faust's own metre (lines 9213 ff.); and the rhymed strophes of Lynceus, which Horst Rüdiger associates with the medieval Minnesang of Heinrich von Morungen, draw her attention to the seductive art of end-rhyme.[16] The rapprochement and the union of Helen and Faust, of Hellenic and Germanic, is prosodically symbolized by her adopting first Faust's metre and finally the device of end-rhyme (lines 9377–84) – which is intensified in lines 9411–18 by the addition of internal rhyming. From this point the verse is dominated by rhymed, modern strophic forms, as the severe classicism of the first part of the act gives way to what Goethe termed the 'operatic' or 'romantic' second half.[17] Certainly, classicizing forms by no means disappear entirely: Faust's lofty assumption of his role as Helen's protector is expressed in trimeter (9435–41); even Phorcyas reverts to trimeter in

lines 9574–81, her following exchanges with the Chorus are in trochaic
tetrameters (9582–628), and the Chorus also retains its unrhymed ode
forms up to line 9678. But the whole section from Euphorion's
appearance to his death (lines 9679–906) consists of an operatic medley
of rhymed verse, in which even the Chorus now adopts the modern
idiom of Faust, Helen and Euphorion: four-beat trochaics (9679–710
and *passim*) or iambic and dactylic lines that defy any regular metrical
analysis (9711 ff.), becoming more pronouncedly dactylic as Euphorion
joins the Chorus in dance rhythms (9745–66). At one point, even, in
lines 9821–6, there are radical rhythmic shifts within the same speech,
while in lines 9835–69 'false dactyls' enclose the four-beat trochaics of
lines 9851–62. The three speeches of lines 9870–90, similar in strophic
structure, are alternately iambic, trochaic and iambic/trochaic. A
quatrain of four-beat trochaic lines (9891–4) is followed by false dactyls
up to the pause after line 9906.

The threnody of the Chorus (lines 9907–38) sustains the four-beat
rhymed trochaics; but the subsequent prosody shows how the classical
and modern elements separate out quite distinctly after the death of
Euphorion. Helen and Panthalis revert to trimeter (9939 ff., 9962 ff.); the
Chorus to its choriambic odes; and Mephistopheles, after a solemn
passage of unrhymed iambic pentameter (9945–54), to seven lines of
rhymed *Faustvers* for his sardonic epitaph to Euphorion (9955–61). The
final dissolving of the Chorus into the elements is expressed in the
dynamic, restless eight-beat trochaics of tetrameter (9992 ff.).

Act IV is relatively undifferentiated, though it does have a distinct
tripartite structure, with unrhymed trimeter and rhymed alexandrines
enclosing a central section of *Faustvers*. The most striking initial feature is
that Faust's opening monologue (lines 10039–66) is in trimeter; his
farewell to Helen reflects the cultural afterglow of his classical experience. With the entry of Mephisto, however, whose seven-league boots
have carried him culturally and geographically north-westwards towards Germany, the familiar *Faustvers* resumes, and, with the exception
of the trochaic four-beat interventions of Messengers and Herald
(10385–92, 10399–406, and 10489–96), this form prevails until the final
scene in the Anti-Emperor's tent. Once again, there is a fairly, though by
no means entirely, consistent distinction between four-beat or mixed-
beat lines of *Faustvers*, comprising the greater part of the dialogue, and
the use of sustained passages of (rhymed) iambic pentameter for the
more formal or sententious set-piece speeches (10198–209, 10407 ff.).
The so-called *Erzämterszene* (lines 10849–11042), however, is entirely in
rhyming couplets of alexandrines: Goethe chooses the metre of the
German Baroque and of mid-eighteenth-century neo-classicism, which

was generally perceived by later writers as stilted and rhetorical, as the appropriate vehicle for the formal pomp and ceremony of neo-feudal restoration.

The fifth act, by contrast, is metrically more diversified. The first scene, 'Offene Gegend', is entirely in four-beat trochaics; the scene 'Palast' opens with uniformly iambic four-beat lines, interspersed with the heavy cadences of the shorter, mixed iambic and trochaic lines of Mephisto and the three thugs in lines 11189–218. The opening lines of Lynceus' hymn in the following scene (11288 ff.) are described by May as 'anapaestic-dactylic two-beat lines';[18] these give way at line 11304 to more urgent trochaics to describe the horrific vision of the fire, after which the dialogue reverts to four-beat *Faustvers*. The four grey women of 'Mitternacht' speak in restless dactylic rhythms; Faust's speeches are in *Faustvers*, which alternates with the four-beat trochaics of Sorge's dismal chanting, until she too adopts Faust's metre for her final lines (11495–8). The following scene is in *Faustvers*, except for the strophic songs of Mephisto and the Lemures. Lines 11531–8 are an adaptation of the gravedigger's song in Act V of *Hamlet* – though the rendering of 'crutch' in line 11536 where Shakespeare has 'clutch' suggests not that Goethe misread Shakespeare but rather that he derived his version directly from Shakespeare's own source, 'The Aged Lover Renounceth Love', attributed to Lord Vaux, which was printed in Bishop Percy's *Reliques of Ancient English Poetry* (I. ii. 2). The 'Grablegung' scene, after the Lemures' opening exchanges, which are also loosely from *Hamlet*, continues in *Faustvers*, alternating from line 11676 with the false dactyls of the Angels' Chorus.

The final 'Bergschluchten' scene, like the marine pageant and the Euphorion episode, offers a shifting and extremely varied metrical pattern, involving some sixteen changes of metre within 267 lines. The opening Chorus and the lines of Pater Ecstaticus (11844–65) are false dactyls, similar to, but distinct from, the Angels' Chorus of the previous scene: the dactylic pattern is more heavily obscured here, especially in the final syllables of the lines, and the rhymes are in couplets as opposed to the fluid rhyme-schemes of the Angels. The iambic four-beat strophes of Pater Profundus give way to the trochaics of Pater Seraphicus and the Blessed Boys; the Blessed Boys break into dactylic dance rhythms in lines 11926–33; the following Angels' lines are alternate four- and three-beat iambics; those of the Younger Angels are four-beat trochaics with consistently feminine endings; the More Perfected Angels have false dactyls, as do the Younger Angels in lines 11966 ff., the Blessed Boys, and Doctor Marianus up to line 11996. Doctor Marianus' hymn to the Mater Gloriosa shifts to alternating four- and three-beat trochaics, interrupted by seven lines of false dactyls (12013–19); the Chorus of Penitents (12032–6) is also largely dactylic, followed by the trochees of the supplication of the three women (12037–68). Gretchen's intercession of lines 12069–75 is a metrical and verbal echo of her prayer in the 'Zwinger' scene (lines 3587–92). The Blessed Boys revert to false dactyls, while the penitent Gretchen's lines and those of the Mater Gloriosa (12084–95) are regular four-beat iambics. Doctor Marianus returns to alternating four- and three-beat trochaics (12096–103); and the Chorus Mysticus concludes with false dactyls. Here, more than anywhere else, the description 'dactylic' is quite inadequate for lines in which varying degrees of stress qualify almost all the syllables of each line; whether, on the other hand, they are adequately described, as by May and Heusler, as 'alternierende Vierheber' ('alternating four-beat lines') is by no means certain.[19]

Such a broad descriptive survey of the prosody of *Faust* can, at best, only hint at the metrical richness and complexity of the work, and is in any case no more than a partial contribution towards an understanding of its poetic texture. Nor can such a survey chart in any detail the shifting irregularities of metrical patterns, the devices that constantly vary the monotony of iambic verse, let alone the problematic scansion of so-called false dactyls and the freer rhythms of the Euphorion episode. While there may not be any innate mimetic or even suggestive value in a given metre or verse form, certain metrical forms – sixteenth-century *Knittelvers*, classical trimeter, neo-classical alexandrines, the forms of medieval religious sequences or of folksong, even blank verse – do have distinct cultural and historical associations, and they are used by Goethe consciously and carefully at appropriate points in *Faust*. His use of metrical forms, and above all the changes from one form to another, are seldom without significance, even if the precise nature or effect of a particular metre is often elusive, and draws its significance primarily from its dramatic context and its verbal articulation – which is then in turn reinforced by the metre. The enormous metrical diversity of *Faust II* becomes at certain points almost anarchic – in the marine pageant of Act II, for example, or in the Euphorion episode of Act III. Most striking, and indeed most innovative of all, however, is the third act, where the archaic forms of Greek tragic drama are gradually superseded by modern prosody, symbolizing the cultural appropriation of the classical heritage by modern Western culture, as Faust instructs Helen in the art of rhymed iambic pentameter.

NOTES: CHAPTER 7

1 For a systematic introduction to and explanation of metrical forms, the reader is referred to Christian Wagenknecht, *Deutsche Metrik. Eine historische Einführung.*

2 For a brief history and description of *Knittelvers*, see David Chisholm, *Goethe's Knittelvers: a Prosodic Analysis*, pp. 5 ff.

3 Andreas Heusler, *Deutsche Versgeschichte*, Vol. 3, pp. 186, 335 ff.

4 Kurt May, *Faust II. Teil in der Sprachform gedeutet*, p. 52.

5 GA. 10. 183.

6 Heusler, *Deutsche Versgeschichte*, Vol. 3, p. 397.

7 ibid., p. 399. See also May, *Faust II. Teil*, p. 291.

8 Wagenknecht, *Deutsche Metrik*, p. 46.

9 Atkins, 'Goethe, Calderón and Faust II', p. 94.

10 See WA. I. 15, ii. 13–14.

11 Wolfgang Kayser, *Geschichte des deutschen Verses. Zehn Vorlesungen für Hörer aller Fakultäten*, pp. 93–4.

12 May, *Faust II. Teil*, p. 75.

13 Druian, 'Note on Faust II'.

14 May, *Faust II. Teil*, p.114.

15 GA. 5. 574.

16 Rüdiger, 'Weltliteratur in Goethes "Helena"', pp. 181 ff.

17 To Eckermann, 29 Jan. 1827 (Biedermann 3. 334).

18 May, *Faust II. Teil*, p. 247.

19 May, *Faust II. Teil*, p. 249; Heusler, *Deutsche Versgeschichte*, Vol. 3, p. 399.

SELECT BIBLIOGRAPHY

Details of standard German editions of Goethe's collected works, correspondence and conversations used for reference in this volume are given above, p. xv.

1   Editions and Reference

Faust-Bibliographie, ed. Hans Henning, 3 vols in 5 (Berlin, 1966–76).

Faust: a Tragedy, ed. and trans. Bayard Taylor, 3rd edn (London, 1890).

Goethes Faust, ed. Georg Witkowski, 9th edn, 2 vols (Leiden, 1936).

Faust. Der Tragödie erster Teil, ed. W. H. Bruford (London and New York, 1968).

Faust: a Tragedy, trans. Walter Arndt, ed. Cyrus Hamlin (New York, 1976).

Faust I and II, ed. and trans. Stuart Atkins (Boston, 1984): Vol. 2 of Goethe's Collected Works, Suhrkamp edn in 12 vols.

Goethe, The Italian Journey 1786–88, trans. W. H. Auden and Elizabeth Mayer (New York and London, 1962).

Goethe, Conversations and Encounters, trans. David Luke and Robert Pick (Chicago and London, 1966).

Eckermann's Conversations with Goethe, trans. John Oxenford, ed. J. K. Moorhead (New York and London, 1971).

The Autobiography of Johann Wolfgang von Goethe, trans. John Oxenford, 2 vols (Chicago and London, 1974).

H. B. Nisbet (ed.), German Aesthetic and Literary Criticism: Winckelmann, Lessing, Hamann, Herder, Schiller and Goethe (Cambridge, 1985).

J. Scheible (ed.), Das Kloster. Weltlich und geistlich. Meist aus der ältern deutschen Volks-, Wunder-, Curiositäten- und vorzugsweise komischen Literatur, 12 vols (Stuttgart, 1846–9).

Siegfried Szamatólski (ed.), Das Faustbuch des Christlich Meynenden nach dem Druck von 1725 (Stuttgart, 1891).

H. W. Geißler (ed.), Gestaltungen des Faust. Die bedeutendsten Werke der Faustdichtung seit 1587, 3 vols (Munich, 1927).

Hans Henning (ed.), Historia von D. Johann Fausten. Neudruck des Faustbuches von 1587 (Leipzig, 1979).

2   Critical Works

Arens, Hans, Kommentar zu Goethes Faust I (Heidelberg, 1982).

Atkins, Stuart, 'Goethe, Calderón and Faust. Der Tragödie zweiter Teil', Germanic Review, vol. 28 (1953), pp. 83–98.

Atkins, Stuart, Goethe's Faust: a Literary Analysis (Cambridge, Mass., and London, 1958).

Bahr, Ehrhard, Die Ironie im Spätwerk Goethes. Studien zum 'West-östlichen Divan', zu den 'Wanderjahren' und zu 'Faust II' (Berlin, 1972).

Baron, Frank, Doctor Faustus: from History to Legend (Munich, 1978).

Bennett, Benjamin, '"Vorspiel auf dem Theater": the Ironic Basis of Goethe's Faust', German Quarterly, vol. 49 (1976), pp. 438–55.

Bennett, Benjamin, *Goethe's Theory of Poetry: 'Faust' and the Regeneration of Language* (Ithaca, NY, and London, 1986).

Beutler, Ernst, 'Georg Faust aus Helmstadt', *Goethe-Kalender auf das Jahr 1936* (Leipzig, 1936), pp. 170–210.

Binder, Alwin, *Das Vorspiel auf dem Theater. Poetologische und geschichtsphilosophische Aspekte in Goethes Faust-Vorspiel* (Bonn, 1969).

Böhm, Wilhelm, *Faust der Nichtfaustische* (Halle an der Saale, 1933).

Borcherdt, H. H., 'Die Mummenschanz im zweiten Teil des "Faust". Versuch einer Deutung', *Goethe. Vierteljahresschrift der Goethe-Gesellschaft*, vol. 1 (1936), pp. 289–306.

Borchmeyer, Dieter, *Höfische Gesellschaft und französische Revolution bei Goethe. Adliges und bürgerliches Wertsystem im Urteil der Weimarer Klassik* (Kronberg/Ts, 1977).

Boyle, Nicholas, 'The Politics of Faust II: Another Look at the Stratum of 1831', *Publications of the English Goethe Society*, New Series, vol. 52 (1981–2), pp. 4–43.

Boyle, Nicholas, '"Du ahnungsloser Engel du!": Some Current Views of Goethe's *Faust*', *German Life and Letters*, New Series, vol. 36 (1982–3), pp. 116–47.

Boyle, Nicholas, *Goethe: Faust, Part One* (Cambridge, 1987).

Brown, Hilda M., 'Goethe in the Underworld: Proserpina/Persephone', *Oxford German Studies*, vol. 15 (1984), pp. 146–59.

Brown, Jane K., *Goethe's Faust: the German Tragedy* (Ithaca, NY, and London, 1986).

Bruford, W. H., *Goethe's Faust I Scene by Scene* (London and New York, 1968).

Bub, Douglas F., 'The Crown Incident in the Hexenküche: a Reinterpretation', *Modern Language Notes*, vol. 73 (1958), pp. 200–6.

Bub, Douglas F., 'The "Hexenküche" and the "Mothers" in Goethe's *Faust*', *Modern Language Notes*, vol. 83 (1968), pp. 775–9.

Butler, E. M., 'Goethe and Cagliostro', *Publications of the English Goethe Society*, New Series, vol. 16 (1946), pp. 1–28.

Butler, E. M., *The Fortunes of Faust* (Cambridge, 1952; reprinted 1979).

Carlson, Marvin, *Goethe and the Weimar Theatre* (Ithaca, NY, and London, 1978).

Chisholm, David, *Goethe's Knittelvers: a Prosodic Analysis* (Bonn, 1975).

Conrady, Karl Otto, *Goethe. Leben und Werk*, 2 vols (Königstein/Ts, 1984–5).

Cronin, Vincent, *Napoleon* (London, 1971).

Danckert, Werner, *Goethe. Der mythische Urgrund seiner Weltschau* (Berlin, 1951).

Dédéyan, Charles, *Le Thème de Faust dans la littérature européenne*, 4 vols (Paris, 1954–67).

Diener, Gottfried, *Fausts Weg zu Helena. Urphänomen und Archetypus* (Stuttgart, 1961).

Döring, Hellmut, 'Homunculus', *Weimarer Beiträge*, vol. 11 (1965), pp. 185–94.

Döring, Hellmut, '"Der Schöngestalt bedenkliche Begleiter". Betrachtungen zu *Faust II. 3*', *Weimarer Beiträge*, vol. 12 (1966), pp. 261–72.

Druian, M. Gregory, 'A Note on Faust II, ll. 6487–6500', *German Quarterly*, vol. 47 (1974), pp. 432–5.

Dshinoria, Otar, 'Das Ende von Goethes "Faust"', *Goethe-Jahrbuch*, vol. 90 (1973), pp. 57–106.

Durrani, Osman, *Faust and the Bible: a Study of Goethe's Use of Scriptural Allusions and Christian Religious Motifs in Faust I and II* (Berne, 1977).

Emrich, Wilhelm, *Die Symbolik von Faust II. Sinn und Vorformen*, 3rd edn (Frankfurt am Main, 1964).

Emrich, Wilhelm, 'Das Rätsel der Faust-II-Dichtung. Versuch einer Lösung', in

Emrich, *Geist und Widergeist. Wahrheit und Lüge der Literaturstudien* (Frankfurt am Main, 1965), pp. 211–35.

Fairley, Barker, *Goethe's Faust: Six Essays* (Oxford, 1953).

Fischer, Kuno, *Goethe's Faust*, 2 vols, 4th edn (Heidelberg, 1913).

Flavell, M. Kay, '"Arkadisch frei sei unser Glück": the Myth of the Golden Age in Eighteenth-century Germany', *Publications of the English Goethe Society*, New Series, vol. 43 (1972–3), pp. 1–27.

Fowler, F. M., 'Goethe's "Faust" and the Medieval Sequence', *Modern Language Review*, vol. 71 (1976), pp. 838–45.

Fowler, F. M., 'Symmetry of Structure in Goethe's *Faust, Part One*', in J. P. Stern (ed.), *London German Studies III* (London, 1986), pp. 22–40.

Franz, Erich, *Mensch und Dämon. Goethes Faust als menschliche Tragödie, ironische Weltschau und religiöses Mysterienspiel* (Tübingen, 1953).

Friedenthal, Richard, *Goethe. Sein Leben und seine Zeit* (Munich, 1963); translated as *Goethe: his Life and Times* (London, 1965).

Friedrich, T., and Scheithauer, L. J., *Kommentar zu Goethes Faust* (Stuttgart, 1973).

Gearey, John, *Goethe's Faust: the Making of Part One* (New Haven, Conn., 1981).

Gerhard, Melitta, 'Faust. Die Tragödie des "neueren" Menschen', *Jahrbuch des freien deutschen Hochstifts* (1978), pp. 160–4.

Gillies, Alexander, *Goethe's Faust: an Interpretation* (Oxford, 1957).

Goebel, Julius, 'Traces of the Wars of Liberation in the Second Part of Faust', *Journal of English and Germanic Philology*, vol. 16 (1917), pp. 195–207.

Graham, Ilse, 'Kompromittierung und Wiedergutmachung. Ein Versuch zu Fausts Schlußmonolog', *Jahrbuch der deutschen Schiller-Gesellschaft*, vol. 26 (1982), pp. 163–203.

Grappin, Pierre, 'Zur Gestalt des Kaisers in "Faust II"', *Goethe-Jahrbuch*, vol. 91 (1974), pp. 107–16.

Grappin, Pierre, 'Faust aveugle', *Études germaniques*, vol. 38 (1983), pp. 138–46.

Gray, Ronald D., *Goethe the Alchemist* (Cambridge, 1952).

Gundolf, Friedrich, *Goethe*, 4th edn (Berlin, 1918).

Hahn, Karl-Heinz, 'Faust und Helena oder die Aufhebung des Zwiespalts zwischen Klassikern und Romantikern', *Goethe. Neue Folge des Jahrbuchs der Goethe-Gesellschaft*, vol. 32 (1970), pp. 115–41.

Hamm, Heinz, *Goethes Faust. Werkgeschichte und Textanalyse* (Berlin, 1978).

Hamm, Heinz, 'Julirevolution, Saint-Simonismus und Goethes abschließende Arbeit am "Faust"', *Weimarer Beiträge*, vol. 38, no. 11 (1982), pp. 70–91.

Hardy, Swana L., *Goethe, Calderón und die romantische Theorie des Dramas* (Heidelberg, 1965).

Hauschild, Richard, 'Mistra, die Faustburg Goethes', *Abhandlungen der sächsischen Akademie der Wissenschaften zu Leipzig, philologisch-historische Klasse*, vol. 54, no. 4 (Berlin, 1963), pp. 1–26.

Hayes, Charles, 'Symbol and Allegory: a Problem in Literary Theory', *Germanic Review*, vol. 44 (1969), pp. 273–88.

Hederich, Benjamin, *Gründliches mythologisches Lexikon* (Leipzig, 1770; reprinted Darmstadt, 1967).

Heller, Erich, 'Goethe and the Avoidance of Tragedy', in Heller, *The Disinherited Mind* (Cambridge, 1952), pp. 27–49.

Henkel, Arthur, 'Das Ärgernis Faust', in Volker Dürr and Géza von Molnár (eds) *Versuche zu Goethe: Festschrift für Erich Heller* (Heidelberg, 1976), pp. 282–304.

Henning, Hans, 'Zur Geschichte eines Faust-Motivs', in *Festschrift für Wolfgang Vulpius zu seinem 60. Geburtstag* (Weimar, 1957), pp. 53–62.

Hertz, Wilhelm, 'Der Schluß der "Klassischen Walpurgisnacht"', *Germanisch-romanische Monatsschrift*, vol. 7 (1915–19), pp. 281–300.

Heusler, Andreas, *Deutsche Versgeschichte*, 3 vols (Berlin, 1925–9).

Hoelzel, Alfred, 'The Conclusion of Goethe's Faust: Ambivalence and Ambiguity', *German Quarterly*, vol. 55 (1982), pp. 1–12.

Höfler, Otto, *Homunculus – eine Satire auf A. W. Schlegel. Goethe und die Romantik* (Vienna, 1972).

Höhle, Thomas, and Hamm, Heinz, 'Faust. Der Tragödie zweiter Teil', *Weimarer Beiträge*, vol. 20, no. 6 (1974), pp. 49–89.

Ibel, Rudolf, *Goethe: Faust I* (Frankfurt am Main, 1972).

Jantz, Harold, 'Faust's Vision of the Macrocosm', *Modern Language Notes*, vol. 68 (1953), pp. 348–51.

Jantz, Harold, *The Form of Faust: the Work of Art and its Intrinsic Structures* (Baltimore, Md, 1978).

Kayser, Wolfgang, *Geschichte des deutschen Verses. Zehn Vorlesungen für Hörer aller Fakultäten* (Berne, 1960).

Keller, Werner (ed.), *Aufsätze zu Goethes 'Faust I'* (Darmstadt, 1974).

Keller, Werner, 'Faust. Eine Tragödie (1808)', in Walter Hinderer (ed.), *Goethes Dramen. Neue Interpretationen*, (Stuttgart, 1980), pp. 244–80.

Kellner, Hans, 'Figures in the Rumpelkammer: Goethe, Faust, Spengler', *Journal of European Studies*, vol. 13 (1983), pp. 142–67.

Kerényi, Karl, *Das ägäische Fest. Erläuterungen zur Szene 'Felsbuchten des ägäischen Meers' in Goethes Faust II*, 3rd edn (Wiesbaden, 1950).

Kobligk, Helmut, *Goethe: Faust II* (Frankfurt am Main, 1972).

Lamport, F. J., *A Student's Guide to Goethe* (London, 1971).

Lamport, F. J., 'Synchrony and Diachrony in Faust', *Oxford German Studies*, vol. 15 (1984), pp. 118–31.

Lange, Victor, 'Faust. Der Tragödie zweiter Teil', in Walter Hinderer (ed.), *Goethes Dramen. Neue Interpretationen* (Stuttgart, 1980), pp. 281–312.

Lange-Fuchs, Hauke, *'Ja, wäre nur ein Zaubermantel mein!'. Faust im Film* (Bonn, 1985).

Levedahl, Kathryn S., 'The Witch's One-Times-One: Sense or Nonsense?', *Modern Language Notes*, vol. 85 (1970), pp. 380–3.

Lewes, George Henry, *The Life and Works of Goethe*, 2 vols (London, 1855).

Littlejohns, Richard, 'The Discussion between Goethe and Schiller on the Epic and the Dramatic, and its Relevance to Faust', *Neophilologus*, vol. 71 (1987), pp. 388–401.

Lohmeyer, Dorothea, *Faust und die Welt. Der zweite Teil der Dichtung. Eine Anleitung zum Lesen des Textes* (Munich, 1975).

Lohmeyer, Karl, 'Das Meer und die Wolken in den beiden letzten Akten des "Faust"', *Jahrbuch der Goethe-Gesellschaft*, vol. 13 (1927), pp. 106–33.

Lukács, Georg, 'Faust-Studien', in Lukács, *Goethe und seine Zeit* (Berne, 1947), pp. 127–207.

Luke, F. D., '"Der nord-südliche Goethe": Some Reflexions on Faust's Dog', *Oxford German Studies*, vol. 15 (1984), pp. 132–45.

Maché, Ulrich, 'Goethes Faust als Plutus und Dichter', Jahrbuch des freien deutschen Hochstifts (1975), pp. 174–88.

Mahal, Günther, 'Der tausendjährige Faust. Rezeption als Anmaßung', in Gunter Grimm (ed.), Literatur und Leser. Theorien und Modelle zur Rezeption literarischer Werke (Stuttgart, 1975), pp. 181–95.

Mahal, Günther, Faust. Die Spuren eines geheimnisvollen Lebens (Berne, 1980).

Mason, Eudo C., Goethe's Faust: its Genesis and Purport (Berkeley, Calif., 1967).

May, Kurt, Faust II. Teil in der Sprachform gedeutet, 2nd edn (Munich, 1962).

Mayer, Hans, 'Der Famulus Wagner und die moderne Wissenschaft', in Käte Hamburger and Helmut Kreuzer (eds), Gestaltungsgeschichte und Gesellschaftsgeschichte. Literatur-, Kunst- und Musikwissenschaftliche Studien (Stuttgart, 1969), pp. 176–200.

Mehra, Marlis, 'Goethes Groß-Cophta und das zeitgenössische Lustspiel um 1790', Goethe Yearbook: Publications of the Goethe Society of North America, vol. 1 (1982), pp. 93–111.

Metscher, Thomas, 'Faust und die Ökonomie. Ein literarhistorischer Essay', in Metscher, Vom Faustus bis Karl Valentin. Der Bürger in Geschichte und Literatur (Das Argument, Sonderband 3, Berlin, 1976), pp. 28–155.

Meyer, Eva A., Politische Symbolik bei Goethe (Heidelberg, 1949).

Michelsen, Peter, 'Fausts Erblindung', Deutsche Vierteljahrsschrift für Literaturwissenschaft und Geistesgeschichte, vol. 36 (1962), pp. 26–35.

Michelsen, Peter, 'Der Einzelne und sein Geselle. Fausts Osterspaziergang', Euphorion, vol. 72 (1978), pp. 43–67.

Molnár, Géza von, 'Die Fragwürdigkeit des Fragezeichens. Einige Überlegungen zur Paktszene', Goethe–Jahrbuch, vol. 96 (1979), pp. 270–9.

Mommsen, Katharina, Goethe und 1001 Nacht (Berlin, 1960).

Mommsen, Katharina, Natur- und Fabelreich in Faust II (Berlin, 1968).

Mommsen, Momme, 'Zu Vers 7782 f. der "Klassischen Walpurgisnacht"', Goethe. Neue Folge des Jahrbuchs der Goethe-Gesellschaft, vol. 13 (1951), p. 296.

Mommsen, Wilhelm, Die politischen Anschauungen Goethes (Stuttgart, 1948).

Müller, Joachim, 'Die tragische Grundstruktur von Goethes Faustdichtung', Zeitschrift für deutsche Geisteswissenschaft, vol. 6 (1943–4), pp. 196–203.

Müller, Joachim, 'Fausts Tat und Tod', Goethe. Neue Folge des Jahrbuchs der Goethe-Gesellschaft, vol. 29 (1967), pp. 139–65.

Müller, Joachim, '"Meiner Wolke Tragewerk". Fausts Abschied von Helena', in Müller, Neue Goethe-Studien (Halle an der Saale, 1969), pp. 209–24.

Müller-Blattau, Joseph, 'Der Zauberflöte Zweiter Teil. Ein Beitrag zum Thema Goethe und Mozart', Goethe. Neue Folge des Jahrbuchs der Goethe-Gesellschaft, vol. 18 (1956), pp. 158–79.

Müller-Seidel, Walter, 'Lynkeus. Lyrik und Tragik in Goethes Faust', in Wolfgang Frühwald and Günter Niggl (eds), Sprache und Bekenntnis. Hermann Kunisch zum 70. Geburtstag (Berlin, 1971), pp. 79–110.

Nollendorfs, Valters, Der Streit um den Urfaust (The Hague, 1967).

Palmer, Philip M., and More, Robert P., The Sources of the Faust Tradition from Simon Magus to Lessing (New York, 1936).

Papst, E. E., Goethe and the Fourth Virtue: an Inaugural Lecture (Southampton, 1977).

Peters, Ilse, 'Das Napoleonbild Goethes in seiner Spätzeit (1813–1832)', Goethe. Vierteljahresschrift der Goethe-Gesellschaft, vol. 9 (1944), pp. 140–71.

Petersen, Julius, *Goethes Faust auf der deutschen Bühne* (Leipzig, 1929).

Pniower, Otto, 'Faust und das Hohe Lied', *Goethe-Jahrbuch*, vol. 13 (1892), pp. 181–98.

Pniower, Otto, 'Pfitzers Faustbuch als Quelle Goethes', *Zeitschrift für deutsches Altertum*, vol. 57 (1920), pp. 248–66.

Politzer, Heinz, 'Der blinde Faust', *German Quarterly*, vol. 49 (1976), pp. 161–7.

Reed, T. J., *The Classical Centre: Goethe and Weimar 1775–1832* (London, 1980).

Reed, T. J., *Goethe* (Oxford, 1984).

Reinhardt, Karl, 'Goethe and Antiquity', in Reinhardt, *Tradition und Geist. Gesammelte Essays zur Dichtung*, ed. Carl Becker (Göttingen, 1960), pp. 274–82.

Reinhardt, Karl, 'Die klassische Walpurgisnacht. Entstehung und Bedeutung', in Reinhardt, *Tradition und Geist*, pp. 309–65.

Requadt, Paul, 'Die Figur des Kaisers im "Faust II"', *Jahrbuch der deutschen Schiller-Gesellschaft*, vol. 8 (1964), pp. 153–71.

Requadt, Paul, *Goethes 'Faust I'. Leitmotivik und Architektur* (Munich, 1972).

Resenhöfft, Wilhelm, 'Goethes Euphorion: August von Goethe', *Dichtung und Volkstum. Neue Folge des Euphorion*, vol. 41 (1941), pp. 78–87.

Reske, Hermann, *Faust. Eine Einführung* (Stuttgart, 1971).

Rickert, Heinrich, *Goethes Faust. Die dramatische Einheit der Dichtung* (Tübingen, 1932).

Römer, Horst, 'Idylle und Idyllik in Goethes Faust II', *Jahrbuch der Jean-Paul-Gesellschaft*, vol. 11 (1976), pp. 137–63.

Rüdiger, Horst, 'Weltliteratur in Goethes "Helena"', *Jahrbuch der deutschen Schiller-Gesellschaft*, vol. 8 (1964), pp. 172–98.

Runciman, Steven, *Mistra: Byzantine Capital of the Peloponnese* (London, 1980).

Schadewaldt, Wolfgang, 'Fausts Ende und die Achilleis', in Schadewaldt, *Goethe-Studien* (Zürich, 1963), pp. 283–300.

Schillemeit, Jost, 'Das *Vorspiel auf dem Theater* zu Goethes *Faust*. Entstehungszusammenhänge und Folgerungen für sein Verständnis', *Euphorion*, vol. 80 (1986), pp. 149–66.

Schlaffer, Heinz, *Faust Zweiter Teil. Die Allegorie des 19. Jahrhunderts* (Stuttgart, 1981).

Schmidt, Johanna, 'Sparta-Mistra. Forschungen über Goethes Faustburg', *Goethe. Neue Folge des Jahrbuchs der Goethe-Gesellschaft*, vol. 18 (1956), pp. 132–57.

Scholz, Gerhard, *Faust-Gespräche* (Berlin, 1967).

Scholz, Rüdiger, *Die beschädigte Seele des großen Mannes. Goethes 'Faust' und die bürgerliche Gesellschaft* (Rheinfelden, 1982).

Scholz, Rüdiger, *Goethes 'Faust' in der wissenschaftlichen Interpretation von Schelling und Hegel bis heute. Ein einführender Forschungsbericht* (Rheinfelden, 1983).

Schöne, Albrecht, 'Über Goethes Wolkenlehre', in Karl Heinz Borck and Rudolf Hensss (eds), *Der Berliner Germanistentag 1968. Vorträge und Berichte* (Heidelberg, 1970), pp. 24–41.

Schöne, Albrecht, *Götterzeichen, Liebeszauber, Satanskult. Neue Einblicke in alte Goethetexte* (Munich, 1982).

Schuchard, G. C. L., 'Julirevolution, St. Simonismus und die Faustpartien von 1831', *Zeitschrift für deutsche Philologie*, vol. 60 (1935), pp. 240–74, 362–84.

Schwerte, Hans, *Faust und das Faustische. Ein Kapitel deutscher Ideologie* (Stuttgart, 1962).

Seidlin, Oskar, 'Is the "Prelude in the Theatre" a Prelude to "Faust"?', *Publications of the Modern Language Association of America*, vol. 64 (1949), pp. 462–70.

238								Goethe's Faust

Seidlin, Oskar, 'Goethes Zauberflöte', in Seidlin, Von Goethe zu Thomas Mann. Zwolf Versuche (Göttingen, 1963), pp. 38–55.

Skwara, Erich W., 'Homunculus und Euphorion', Literatur und Kritik, no. 131 (Salzburg, 1979), pp. 19–24.

Smeed, John W., Faust in Literature (London, 1975).

Sørensen, Bengt A., 'Altersstil und Symboltheorie. Zum Problem des Symbols und der Allegorie bei Goethe', Goethe-Jahrbuch, vol. 94 (1977), pp. 69–85.

Staiger, Emil, Goethe, 3 vols (Zürich, 1952–9).

Theens, Karl, 'Geschichte des Faust-Motivs im Film', Blätter der Knittlinger Faust-Gedenkstätte, no. 11 (1960), pp. 425–47.

Theens, Karl, 'Faust in der Musik', Faust-Blätter, no. 4 (1968), pp. 106–14, 115–23.

Vaget, Hans Rudolf, 'Faust, der Feudalismus und die Restauration', Akten des VI. Internationalen Germanisten-Kongresses Basel 1980 (Berne, 1980), pp. 345–51.

Viëtor, Karl, Goethe. Dichtung, Wissenschaft, Weltbild (Berne, 1949).

Vincent, Deirdre, ' "Die Tat ist alles": a Reconsideration of the Significance of "Faust II", Act Four', Seminar, vol. 18 (1982), pp. 125–41.

Vischer, Friedrich Theodor, Faust. Der Tragödie dritter Teil. Treu im Geiste des zweiten Teils des Goetheschen Fausts gedichtet von Deutobold Symbolizetti Allegoriowitsch Mystifizinsky (Tübingen, 1862).

Wagenknecht, Christian, Deutsche Metrik. Eine historische Einführung (Munich, 1981).

White, Ann, Names and Nomenclature in Goethe's 'Faust' (London, 1980).

Wiese, Benno von, Die deutsche Tragödie von Lessing bis Hebbel, 2 vols (Hamburg, 1948).

Wilkinson, Elizabeth M., 'The Theological Basis of Faust's "Credo"', German Life and Letters, New Series, vol. 10 (1956–7), pp. 229–39.

Wilkinson, Elizabeth M., 'Goethe's Faust: Tragedy in the Diachronic Mode', Publications of the English Goethe Society, New Series, vol. 42 (1971–2), pp. 116–74.

Williams, John R., 'The Festival of Luna: a Study of the Lunar Symbolism in Goethe's Klassische Walpurgisnacht', Deutsche Vierteljahrsschrift für Literaturwissenschaft und Geistesgeschichte, vol. 50 (1976), pp. 640–63.

Williams, John R., 'The Flatulence of Seismos: Goethe, Rabelais and the "Geranomachia"', Germanisch-romanische Monatsschrift, Neue Folge, vol. 33 (1983), pp. 103–10.

Williams, John R., 'Faust's Classical Education: Goethe's Allegorical Treatment of Faust and Helen of Troy', Journal of European Studies, vol. 13 (1983), pp. 27–41.

Williams, John R., 'Die Rache der Kraniche. Goethe, Faust II und die Julirevolution', Zeitschrift für deutsche Philologie. Sonderheft Goethe, vol. 103 (1984), pp. 105–27.

Willoughby, Leonard A., 'Goethe's Faust: a Morphological Approach', in Elizabeth M. Wilkinson and L. A. Willoughby, Goethe: Poet and Thinker (London, 1962), pp. 95–117.

Wittkowski, Wolfgang, 'Faust und der Kaiser. Goethes letztes Wort zum "Faust"', Deutsche Vierteljahrsschrift für Literaturwissenschaft und Geistesgeschichte, vol. 43 (1969), pp. 631–51.

Wittkowski, Wolfgang, 'Irrestorable Destruction and Tragic Reconciliation in Goethe's Faust', in Clifford A. Bernd et al. (eds), Goethe Proceedings: Essays Commemorating the Goethe Sesquicentennial at the University of California, Davis (Columbia, SC, 1984), pp. 93–106.

Zweig, Stefan, Marie Antoinette, trans. Eden and Cedar Paul (London, 1952).

INDEX